Avraham Dardashti (اوراهام دردشتی) holding Nemat in his lap, only a few months old

Nematollah Shakib

نعمت اله شکیب

Dardashti

دردشتی

By

Nematollah Shakib

نعمت اله شکیب

Translated from Farsi to English

By

Iraj David Shakib

Acknowledgements

I am currently about the same age my father was when he began writing this book. I am in awe at the extent of his knowledge, his memory about his life and all of his experiences. On behalf of my brother, my sisters and my entire family I thank my enormously gifted father and the treasure he left behind. We are all very proud of him for spending several years researching to write this book in such detail and accuracy.

Many thanks to my beloved wife, Phyllis, whose support and her final editing are the reasons I completed the translation and publishing of this book. This book entails many family members and their relationships to each other with unfamiliar names and cultural nuances. Her editing made the book easier to follow. Phyllis's encouragement helped me to continue the translation during the eight year period that I was fighting terminal cancer; translating my father's manuscript was a helpful distraction. She was also instrumental in hiring her high school friend, Peter Mathew, a journalist, to do the editing following my initial translation from Farsi to English; my many thanks to Peter.

Many thanks to my cousin, Keyoomars (Robbi) Azizian (کیومرز عزیزیان), he assisted my father in typing the original manuscript in Farsi. He had just arrived from the United Kingdom to Lexington, KY, and was residing with my parents for a short time.

My mother Yafa was also a great supporter and she continually inquired about the progress of the book until she died in 2007.

Finally, I thank my family for their support and sharing their family photos with me. Due to the size of the family and the many locations around the world where they have settled some of the Family Trees are incomplete and it was impossible to have every picture included.

Contents

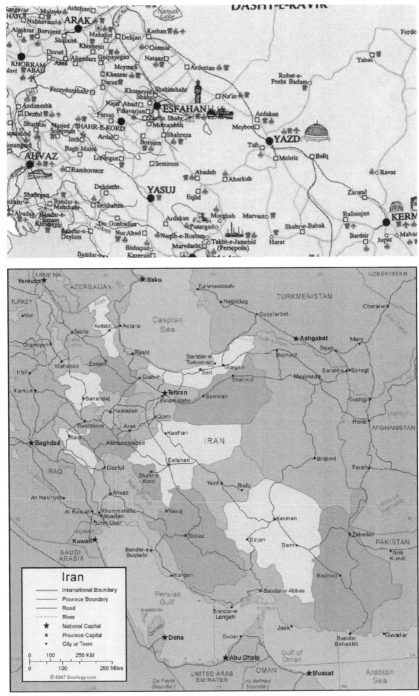

(Courtesy of Bing)

Prologue

My name is Iraj David Shakib and I am the first born of
Nematollah Shakib (نعمت اله شكيب). Nemat wrote this book while
in his early seventies. He was a self-taught scholar with only an
eighth grade education. After he retired in 1970 with forty years
of service with the National Iranian Oil Company (NIOC), he
traveled to the United States to visit with his four children. The
two older children, Iraj David and Jahangir John were college
graduates working for IBM, married and each had a son. His
two daughters were in college and unmarried. He returned to
Iran after two years. He then translated a book written by Abba
Eban, "My People" (a history of Jews), from English to Farsi
(the language of Iran), he returned to Iran to publish his Farsi
version of "My People". My father's version of "My People"
was extremely successful in Iran, especially among the Jewish
Iranian community.

He revisited the United States two years after publishing
"My People" and several years later he began writing this book,
a book regarding a Jewish family in the ghettos of Esfahan, Iran
during the 19th and 20th centuries. He was an avid reader and his
major interest was in history. He was knowledgeable
concerning the Bible and he wrote several commentaries about
it. He had tremendous comprehension of many that authored the
Bible and he disputed many of their interpretations as well.

He finished this book in the late 1970's and he sought to
interest me in reading and publishing it, but my life was too
hectic with work and personal involvements. To my misfortune
and regret, I waited until my father passed away and it was in
the early 2000's when I began reading his book and I realized

and appreciated the treasure my father had left behind. That is when I unquestionably decided to translate this book to English so the events and historical aspects that are contained within could be shared with a much larger audience, including his grandchildren and the future generations of our family. To my dismay, concurrently I was diagnosed with terminal cancer and after an eight year struggle I am well now and I proceed with great enthusiasm to publish his book.

Among my father's papers I found the following half page of notes where he began to translate his book from Farsi to English. Below is his hand written draft translation. The

following is a transcribed version of my father's draft.

Every one human being arrives in this earthly world and lives for a period of time and dies and makes for his own a history. Some are interesting and some not attractive. Mine is so, and I believe, my life also is a history which now I like to describe it as much as I remember. It means a long story and I believe it is interesting to read it. Most of us living have stories that have grief and sympathy and I like as much as my remembrances help me and I can help it and my remaining life is sufficient to fulfill is to write and leave it behind and go.

The 1st Chapter: My name is Nemat. My father's name is Yaeir and he was born in Isfahan, one of the very famous cities in Iran. I am a Jewish born boy, of this town. Isfahan is very famous in the whole world, because of its most famous old buildings and monuments throughout the world. These old buildings attract millions and millions of visitors and tourists to visit this city every year.

My greatest concern is that my translation might not do justice for his book—my father's writing in Farsi was poetic and literary. My father was a very loving man who was dependable and steadfast for anyone in the family in times of trouble. My siblings and I had a very loving and attentive childhood, except the occasions that my father dragged us into everyone else's misery while he was attempting to lend support to them. But I understand that my siblings and I were very fortunate being raised by my father and mother—my childhood memories are some of my happiest times. My father was very compassionate and tried to assist anyone in the family. I remember during my childhood we always had one of my father's nieces or nephews living with us. We even had my father's sister's granddaughter live with us. I discovered from my cousins that for many years at Passover my father bought those nieces or nephews shoes but he never disclosed this to anyone.

He was a self-made man who strove to ensure his children would do better in life and be even more independent and self-actuating than himself. He emphasized the importance of a good education by sending his children to the best schools in Iran and overseas. I was the first of my family to come to the United States to continue my education. At that time my father was earning a respectable wage with the NIOC (National Iranian Oil Company), about $110 per month. However, the Iranian government minimum monthly requirement was about $160 to allow a student to study abroad. My parent's entire savings was spent on my airline ticket and a couple of months of the required expenses. He and my mother were incredibly brave people. They educated their daughters as well as their sons. Unlike my father's contemporaries, he wanted exactly the same level of education for his sons and daughters. He was vastly ahead of his time in his thinking.

He was a compassionate conservative but he believed in a national safety-net. He had come across many people, especially women that became destitute after the death of their bread winners. He had experienced firsthand the hunger of famine, extreme discrimination and the loss of his father at a very young age. He was a very hardworking man who did not believe in free handouts and that everyone should work hard in order to receive assistance—he believed the safety-net should be there for extreme situations only. After my father lost his pension with the National Iranian Oil Co. after the revolution, he was offered Food Stamps from the State of Kentucky. Not only he refused the offer, he thanked them and walked out the building.

He loved Iran even though he experienced much hardship and discrimination, and he rejected the belief of some Muslim Iranians that the Jewish populace cannot be considered Iranians because of their religion. His ancestors had lived in Iran for centuries; therefore he was as Iranian as anyone in Iran. His experience with a lot of Iranian Muslims was mostly humiliating and prejudicial. But like my own experiences, there were many kind and decent Muslims. I do not know how my grandmother could have managed to feed several hungry children during a horrible famine, when her husband was away on business for several years, if it were not for the generosity of several wealthy Muslim customers of my grandmother.

My father's generous retirement was confiscated after the revolution of 1979 in Iran. Thereafter, he and my mother applied for citizenship in the United States and in 1983 they were sworn in as United States citizens. My father was proud to be a citizen of this great nation and he was very patriotic.

Similar to me, he and my mother received their citizenship in one courthouse and walked to another courthouse registering to vote. This was their first experience in their lives voting in an election. He was a great defender of the United States and Israel. He believed that the United States and its Constitution was an asset for the world and the human race. He also believed in his heart that Israel's independence was a turning point for all Jews worldwide, and its existence was critical for the survival of the Jewish race. He had more appreciation of his "Jewish" heritage after translating the book "My People". He translated numerous books written about the struggles of Jews who fought for Israel. He was hawkish concerning Israel and he was a supporter of the late Rabbi Meir Kahane.

My father was respected and loved by most everyone he came in contact with. He was unselfish and full of pride. The love of his wife, children, grandchildren and his family was to a fault. He fretted over anyone involved in a dilemma due to of his own harsh childhood and the prejudicial environment he was brought up in. I feel honored to translate his book to English and I am very proud of him.

I have included numerous pictures and footnotes so the reader may easily have a better understanding of the many unfamiliar names and places. My father has delved quite a bit into history and it was necessary to elaborate further to show the connections. Again, I am in awe at his depth of knowledge of history.

Before Reza Shah's Dynasty everyone was identified as the child of their father and no one had a last name (ex. Nemat-e-Yaeir). In the mid 1920's after Reza Shah came to power, he declared an edict that everyone must select a second name (family name). Therefore, our family chose the name "Shakib", meaning patience.

I, Iraj David Shakib, the son of Nematollah, feel honored to have the privilege of translating my father's book, "Dardashti".

CHAPTER **1**

Background

My name is Nemat (نعمت), son of Yaeir (یائیر), and I was born in Esfahan, one of the most famous and important Iranian cities. I am a Jew from a relatively prominent family from the ethnic Jewish minority in this town. Esfahan is a large tourist city that has historical significance and contains many monuments and ancient palaces. Every year several thousand people visit from all corners of the world, and it is hard to find anywhere in the world that someone has never heard or read about this city. This city was the capital of Iran during the Buyid[1] (ال بویه) Dynasty and later in the reign of the Safavid[2] (صفویه) sultans. According to what is written and has been preserved on ancient tablets of stone and tombstones, the Jews

---

[1] Būyid Dynasty, , also called Buwayhid, (945–1055), Islāmic dynasty of pronounced Iranian and Shīʿī character that provided native rule in western Iran and Iraq in the period between the Arab and Turkish conquests. Of Daylamite (northern Iranian) origin, the line was founded by the three sons of Būyeh (or Buwayh), ʿAlī, Ḥasan, and Aḥmad.

ʿAlī, appointed governor of Karaj about 930 by the Daylamite leader Mardāvīz ebn Zeyār, seized Esfahan and Fārs, while Ḥasan and Aḥmad took Jibāl, Khūzestān, and Kermān (935–936). In December 945 Aḥmad occupied the ʿAbbāsid capital of Baghdad as amīr al-umarāʾ (commander in chief) and, reducing the Sunnī caliphs to puppet status, established Būyid rule (January 946). Thereafter the brothers were known by their honorific titles of ʿImād ad-Dawlah (ʿAlī), Rukn ad-Dawlah (Ḥasan), and Muʿizz ad-Dawlah (Aḥmad). (from Encyclopedia Britannica Facts matter)

[2] Safavid Dynasty, (1502–1736), Iranian dynasty whose establishment of Shiite Islam as the state religion of Iran was a major factor in the emergence of a unified national consciousness among the various ethnic and linguistic elements of the country. The Ṣafavids were descended from Sheykh Ṣafī od-Dīn (1253–1334) of Ardabīl, head of the Ṣūfī order of Ṣafavīyeh (Safawiyah), but about 1399 exchanged their Sunnite affiliation for Shīʿism.

have resided in this city for more than a thousand years. The

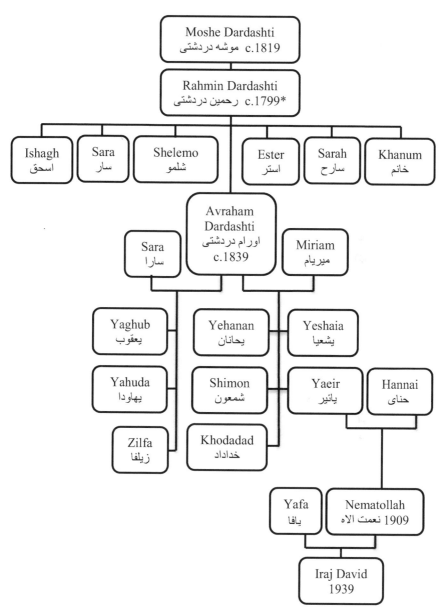

*Birth Year

language that the Jews of Esfahan speak is a mixture of ancient Persian language and today's Farsi. These Jews are the descendants of the Jews that migrated to Persia after the defeat of Babylon by Koresh[3] (كورش كبير, Cyrus) the Great. Near Esfahan there is a string of villages by the name of Seddeh Beneh (سده بنه) of Esfahan whose inhabitants speak with a very similar dialect as the Jews of Esfahan. Whenever any of these inhabitants comes in contact with Jews from Esfahan, they are able to converse with each other easily and no one could tell which one is Jewish and which one is a Muslim from Seddeh. One could conclude that these farmers from Seddeh at one time were Jewish and because of the pressures of the majority have all converted to Islam. Their social and cultural behavior is very similar to the Jews of Esfahan. These farmers lit a candle in their homes every Saturday night without knowing why. Therefore, the Jews deduce that these lights are the same lights that the Jewish ancestors of the farmers used and blessed during Sabbath — a custom that is practiced by Orthodox Jews.

The Esfahani Jews live in three ghettoes, in three locations in Esfahan. The first one is Jahanbareh[4] (جهانباز) or Juybareh, the

---

[3] Cyrus II of Persia (Old Persian: Kūruš; c. 600 BC or 576 BC–530 BC), commonly known as Cyrus the Great,, also known as Cyrus the Elder, was the founder of the Achaemenid Empire. Under his rule, the empire embraced all the previous civilized states of the ancient Near East, expanded vastly and eventually conquered most of Southwest Asia and much of Central Asia and the Caucasus. From the Mediterranean Sea and Hellespont in the west to the Indus River in the east, Cyrus the Great created the largest empire the world had yet seen. His regal titles in full were The Great King, King of Persia, King of Anshan, King of Media, King of Babylon, King of Sumer and Akkad, King of the four corners of the World. He also pronounced what some consider being one of the first historically important declarations of human rights via the Cyrus Cylinder sometime between 539 and 530 BC. (from Wikipedia)

[4] The forgotten district of Juybareh (jūybārɘ) in the ancient city of Esfahan is one of the oldest residential quarters in Iran that has been occupied since the time of Cyrus the Great, the founder of the second Iranian dynasty, the Achaemenids (550-330 BCE), which has received no attention whatsoever from the cultural authorities.
"According to historical accounts, the Jews from Babylon were brought here when Cyrus the Great freed them from captivity in 6th century BCE, and were settled here since then", according to Mehdi Sajadi-Naeini a researcher and local historian. (from London CAIS)

second one is Dardasht[5] (دردشت) and the third one is Golbahar
(گل بهار). Juybareh is the main ghetto where the majority of
Esfahani Jews reside; Dardasht and Golbahar were second and
third, respectively. The population of all the Jews in Esfahan for
all three ghettos during 1920-1940 was estimated in the tens of
thousands. A major portion of them immigrated to Israel after it
gained independence, and another group moved to Tehran, the
capital of Iran. As I write this book (10th day of Ordibeshet,
1356, or April 30, 1977), the population of Esfahani Jews has
reduced drastically, and just about all of them have moved out
of the ghettos into modern homes in the more affluent sections
of Esfahan similar to Muslim neighborhoods.

Entrance to Juybareh   *Shopping Area in Juybareh*

The Jews that lived in Dardasht spoke with the same dialect
as their Muslim neighbors. The Jews of Dardasht did not fully
understand the language, the language that is similar to the old
Farsi, of the other two ghettos. My ancestors lived in Dardasht,
but my grandfather, Avraham Dardashti (اوراهام دردشتی), moved
to Juybareh. He constructed a home there and married and lived

---

[5] Dardasht (Persian: دردشت) is the name of a neighborhood in Isfahan, Iran.
Dardasht is the name of a quarter (formerly known as Babol-Dasht) and a historical
minaret in Isfahan Province of Iran. Dardasht is well known for its outstanding
cemetery and shrine architecture as the Darb-i Imam Shrine. The Dardasht quarter of
Isfahan was one of the major Jewish quarters of the city. Unlike other Jewish
quarters, Dardasht was in closer proximity to the city center and its Jewish residents
had a closer contact with Muslim areas of the city. Unlike Jews of Mahlleh--
Juybareh--Dardashti Jews could not converse in the Judæo-Persian language. A
family that comes from the Dardasht area often has "Dardashti" as it's last name to
characterize where you came from. (from Wikipedia)

there for the rest of his life. Even though he and his family lived in Juybareh, they continued to speak the dialect of Dardasht. The Jews of Juybareh looked upon my grandfather's family, the family of Avraham, as outsiders because of the similarity of their dialect to that of the Muslims.

We, the children of this family, were treated with prejudice and were considered to be lower class Jews. I remember at the age of eight when I was going to Alliance Israelite Universelle[6]

Kosher Butcher Shop in Juybareh   *Juybareh in 1973*

(AIU), I was the subject of ridicule and abuse of other Jewish schoolboys. We were considered outsiders and looked upon as not their equal. However, we had some very good friends amongst them. Even after sixty years, when I meet with the surviving ones, the old feelings are still there and we feel that we have been near one another always.

The other Jewish ghetto that I mentioned before, Golbahar is in two sections, located in the heart of the Bazaar not too far

---

[6] The AIU was established by wealthy French Jews in 1860 as a means to provide western education to poverty stricken Jews in Islamic countries in North Africa and the Middle East. The goal was for these educated Sephardic Jews to improve their lives and livelihoods by means of using their education. However it was not until 1898 that the Qajar monarch of Iran permitted the AIU establish schools in Iran for the Jewish community. In total between 1898 and 1929, 11 boys and girls schools were set up throughout Iran in the following cities; Tehran, Hamedan, Esfahan, Sanandaj, Shiraz, Nahavand, Kermanshah, Bijar, Bourjerd, Yazd, and Kashan

from the others. I visited these ghettos a few times in my
childhood, and from what I remember these areas were the
poorest places on earth and the inhabitants were the most
unfortunate and forgotten Jews of Esfahan. The homes these
people lived in resembled sheep stoles or pre-historic
cavemen's dens. The homes were at the end of a very dark,
filthy and narrow alleyway. They were always dusty with
cobwebs and lacked any means of sanitation.

Overall, one cannot say that the Esfahani Jews had even a
poor man's life. These people as of sixty or seventy years ago
had no access to education, arts or trades. The Iranian Muslims,
who were and are the majority, considered the Jews strangers
and foreigners and were always suspicious of them and looked
at them with vengeance. They did not allow this minority, the
Jews, to work in any governmental or other meaningful jobs.
They obstructed all roads to any successful path that could lead
to the betterment of their Jewish lives. There were only two or
three jobs available to them for a meager existence for
themselves and their families. The first was garbage collection
or collection of human excrement, which was the lowest,
dirtiest and most unspeakable job. The second job was spinning
yarn, and the last one was selling bolts of fabric (cloth) to
farmers in remote villages. Very seldom did the Jews have other
jobs. Farming and tending cattle or sheep were out of the
question, especially for the Esfahani Jews. A very small group
of them dabbled in gold and silver jewelry. In Esfahan there
were no Jewish doctors. After the Alliance Society opened a
relatively modern school in Esfahan and the Jewish children
were exposed to education, little by little there were
shoemakers, carpenters and tailors and they began working in
the Jewish community. At the beginning of this century, when
Alliance School (AIU) opened, the graduates of this school that
had the command of Farsi and French were able to secure some
jobs in the Department of Customs. Little by little, Alliance
School (AIU) became famous to the point that the affluent

Muslims had their children attend this school. Some of these Muslim students became merchants, bankers, and members of parliament and even members of the king's court.

My oldest brother, Aziz (عزیز), was one of these students. His command of Farsi was excellent, and he could speak French somewhat fluently and he knew enough French to write and correspond. I myself was a student at this school until I was 12 years old, and I also learned some French. The foundation of my education was established in this school. Because my grandfather was raised in Dardasht, my whole family was known as Dardashti.

CHAPTER **2**

Avraham (אברהם) Dardashti's (اورام دردشتی) Family

My grandfather was Avraham (or Abraham), and he was known as Mullah[7] (Rabbi) Avraham Dardashti, eldest son of a man by the name of Moshe (موشه). Avraham had two brothers and four sisters. Their names were Shelemo (شلمو), Ishagh (اسحق), Ester (استر), Khanum (خانم), Sara (سارا) and Sarah (سارح). Grandfather left home and began working after reaching puberty. He also left Dardasht and resided in Juybareh, where the majority of Esfahani Jews lived. There he married a girl named Sara from a relatively poor family. They had two sons and one daughter, by the names of Yaghub (يعقوب Jacob), Yahuda (يهودا) and Zilfa (زيلفا). After some time he divorced her for reasons that I will write about later. Shortly after, he married a very modest and virtuous woman, Miriam (ميريام). From this wife he had five sons and one daughter who died in childhood. The sons' names were Yeshaia (يشعيا), Yaeir (يائير), Yehanan (يحانان), Shimon (شمعون) and Khodadad (خداداد).

My grandfather bought a relatively large parcel of land in the middle of Juybareh ghetto. He built two homes on a portion of it and sold the remaining parcels to other Jews.

The purchase of this land from a group of Muslims in the Jewish ghettos created hardship for my grandfather. The trouble was so complex and dangerous that he almost lost his life. This is how my grandmother recollected and explained how the

---

[7] The title has also been used in some Sephardic Jewish communities for a Rabbi.

problem began. When I was 10 or 12 years old, I would finish
my homework, and when I had some spare time I would go to

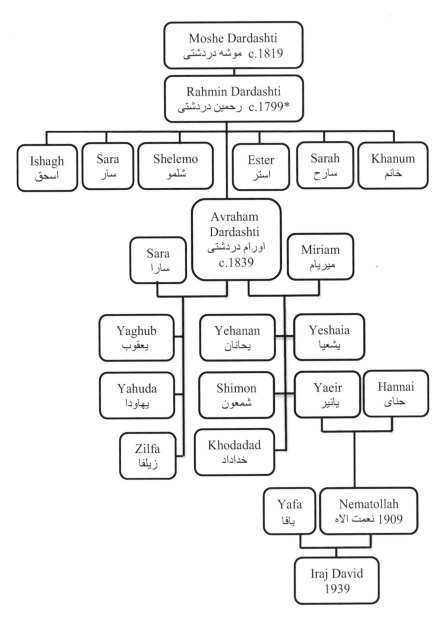

*Birth Year

my grandmother and would ask her to recite stories from the past. She would put my head in her lap, caress me tenderly and then she began telling me stories of her life. She was so interesting and sweet that I would fall asleep in her lap.

My grandmother explained that after my grandfather paid for the land, a group of Muslims protested to the local mullah and requested a Fatwa (فتوی, judicial decree) that this piece of land was Takieh[8] (تکیه) of Muslims and that the parcel of land should not have been sold, especially to a Jew who is Nejes (نجس, unclean or impure, a demeaning title given to Jews) an unbeliever and the sale of this type of property is unlawful according to the Sharia[9] (شرعیات, book of Muslim laws). After the judicial decree and the mullah's document reached the Muslim populace, there was no power on earth to get the land back. However, the only one that could reverse the decree was the King of Iran.

My grandfather was not one to easily forgo his legal right and forget about property that was legally his. He was a wise, brave and educated man, and very persistent. After his exhaustive appeal to all local officials for justice, and after he realized that no one had the power to help him, he decided to

---

[8] Takieh is a square where in ancient times people would hold a religious play and reenact the Karbala incident. Karbala incident was a war that happened between Hussein, the grandchild of Prophet Mohammed, one of the 12 Shiite disciples, and Yazid bin Moavieh. The battle happened at Karbala where Hussein lost his life. I myself had seen these plays that were similar to a Hollywood film. The Muslims consider this sacred ground.

[9] Sharia is the moral code and religious law of Islam. Sharia deals with many topics addressed by secular law, including crime, politics, and economics, as well as personal matters such as sexual intercourse, hygiene, diet, prayer, and fasting. Though interpretations of sharia vary between cultures, in its strictest definition it is considered the infallible law of God— as opposed to the human interpretation of the laws (fiqh).
There are two primary sources of sharia law: the precepts set forth in the Quran, and the example set by the Islamic prophet Muhammad in the Sunnah. Where it has official status, sharia is interpreted by Islamic judges (qadis) with varying responsibilities for the religious leaders (imams). (from Wikipedia)

 travel to Tehran and personally explain the situation to the king, Mohammad Ali Shah. Mohammad Ali's father, Mozzafar-al-Din Shah, ratified a new constitution but in 1907 Mohammad Ali dissolved Majles (Iranian parliament/National assembly) claiming it was contrary to Islamic law. In July 1909, pro-Constitution forces marched from Iran's province of Azerbaijan to Tehran led by Sattar Khan, Bagher Khan and Yeprem Khan, deposed the Shah, and re-established the constitution. On 16 July 1909, the Majles voted to place Mohammad Ali Shah's 11 year old son, Ahmad Shah on the throne. Mohammad Ali fled to Odessa, Russia (present day Ukraine). He finally died in San Remo, Italy in April 1929.

Upon hearing of his impending journey, all his friends tried to point out to him the awesome and dangerous task he was about to embark on and tried to change his mind. They also tried to advise him that this bold gesture could possibly have him killed on the way to Tehran and that he may have to stay there for a lengthy time without any result. Nevertheless, he was determined and he began his journey to Tehran.

Back in the day this journey was not like today, easy and quick. One had to have enough supplies for a month of travel in the desert. The journey was with donkeys and horses in a caravan or in a four-wheel mail buggy. He quickly collected some supplies for a journey to Tehran along with the four-wheel mail buggy. After 18 days on the road, he arrived in Tehran. On the 19th day he arrived at the house of an old friend, and he stayed there. The next day he prepared himself for an audience with the king. After two months and overcoming many obstacles and paying numerous bribes, he received permission to have an audience with the king. My grandfather was full of confidence, unafraid and an astute Jew. He presented himself at the designated time for his audience with king. He was led into the palace to the king's court. The king had expected a foul and poorly groomed Jew; instead, he found a distinguished, courageous and cultured grandfather.

Mullah Avraham (as he had introduced himself) took a splendid bow. He spoke very calmly, clearly and with amiable words explained his situation in detail. The king, who by now was taken by this man's charming encounter, asked him, "Where were you educated and under which mullah were you trained?" He replied, "I went to Maktab[10] (مکتب, an old-fashioned grammar school) for a few years and then a Jewish rabbi taught me for a few years. There I learned some Hebrew so I can read the Torah. Other than that I have taught and educated myself because of my burning desire for knowledge, as your majesty has noticed." The king calmly and affectionately told him that he would clear up the problem, and he should go and, receive his request from the minister of the king's court.

Grandfather left the palace after thanking the king. The next day he received a package addressed to the local governor in Esfahan. He left Tehran ecstatic and on his return to Esfahan, he presented the documents to the local governor. Upon reading the king's decree, the governor ordered the people who occupied the land to his office and had them vow that there would not be any other problem for Mullah Avraham. The king stated to them that they would be severely punished if anyone disturbed Mullah Avraham.

Mullah Avraham accepted his triumph of receiving his lawful justice with dignity, and the Esfahani Jews realized that they had a very prominent man amongst them. Thereafter, many of the Jews looked upon grandfather as being heroic and grandfather's enemies begrudgingly respected him.

Avraham Dardashti divided the land and sold a portion of it to Jews because they were not allowed to buy land, and that is why they were always in such constricted quarters. The two

---

[10] Islamic world, an elementary school was known as a *Maktab*, which dates back to at least the 10th century.

houses that grandfather had built were on a portion of this land. He also gave a portion of this land to his son-in-law, the husband of Zilfa. Zilfa's husband also built a house next to his father-in-law. I remember one could hear people speaking in Aunt Zilfa's (Doda Zilfa's) house and vice-versa. Other children and I played on top of the flat roofs of our home and Aunt Zilfa's.

As it was explained before, my grandfather had seven sons and one daughter. The two oldest sons, Yaghub and Yahuda, and Zilfa were from his first wife, Sara, and the other five sons, Yeshaia, Yaeir, Yehanan, Shimon, and Khodadad, were from his second wife, Miriam. Grandfather gave one house to Yaghub and another to Yahuda for as long as they were living. He, his wife and five sons lived in the other house, which was much more substantial. This house had enough bedrooms, closets, basements, secret rooms and interyards that could house grandfather and grandmother separately from their sons and their families. When I say separate quarters I do not mean each had an apartment. Each had one bedroom, one walk-in closet and one room in the basement. In this house there were two so-called kitchens. Everyone shared the larger kitchen and one family used the small kitchen. Yeshaia, my oldest uncle, moved out in his youth and sold his share of the house to his brothers and in return received cash from my grandfather. He bought a dilapidated old house in another famous neighborhood called Sangbast (سنگ بست) , where he had finished and remodeled half of the house, and he lived there with his family. My youngest uncle, Khodadad, also left after he finished his schooling at Alliance School (AIU) and moved out of town. After my grandfather died, my grandmother lived in one room, and the three sons and their families shared the rest of the house, where they all lived comfortably.

My grandmother, Miriam, to the extent that I knew her, was a very kind, loving and easygoing elderly woman who got along with her daughter-in-laws very well and treated them with kindness. She lived by herself, simply and modestly. When I was four or five years old and I had begun to comprehend my surroundings, I would approach my grandmother in her room or on her small porch and ask if she had a free moment for her to tell me stories about the past. I enjoyed these stories very much. She was a very sweet and loving woman. She first hugged me and showered me with kisses and then she would say, "All right, come and sit in my lap so I may tell you a story." This went on for several years, and this is the source of my knowledge contained in this family history. This ended when fate turned its back to this woman and her first son, Yeshaia, died in his youth. Not long after, her second son Yaeir, who was my father, died. These deaths were great blows to her spirit and robbed her of her energy and her inner peace, and she had no desire or time to continue her interesting stories.

Grandmother managed to get by with matchmaking and peddling to low and middle income Esfahani Muslims. She continued doing this as long as she was physically able. After the death of her two sons, she became completely disabled and homebound. Her sons financially supported her, buying her clothes and other necessities, and she resided with each son for a while. She put up with this for years until her son Khodadad returned to Esfahan after living many years in Khuzestan[11] (خوزستان).   She lived with him until he was married. The marriage of Uncle Khodadad and the future of grandmother will be explained later.

---

[11] Khuzestan is located in SW Iran, bordering on Iraq in the west and the Persian Gulf in the south.

CHAPTER **3**

The Lives and Social Standing of Iranian Jews in the Early Twentieth Century

Iranian Jews were an insignificant and weak minority and lived amongst the Muslim majority in most of the Iranian cities. Wherever the Jews lived, they relegated themselves to one area. Very seldom did any Jew venture to live outside the Jewish ghettos. The reason was that they were always uncertain and fearful of their future, because fanatical religious Muslim mullahs would attack and would often massacre a great number of Jews. For this reason, the Jews tried to be in one area to help one another in case of a threat of an attack.

I should remind you that the Jews built their homes at the end of narrow and covered alleyways. The ceilings of these alleys were very low and dark. This was so enemies on horseback and mobs could not attack, raid and kill the occupants of the homes. The doors of homes were always closed and had very heavy steel locks and latches.

The majority of Iranian Jews lived in Tehran, Esfahan, Shiraz, Hamedan, Yazd, and Kerman. Tehran had the vast majority of Jews and Esfahan had the second-largest population. The Esfahani Jews were destitute because, as was mentioned before, they had no access to any education or trades and had poor knowledge of Farsi. There was a small group of Esfahani Jews who managed to open a dialogue to foreign lands and had some transactions with outsiders and expertise of jewelry. They were relatively well off. Other than this small group, the rest were the poorest of poor and merely just existed.

The Jews always tried to save some of their meager income for fear of their uncertain future and not having anyone to lean on or depend on. After fifty or sixty years, I still shudder when I think back to those dark days of some of my relatives. I remember behind my maternal grandfather's house, there was a broken-down shack that its occupants called this place their home. This home had two archaic rooms made of mud with no door. This so-called home was similar to a hole in the ground; in the center of it there were a few old tin cans, a few broken clay pots, piles of paper and cardboard, and finally a pile of dirty rubble. Inside the two rooms in one corner there was cow dung and horse manure, and in other corners there were torn papers and other similar things. In the center of one of these rooms was a pile of old pieces of clothes and a torn-up filthy old comforter and this was the bed that the occupants slept in. In the morning, to leave this hellhole, one would pass through a very

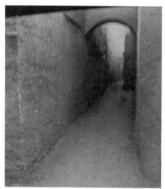

long narrow and dark alleyway, where the owner of this home had dug a hole that the occupants used as their bathroom. If anyone in broad daylight would walk through and was not familiar with this hellhole, he would fall into this hole without a doubt and would be covered all over with human excrement. One day

Daloon (دالون, narrow ally way) when I tried to fetch my soccer ball that had fallen over the roof in this yard, I met the same fate and fell in the hole. I had to disrobe completely and take a bath. Perhaps no one would believe that this hellhole for years had accumulated cobwebs and termites and there was no one to care for the occupants and their cleanliness.

I knew these people very well; they had a daughter by the name of Tuti (طوطی) who had two brothers, one named Shemuel (شموئیلی, nicknamed Shamehii) and the other named Haii (حائی) whose job was collecting human manure and rubbish. He also sold live chickens at times. Shamehii had no real job; he worked at odd jobs from porter to street vendor, and at times gambled. These three had given up on getting married.

Tuti worked in the Jewish Women's Public Bath washing women for her income. She was not pretty; instead, she was very kind and had a pleasant disposition. All the ladies liked her, and she was invited to people's homes.

Iranian Jews were so poor and destitute that there were many families such as this family. Yazd probably had the poorest Jews in Iran and most of them lived like that. Even though these people were destitute, they never lost their faith, and eventually became independent and established their own country and willingly gave their lives for its safety. The Jews that were born after these dark years and were freed from these misfortunes and toils are obligated to read their ancestors' story and to learn a lesson so they do not lose their freedom again.

CHAPTER **4**

Avraham Dardashti's Family Traits and His Family

Everyone in Avraham Dardashti's family, man or woman, was highly respected, kindhearted and intelligent. Their behavior was completely different from that of other Esfahani Jews. Anyone who had any association with them admired the intelligence and wisdom of these brothers and sisters. Friend and foe accepted the bravery, fearlessness and distinguished work of the members of this family. I myself had overheard people praising them for unusual and heroic deeds. My great grandfather Moshe had six sons and daughters. His father's name was Rahmin (رحمین), and he was known as Moshe Rahmini (my great-great-grandfather).

After his father, my grandfather literally ruled the rest of the brothers and sisters and they accepted and respected him in that position. They carried out his orders without question because they had faith in his knowledge and wisdom. It was customary for younger sisters and brothers to call the elder brother "Aghachi" (آقاچی small sir). Unfortunately, I do not know the order of my grandfather's siblings. Shelemo (شلمو), one of grandfather's brothers, became blind and passed away when I was seven or eight years old. Unfortunately I never met him. Ishagh (اسحق), another brother of my grandfather, was alive until I was in my early twenties. He visited us frequently and I enjoyed listening to his interesting stories.

Grandfather's sisters were as follows, Sara, who was Nissan's mother, the husband of my sister Sinoor (صینور), Sarah, was the next younger sister who was Mordekha-Metat's (مردخامتا ت) mother who was uncle Yahuda's son-in-law, the last sister was Khanum who was Zelkha's (زلخا – زلیخا, Zelikha) mother who was Uncle Yaghub's wife.

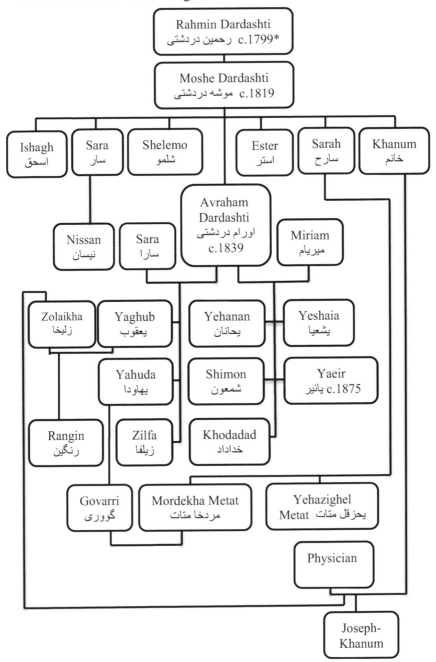

*Birth Year

It has been told that Shelemo, my grandfather's brother, had a young and handsome son who became ill and died. This young man's name was Shalom, and everyone called him Shalomi (شالومی). His mother nearly went mad because of her son's death and gradually people called this ill-fated mother by the name of the son, Shalomi. The father also grieved his son's death and wept so much that he eventually went blind and became confined to his home.

Khanum, the youngest sister, was married off to a Jewish physician from Khonsar (خونسار), one of the villages near Arak that is famous for pleasant weather and a resort for summer vacation and relaxation. My family and I vacationed there several times and enjoyed the wonderful fresh air. She left Esfahan at age thirteen or fourteen to marry the doctor. She was away from her family for many years and no one had any news of her until (as my grandmother explained) one day a young farmer boy appeared at the door of my grandfather. He was dressed in a torn and weathered farmer's robe, baggy and dusty pants full of patches and a pair of Giveh (گیوه, sandal or summer shoes) shoes. He had an exceptionally tanned face with tangled and uncombed hair. My grandmother was surprised and puzzled who this farmer boy might be and asked him who he was and what was he doing there. He explained that he was Khanum's son, and his mother had sent him because his father had died and his mother was widowed and destitute. Being poor forced his mother to send her son on foot to her brothers to ask for their help.

Upon grandfather returning home that evening and hearing of his sister's story, grandfather summoned his younger brother, Ishagh (اسحق), and ordered him to go and bring his sister Khanum (خانم) and her family to Esfahan. Grandfather found a home for her and her family and took care of their expenses. This farmer boy was sent to school and he became a scholar of the Farsi language because he was very intelligent and learned. This was unusual because this type of education was hardly available to Jews. Later this farmer boy came in contact with English Christian missionaries and converted to Christianity. I remember this man well; he was an uncle our family used to call Joseph-Khanum, who had joined the missionaries and became a very serious spokesman for the church. He had rented a small storefront in the middle of Juybareh ghetto and had furnished the storefront with very dignified wall-to-wall bookshelves full of Christian and religious books. He was always sitting behind the desk reading or discussing with patrons about religious subjects. A few times when I had a chance I watched him with reason trying to debate a point with someone. He sounded very wise, respectful and knowledgeable.

I observed that people who were passing by looked at him with jealousy and contempt while quietly cursing the owner of the store. The Jews disliked other Jews who had a good knowledge of English and had any dealing with the missionaries, especially Mr. Garland, the renowned Christian priest, and they tried to shun him. For the same reasons, most Jews did not like my grandfather and they considered him almost a backsliding atheist. The Jews had heard that at times grandfather visited Mr. Garland. Unfortunately, the common and uneducated Jews of that time had no comprehension of countless problems and could not appreciate and value of knowledgeable and wise people.

Grandfather, unlike others, always sought out accomplished people. He had opened a dialogue with this knowledgeable man of God without fear of what others might say or think. Grandfather knew that this man was from an aristocratic and wealthy family in England, and that this noble man had given up the comforts and riches of this world in his youth to dedicate his life for service to God and his fellow man. He had left behind all that attention, security and love in England.

Grandfather knew that this man had departed one of the most civilized countries of the time to come to Esfahan and reside in the most dreadful areas to help and direct to God, day or night, these extreme fanatical people who had no real idea of God. He totally had immersed himself in his faith and spiritual pleasures. This man, who had come to Esfahan in his youth and resided until his mid-eighties, spent all the riches from England and any other money he could acquire, to help others and pursue his faith with sincerity and purest intentions, and he passed away to the heavens in Esfahan in the English Hospital.

One of the people who were present at his deathbed told me of the night that the infamous Khadijeh (خديجه) that came and spent quite a long time at this great man's bedside. Khadijeh was a forty five year old red faced, plump woman who had breached Garland's inner group and pretended that she was accepting Christ. She was illiterate, common and worshipped money and that was why naive and trustworthy Garland was deceived and with various concocted reasons money was pilfered from him. This woman had a daughter who also had a red face, was big boned, tall and somewhat plump with black hair. She was somewhat attractive. She had her face covered with layers of powder, rouge, and beauty creams. She, similar to her mother, had acquired the art of extracting money from this English man. She would participate in prayers and sermons and would not leave until she received some money. These two women had demonstrated so much interest in Mr. Garland that some people wrongly accused him of having a sexual relationship with them. This was completely false and unfounded. Mr. Garland was totally celibate and had no interest in sex. Perhaps, he was not capable of this feeling. This dying man, who was unconscious, came to and saw Khadijeh at his bedside. He looked at her and said, "I tried very hard to guide you to a path of righteousness; however, I failed. I know you have not come to see me; you are here to obtain money from me, very well." He reached under his bed and took out a small bag of money and stretched his arm toward her and said, "I will give you my last bit of wealth. But try to accept God and realize that God is worth much more and better than worldly wealth."

He said this and calmly, as if going into a deep sleep, went to his savior in the heavenly kingdom according to his belief. The person that was telling me this said, "I and the others that were at the bedside were lost in the moment, we were absorbed in what happened in front of us. A holy man fell asleep and everyone fell into a trance and no one made a sound."

Joseph-Khanum had a home in an alley in Juybareh that had rooms on three sides and all of his family lived there. However, his elderly mother did not live with him because she did not get along with Joseph-Khanum's wife. He had left her at one of the rooms at Garland's school. I was at this school until I was 8 or 9 years old. I remember well, Khanum, my grandfather's sister, who was by now quite elderly, at times would call me to her and after doting on me would give me a few shahi (equivalent to a few pennies) and ask me to buy her some cheese. She was very particular about her favorite cheese and at times she would send me back to change the cheese. She would always say, "Make sure the cheese is like a honeycomb with many holes."

I never saw the second sister, Sarah, who had two sons, Mordekha and Yehazighel (يحزقل). I was more familiar with Mordekha because he was married to a daughter of my Uncle Yahuda, and in the latter years he and I were good friends. These two brothers were known for their intellect. I never will forget when Mordekha Metat (موردخا متات) was telling me, "Nemat, I am so unfortunate that if I take a gold lira or a gold English pound which are the most dear coins in the Bazaar to sell, even lower than the market price, everyone who knows me will right away question and become suspicious and wonder if there is something wrong. They will ask why a smart and knowledgeable Hajj (حاج, a person who has made a pilgrimage to Jerusalem or Mecca) Morad (his nickname) is trying to sell a gold lira and they hesitate buying my coins. No matter how much I plead to people that I need money and that is the only reason that I am selling these coins, no one would believe me."

He told me, "Nemat, now you can see how intelligence and knowledge can cause a headache and create problems for me." Hajj Morad Metat was profound. He was a smart and skilled world traveler, a very interesting and gifted speaker. Whenever one began listening to his stories one could not stop because it was so pleasurable and addictive. He was a riveting, eloquent and thought-provoking orator who captured your attention with sideline stories and examples and would keep you guessing at where he was leading you.

He was our neighbor in Esfahan, and one summer afternoon my mother and I went to his house. Hajj Morad was on his mahtabi (a balcony used for watching the moon) on the second floor, sitting on a small mattress on a carpet with a pillow behind him. In front of him he had a samovar that was old, it looked as if for some time no one had washed or polished it and one could hear water boiling. Next to a pile of red charcoal in a manghal (a grill-like container with two inches of ashes and red hot charcoal atop it) there was an old and mended ghoori (tea pot) full of the best Darjeeling tea. As soon as Hajj Morad saw us he became jubilant and said, "Hannai (حناى, my mother's nickname), welcome," come and sit down and let's talk. My mother sat near him on the small mattress. He called for his wife, saying, "Hannai is here." "Govarri (گوورى, our cousin and Hajj Morad's wife), bring the Kaleh Ghand[12] (قند) Hannai is here." It appeared that this was an extraordinary event that had made him so happy and he was relaying this good news to his wife.

In any case we sat down and Govarri brought a whole ghand with a ghand hammer and placed them on top of a cloth napkin in front of Hajj Morad to break up the ghand. Then with pleasure and laughter he directed his attention to my mother, saying "Hannai, what gives us the pleasure of your company and brings you to us?" My mother in return said, "I have missed

---

[12]Kaleh Ghand is a Sugar Cone wrapped in a decorative sheet. It is a perfect gift for any occasion but it is widely used in Persian Weddings. (from kalamala.com)

you and I have come to see you." We sat down and Hajj Morad poured us two teacups of the strong and very fine fragrant tea and placed them in front of us with a few pieces of the ghand that he had broken. Then as he was breaking the rest of the ghand he began talking. He mostly spoke of current news and subjects and made us fall in love with his gift of gab. For example, he told us about what happened during World War II and how he got out of a dilemma by trickery. It would be interesting for you to know about this world traveler's ruse and cunning politics.

Nemat's mother, Hanna (nicknamed Hannai, حناى)

Hajj Morad was saying, "During the World War II, Iran in reality was under the control of allied countries. Secretly, Iran had to do what the allies demanded. Because of this and a great need for grain, the allies had forced the Iranian government to pass a law that Iranians must report to the government any storage of grain or flour. Violators would be jailed and their products would be confiscated and subject to a cash fine." Hajj Morad continued, "I had stored a lot of wheat for a long time and I was very afraid because it was not in my interest to report to the government that I had this great amount of wheat in the silos. The government would pay only one-tenth of the black market prices. This subject completely occupied my thoughts for a few months and even though I secretly sold some of the wheat, I still had a lot more in storage.

Now it was the time for harvesting and transporting to the market their products. Most of the farmers and farm owners were busy gathering the new crop and storing it. One day in the middle of all of this, a Department of Treasury official asked me to go to their office. I went to the Department of Treasury and met with a very gruff and frightful agent. I was told, 'News has come to our attention that you, Hajj Morad, have been storing wheat for some years and you have violated the laws and you have ignored the many repeated general announcements about reporting your total wheat storage, and you have hidden away the staple that hungry people need in storage to sell in the black market and reap huge profits. If this happens to be true, God help you!' "

Hajj Morad continued, "When I heard this, my heart leapt in my mouth and I knew that my fears of the last few months were coming true. However, even though I was very frightened, I kept my composure and I calmly replied, 'No, sir, the news that you have heard is not true and is nothing but a bunch of lies. I have some new crop and I am waiting until all the crop is collected at which time I am going to report promptly to the government and I urge you to send agents to inspect the wheat crop.' " Hajj Morad was saying, "When I entered this office I recognized the man behind the desk and I knew that I was dealing with a very tough, scrupulous and uncompassionate man. I knew his name and I even knew his parents but I did not think it was to my benefit to let him know that. After our discussion ended and after we set up a time for the next day for inspection and verification of the new crop, the time came for me to leave. But I did not leave, I sat there and told the man, 'Excuse me, may I tell you something before I leave?' After receiving permission, I said, 'Your Excellency, do you know Mr. Taghikhan Mostavafi Olmamalek (تقی خان موستوفی الممالک), the son of God bless his gracious soul Hajj so and so of so and so dynasty?' He was the father of this man, but I acted ignorant of that; I was trying to show that I did not know him. The agent bought my story, that I did not know him and acted ignorant of that himself and said, 'No, I don't know him, what is the connection?' I told him, 'This man, Mr. Taghikhan (تقی خان), was a God-fearing religious and very conscientious person who was from a very respectable and prominent family. He always was very concerned about other people's welfare and he tried to help people out of a jam. I never met this man's son and I don't know what kind of a man he is, but the father, God bless his soul, I knew him and for years I had dealings with him and often he helped and freed me from a few precarious situations. God be with him, he was such a wonderful man. I am sure that his son, that I have heard is in high places, is also walking in his father's footsteps and is doing the same good work in helping people.' I told him 'how nice it would be if the son could be here right now so he may put in a few good words for me with your Excellency. Who knows, you are probably no less than him. I wished this was so and you were as nice and charitable.' With these praises the agent's faced changed and like a blossom opened up and he became delighted and jovial and with a smile said, 'Hajj Morad, be assured I promise you I will not be a bad man.' With these words, he sent me away."

Hajj Morad continued, "I well prepared this man of authority and had him ready for cooperation and left the office and waited impatiently for the next day. They told me whom they were going to send for the inspection and I knew him and I knew how to deal with him."

"The next day, a short time before noon, someone knocked on the door at my home and I went to see who was at the door. When I opened the door I found the inspector in front of me. Even though I knew him, I pretended that I did not know him and asked him who are you and what do you want from this humble man (meaning himself, Hajj Morad). The inspector replied to me, 'Hajj Morad, you know me well and you know

what I do for a living.' I immediately told him I am sorry but I
do not remember you. The inspector, surprisingly, looked at me
and said, 'I am the person who is supposed to inspect the wheat
crop.' I still acted like I did not know him and no, you are not
that person, I know that man. He is a very nice, kind,
respectable and God-fearing person. I do not allow anyone else
other than him to inspect my wheat. He kept insisting and I kept
denying that he is the same man until many assurances and
swearing to God I reluctantly with a skeptical look allowed him
in. The inspector who was pumped up with my repeated and
redundant praises and he had come to believe them entered the
wheat storage and after grabbing a handful of wheat in his fist
and looking at it said, 'Hajj Morad, you are right, this wheat is
this year's crop. The report is false and unjustly accused you,
created a headache for you and slandered your name.'

"The distracted inspector took his pen and paper out and
wrote a verification note that the stored wheat is a recent crop
and gave it to me to put my mind at ease. On the way out I
slipped a 10 tumon bill (Iranian currency, approximately $1.50
which is equal to a week's pay) in his pocket and let him out
with a sigh of relief." Years later I realized that Hajj Morad
prevented months of jail time and a hefty fine for storing and
selling wheat illegally with his wise and clever disposition.

When I was a very young child my father was bankrupt and
he fled Esfahan to Khorramshahr to collect some of the lost
investment to pay off several of the big creditors in Esfahan.
During this time, Hajj Morad Metat was a great help to my
mother to ward off the harassing creditors. His experience and
shrewdness calmed them and convinced them not to take legal
action against my mother so it would give my father a chance to
send her some money. I remember often, late in the evening
when Hajj Morad was coming home from his office tired and
exhausted, my mother was waiting anxiously at his house
asking for guidance and help--one should always appreciate the
good deeds of others because it is connected to God's mercy. In

return Hajj Morad was explaining at one time he was persuaded to go to Khuzestan to rescue his investment from a few clever and angry partners and he was frustrated and helpless. In

Haiem Hanna & his two sons Shokri & Rabie

Khuzestan he asked my brother for help. My brother, who knew of the help he had given to my mother, offered his assistance with pleasure and tried very hard to recover his money and returned Hajj Morad happily back to Esfahan. Another time my brother gave invaluable help to him that I will write about in detail later.

Sara, the other sister of grandfather, was the wife of a man called Haim-e-Hena and she had five sons by him. The youngest, Nissan, married my sister Sinoor. In my opinion Nissan was not motivated to work hard and had very poor personal and business judgment. He kept producing children he could not provide for. My sister was continually impoverished and her children had hardly any food to eat. Sinoor was a very proud, brave and kind woman who valued her family's reputation and respect. When her husband was out of work and unable to provide for his family of eleven, my brave and proud sister never asked for handouts or help. Unbeknownst to us brothers and sisters, we were not aware of the depth of her desperate situation. Rather she bore the responsibility patiently and accepted her misfortunes and worked very hard with many sleepless nights to earn a portion of their expenses. She also tried to teach her sons hard work and make them labor in odd jobs until the boys grew up and saved the family from devastation. My sister's situation and worrying about her and her family spoiled and ruined a portion of my life.

Musa, a relative, himself has an interesting story and maybe I should write about him as much as my memory allows. Before Musa was married, until the age of 30, he was a peddler of bolts of fabric and covered many areas in Esfahan. This was mostly the profession of Esfahani Jews. Because of the nature of this profession, most of the interactions of these peddlers were with housewives, Jew or Muslim, and they had very little contact with men. Some of these peddlers had created intimate relations with a few of the female customers. Musa, who was going through puberty and was single and unattached during this time, had also started an intimate relationship with a Muslim female customer. One day on a routine visit to this Muslim woman, maybe even in the couple's bed, he was caught in the act by the woman's husband, a devout Muslim man. The husband found his wife with a strange man in his bed in a dark room and to make matters even worse, the strange man happened to be a Jew. Musa managed to get his clothes on and vacate the house before this man had a chance to put a hand on him. But on the way out, because of the man's cries for help, he was subdued by other Muslim men in the street. Soon after, a crowd gathered and they decided to kill Musa. However, in the crowd someone who was a friend of Musa's father recognized him and realized the situation was very grave. The only thing he could do was to run to the middle of the crowd and say "We should not commit this murder and get our hands bloody, we should follow the laws of the Koran, Sharia and our religion and we should get a Fatwa (فتوى, a judicial decree) and official permission from a mojtahed (مجتهد, a clergyman competent to practice divine science or religious jurisprudence) and an elder of our religion. Then we can punish this man who has committed this obscene act."

This reasoning made good enough sense to most, and it calmed down the angry crowd. The unfortunate Musa was taken to the local mojtahed after a good beating, bloody and barefooted, who heard of the shameful and ugly sinful deeds of Musa and asked for an immediate decree of death. The mullah was a wise man and knew that he could not sentence anyone to death without reporting to government officials and having a formal trial and he knew that he would have to answer for his actions to authorities later. He stepped in the middle of the crowd and said "Give me this filthy Jew who should be hanged, and after he is convicted according to Sharia, I and other religious leaders will declare his death sentence and will give him back to you to punish him. Leave him to me and get out of here before you do something that is not in accordance with the Koran."

After listening to these words from the mojtahed, the crowd left Musa with him and dispersed. The mojtahed ordered Musa to be jailed in a room in his house until he figured out what to do with him. Then he gathered a few of the clergy to get advice. He also contacted the authorities and told them that if he let them take Musa, he would lose face with people and they might kill him. He requested that the government let the mullahs have a trial themselves for Musa. In the meantime, Musa's parents and brothers began trying to find a way to free him. Finally, after a few days of trial and bribing every mullah known to Nissan's parents, they unanimously voted to exercise one of the Koran's and Sharia's laws in order to determine the real guilt or innocence of Musa. It was necessary when a man is atop a woman to pass a string between the two. If the string moves freely between the man and woman, there was no crime and if the string experiences any resistance then a crime was committed. Since no one actually had seen Musa committing adultery, this test was necessary. The test was done and the string moved freely and this proved Musa's innocence; however, since he had seen a Muslim woman naked, he was given a punishment of 100 lashes. Musa was strapped on a board tight and two of the most fanatical Muslims from the crowd were elected to perform the punishment. His mother said, "He was delivered to us still strapped to the board, blood dripping from his wounds and passed out. Even though the family was very sad and heartbroken to see him in that shape, we were all very glad in our hearts that he was not killed and escaped this great danger."

Musa's mother said, "We prepared all kinds of remedies for his wounds. We covered his wounds with egg yolk and other medicines and took him home. After resting for a while and gathering his strength, he got out of bed. "We knew if the Muslims happened to see Musa recovered and well they would not give up until they killed him. Because of this we thought it's best to send him out of Esfahan for a while and we sent him to Tehran."

Musa left Esfahan in the middle of the night and went to Tehran and remained there for some time until his parents sent word all the uproar had settled down and most people had forgotten the incident and he returned to Esfahan.

In those days, a journey was not as simple as it is today. A journey either was made on a donkey or in a buggy that was for transporting mail that also would carry a few passengers. Mail buggies, called a delijan, were pulled by several horses (a coach drawn by two, three, or six horses) and usually these vehicles were reliable and on time and would reach their destination more predictably because the post office had designated areas for a change of horses and repair of delijans. A delijan was also more secure from robbers because the post office was transporting the mail and had the proper protection for each delijan; the driver and his helper were armed and had a couple of armed guards. Even with this, at times one would hear the mail was robbed, and the driver or his helper were killed or ran off.

In reality in those days going on a trip meant putting one's life in harm's way. Most people were aware of road danger, but still journeyed about. Usually to travel with a caravan a distance of 420 kilometers (about 260 miles) would take 20 days and nights and would present many problems. One would travel in the middle of winter only in an emergency or absolute necessity. Summer travel had its own difficulties, such as running out of water and dying from thirst or heat exhaustion. Because of past experiences, people would say, "So and so endured the pain of travel" even though the travel was on a plane and took only a few hours.

Rainfall usually is very scarce in Iran, and because of that most of Iran is a desert and not suitable for farming. Most of the land is covered with rock and pebble without any vegetation. People who travel from Kerman to Yazd or from Yazd to Esfahan or many other areas of Iran know what I am referring to. All that the travelers saw for days was desert, no water and no trees. Because of this, before today's motorized vehicles were available; one had to make extensive preparations to venture on such a journey, especially a lengthy journey.

When I was very young, every spring the Esfahani Jews would make a pilgrimage to the cemetery, about 22 miles away. People would take advantage of this gathering and vacation a few days there and try to enjoy themselves. The cemetery was located in an area that was also a place of pilgrimage for very fanatic and superstitious people.

Hebrew inscription, c. 500 BCE

To go to the cemetery, people prepared themselves days before, and on the way they sometimes stopped for one night even though today it takes approximately half an hour by car.

Legend has it that during Shah Abbas II[13] (1642-1666) the Jews
miraculously were given certain rights. It is alleged that the
shah experienced a miracle inside a cave called Sarah bat Asher
(house of Mama Sarah).

Musa started his journey back to Esfahan and after many
days of hardship he arrived at his home. This time, rather than
returning to being a peddler, he began to trade local goods with
other cities in Iran. He became a respectable merchant; he was
the talk of the town and he was often called "Businessman
Musa". Now that Musa was considered one of the renowned
businessmen, he was looked at and accepted differently.

Cemetery at Mama Sarah

Ishagh Dardashti was another of grandfather's brothers. He
must have been many years younger than grandfather, because
even when I was in my twenties, he was still not too old. He
often visited my older brother Aziz and they had hours of
discussions. He was a medium built person with light colored
hair and a gray beard that he colored with henna. His beard
would turn a shade of dark red whenever he freshly applied

---

[13] During a polo match, Shah Abbas noticed a white fawn and he chased it to a
cave at Lenjan (where Mama Sarah is located). Inside the cave the fawn was
transformed to the ghost of Mama Sarah, who told the Shah "you will die unless you
promise to grant the Iranian Jews many freedoms and land". Shah Abbas was allowed
to leave after giving his promise.

henna, but when his beard was partially gray and partially red you knew that he had not paid any attention to his appearance. His beard was very full and it covered his cheeks all the way to under his chin, and it gave him an interesting look. However, Uncle Ishagh never let his beard get out of hand or get too long. I saw him no more than thirty times during his life, but he never looked any younger or older. He was a very intelligent person and it was interesting to hear him speak. His handsome face and full beard made him distinguished and respectable.

Whenever Uncle Ishagh began speaking, one immediately would recognize that he was experienced, wise and a world traveler. People who came in contact with him would be extremely cautious around this clever man. They were even more careful after they learned that he was the famous Ishagh Dardashti (اسحق دردشتی).

I was lucky to have the pleasure of being able to hear his delightful speeches. He often spoke of how people hesitated to make contact with him because of his intelligence and cleverness and it had brought him nothing but misfortune — people were simply fearful of him. He may have had a point, because he never cashed in any wealth as a result of his intelligence. He was always bitter and often complained about people and this world. He asked God, why with all that wisdom and knowledge he was not blessed with any wealth so he may live the lifestyle that was worthy of him and the way he desired to live.

He always spoke of his bad luck, but his life was not all that bad. Uncle Ishagh was married several times and he had children by every one of his wives. His first wife was Ester(استر) ; Heli (حلی) was the second and the third one was Khorshidi (خورشید, he might have had other wives that I do not know about). He had a daughter by the first wife; she was married to Moshe (موشه) , the son of Hezghia (حزقیا). There was talk that my uncle had a son by a wife who died in childbirth. He had two sons and one daughter from the second wife and three sons and two daughters from the third wife. The husband of Tubai (طوبای), his oldest daughter, went mad after they were married and stayed that way for the remainder of his life.

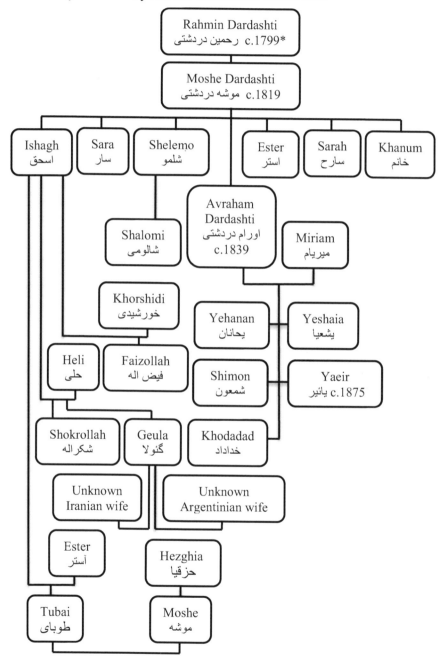

*Birth Year

This man, whose name was Moshe, would walk around
carrying a container full of pens made out of cane, an inkwell
full of the best ink and a few sheets of large paper under one
arm where on some of the sheets the Hebrew word "Sipurah"
(סיפורה ,سیپورا) was beautifully handwritten. This harmless
madman would walk the streets and alleyways with an escort
called Ishaghi who was hired by his wife to watch over him. As
long as he did not cause anyone trouble and no one bothered
him, Ishaghi would follow his master Moshe without any
interference. Moshe always dressed well and very seldom
caused trouble for anyone. Sometimes naughty children would
play tricks on him and mock him; that is when Ishaghi would
intervene and run off the intruders. However, when these
children persisted and continued bothering Moshe, he would run
away from them and wander the streets, finally stopping at
some Jewish home where usually they would know him. After
going into the house he would try to find someone he knew and
politely would greet them and ask them to spread a rug. Usually
no one would create a problem for him because his father was
the wealthiest Jew in Esfahan, and most would try to comfort
him. He would sit on the rug or a small pillow that people
provided him. He then would take out his pen and paper and
write the name Sipurah (סיפורה) in Hebrew. No one knew why
he would write this word.

Early in the 20th century, the charitable organization known
as Alliance Israelite Universal (AIU) started schools in large
cities with high concentrations of Jews. This allowed for the
first time the sons and daughters of Jews to have a chance to
learn Farsi, Hebrew, French or technical skills. One of these
schools was in Esfahan. After a few years, the second person
that was sent to Esfahan was a Jew from Paris, France, who
resided near the school in the center of the Juybareh ghetto with
his wife, called Sipurah. This educated woman was responsible
for the females of the school. She had a light complexion, was
overweight and somewhat pretty. This plump French woman,

clean-cut and without any head covering, was attractive to Moshe, and it was rumored that he was so deeply in love with her that it drove him to madness. Because of this, there was nothing else in his mind other than the memories of this woman Sipurah. Unfortunately, at that time there was no one to diagnose his disease and no medications to alleviate his condition.

Now is a good time to tell you about Moshe's father, Hezghia (called Hezghia-Abba-Yagho حزقیا ابا یاقو, meaning son of Yagho). Hezghia was an illiterate, unskilled person and quite poor; however, he was a very clever and a hardworking man. After working for a jeweler and a gemologist and learning the trade, little by little he entered the jewelry business. Because of his hard work and perseverance he accumulated a small fortune and established his name and a place in the Jewish community and became known as Mr. Hezghia. Mr. Hezghia, was knowledgeable regarding human psychology and knew how to misguide people, he had managed to create a following for himself with simple and naïve people. By the time he reached his forties, his following had grown to a point that a large group of Jews looked to him as a leader and governor of Esfahani Jews.

While trading with foreign countries, especially within Europe, he learned that there are generous people that out of the goodness of their hearts would help needy and unfortunate Jews of other countries in the East like Iran. He also learned that there was a wealthy and generous Jewish man in England that every year would donate a large sum to charities. This money-worshipping and opportunistic man, Hezghia, immediately asked himself why his poor and unfortunate fellow Jews should not benefit from this large monetary sponsor. Therefore, he ordered his English-speaking employee to draft a letter to this man, called Moshe Montfivar, about the misfortunes and difficult conditions of Esfahani Jews. After the letter was prepared, he included an attachment requesting in the event Mr.

Moshe Montfivar wanted to send any funds, it would be better
to send the money to his personal address so he may distribute it
to the needy. Shortly later he received a favorable answer and a
bank draft. No one ever knew the amount, because Hezghia
deposited the draft in his own account rather than giving it to
the people who were supposed to receive it. Some time passed,
and after he was assured that no one knew and had any
objections, he worked on the second payment. This went on for
a long time and no one ever found out how much was funneled
to this greedy man.

Previously I wrote how I enjoyed my dear grandmother's
stories during my childhood and how I often persuaded her to
tell me more about the past. My grandmother said, "My dearest,
this Mr. Hezghia has accumulated all this fortune from Moshe
Montfivar (موشه منتفیور), if not from him where else can Hezghia
make this much money in such a short time?" At that time I was
asking myself who is this Mr. Moshe Montfivar who can afford
making other people well-off. This was a puzzle that I could not
solve. Often I had asked my grandmother who was this man and
she also had no idea and she never had a direct answer for me.
Later I learned that my grandmother's knowledge of this matter
is what she had heard from grandfather. Apparently he knew
more and he had not told grandmother the whole story. Many
years went by, my grandmother and Mr. Hezghia both passed
away and his family was scattered all over. Most of the fortune
was gone and some of the grandchildren and great
grandchildren were poor, almost destitute.

When I was translating the book "My People," the history of
Jews into Farsi, I realized who Moshe Montfivar was, what he
did for a living and after doing some more research I finally
found out that my previous guesses about the situation were not
far from the truth.

Another interesting story that I heard from several sources
was that Mr. Hezghia often would gather some of the Esfahani
Jewish heads of households and have an impromptu session

similar to a political rally. The meeting, however, always turned into honoring and praising him with the hope of winning Mr. Hezghia's favor.

One day when Rahmin Elia (رحمین الیا), father of famous Hajj Elyahu Rahmin, was present at one of these impromptu sessions, someone knocked on the door of Mr. Hezghia's home and informed him that there was a representative from Zell-e Soltan (ظل السطان), son of Nasser-al-Din (ناصرالدین شاه) the Qajar Shah, and handpicked by his father to be the governor of Esfahan, asking for him. Mr. Hezghia immediately ordered that he be let in and led the agent to him. The agent came in showing his respect and said, "Mullah Hezghia (years ago the Muslims called the Jewish leaders Mullah begrudgingly), I have a package from the divine protector" and he gave it to him. Mr. Hezghia took the package and opened it. To his surprise he found the package full of jewels, such as diamonds, jades, sapphires, and other ladies' gold ornaments. He lifted his head with amazement and said, "Well, I see them, what do you want?" The agent said, "His Excellency the divine protector has ordered you to appraise these jewels because he wants to sell them." Hezghia said, "Of course, it would be my utmost pleasure to appraise these jewels, his Excellency Zell-e Soltan[14] could ask for my unworthy life or anything else".

He began examining the jewels by running his hand through them and looking at each piece. In the meantime, he told Rahmin Elia in the local colloquial dialect, the language that the agent could not understand, "Rahmin, why are you just sitting there, 'begnev' (بگنو כגנז) meaning take one of the jewels." Naïve Rahmin, unaware of what Mr. Hezghia was up to, stole

---

[14] He was eldest son of Nasser-al-Din Shah and Efet-od-Dowleh, and the brother of Kamran Mirza Nayeb es-Saltaneh and of Mozzafar-al-Din Mirza (who eventually became Mozzafar-al-Din Shah), but Mass'oud Mirza could not ascend as Shah as his mother was from outside the Qajar dynasty's family group. He was governor of Esfahan from 1872 to 1907 and governor of Fars from 1907 to 1908. Mass'oud Mirza died in Esfahan in 1918. He was buried in Mashhad. He had 14 sons and 11 daughters. (from Wikipedia)

one of the diamonds and hid it in his mouth. Soon after Mr. Hezghia slapped Rahmin hard, clearly and loudly told him, "Rahmin, you miserable man, don't you know whose jewels are these, don't you know that committing a crime against his Excellency Zell-e Soltan, the Shah's agent, bears a great punishment? Don't you know that we should be willing to sacrifice even our lives for Excellency Zell-e Soltan and be willing to offer him all our wealth, much less stealing from him? You despicable man, this crime is punishable by death and what were you thinking, do you think I would allow this crime past me?" Then he reached in Rahmin's mouth and pulled out the diamond and showed it to the agent.

Rahmin was shocked and did not know what to say or do. When the agent saw this happening, he proceeded to handcuff Rahmin to take him in. If this had happened, God help Rahmin, but Mr. Hezghia interceded and said, "No, it is not necessary for you to bother with this, I myself will punish his despicable action," and led the agent away from Rahmin. He said, "It is not necessary for you to speak about this to Excellency Zell-e Soltan". Of course Mr. Hezghia knew that the agent would not pass on this incident and keep quiet.

Finally, Mr. Hezghia appraised the jewels and told the agent, "Please tell Excellency Zell-e Soltan that my appraisal is much higher than they should be and in order to be a service to his Excellency, I am ready to buy them myself, even if I may sell them for a loss." The agent, who was very impressed with the fictitious scene he had witnessed, returned to Zell-e Soltan and told the story back to him with some of his own exaggerations. He added that in his whole life he had never seen anything like it or met anyone more honest, sincere or loyal to the shah's family.

Zell-e Soltan, after some pondering, ordered the agent to "take back the package and tell the Jewish Mullah Hezghia that thereafter he would be under my special attention and take the jewels and pay me what he thought they were worth. Also tell him that thereafter he will be receiving our special blessings."

There were many other stories about this charlatan. In the year of 1296 (1917) about 60 years ago, when there was a great famine in Esfahan and hundreds died of hunger every day, this man sold a great deal of stale, old and almost inedible almonds to hungry people at a very inflated price. My mother bought some of these almonds to supplement the food for her hungry family and I remember how bitter and bad these almonds were, but because we were so hungry we ate them. Later it was said that Mr. Hezghia pocketed a great deal from the governor's jewels and the sale of the stale and rotten almonds.

The only time that I met this charlatan was when the Jews were congregating at his house for a sermon. I remember his yard was full of Jewish men and Nissan, the great mullah, was busy with his sermon. On one side of a patio, on top of very fluffy mattresses and among many pillows there was an overweight, pale, red man in his eighties. Further, I noticed a man with a gray goatee and a bald head with just a few gray hairs. His very pale and red face was quite plump and he had stretched his legs on the mattresses and he could not cross his legs because he was overweight. It was also apparent that he had a very difficult time breathing. A few days later I heard that he had died.

Mr. Hezghia had two sons, Ydidia and Moshe. The younger son, Moshe, was Tubai's husband, the man who became mad and had nothing to do with his father's wealth. After the death of Mr. Hezghia, all the wealth that remained was in the care of Ydidia, the oldest son, who was managing his father's businesses during his father's living years. According to her departed husband's power of attorney, Tubai claimed her husband's inheritance for herself and her children. One day Ishagh Dardashti told my brother that Ydidia hesitated to reveal the amount of the inheritance. Other than a small amount, he had hidden all the real estate and the tangible and non-tangible wealth, and the part that he could not hide he denied ever existed. Because of this, Ishagh Dardashti came to the aid of his daughter and sued him in court. This made big news, and most people were saying that Hezghia's wealth was in the millions. The government also was interested in getting to the bottom of this and finding out where the millions were so they could collect their portion of taxes, and this contributed to the lengthy duration of the lawsuit. A major portion of the inheritance was spent during the long legal battle. This went on for years until both sides became weary and realized that there were many advantages in settling the lawsuit.

Sometimes Ishagh Dardashti would come to my older brother Aziz for advice and direction, and discuss the happenings of the day, the discoveries, the disappointments, the wins, the losses, the delays in court and the government worker's hunger for some of the wealth. Sometimes I would join them and listen to their conversations. Uncle Ishagh explained that the court had ordered us to go for arbitration to a great Esfahani Islamic jurisprudence and reluctantly we had to agree with whatever the judgment would be.

Hence Mr. Ishagh Dardashti did not sit idle and he told my older brother, "Aziz, I thought a lot about what to do to make sure that my daughter receives her fair share. One day I came to the conclusion that the only way we will receive justice is to corrupt Mr. Islamic jurisprudence by bribing him so he would judge in my daughter's favor. So without any hesitation I bought a plateful of gold coins and took it to his Anderoni[15] (اندرونی) house with my daughter. We sent word that Ishagh Dardashti requests a private audience with him for a private matter. After a while a man appeared and led us to a room to him. We expressed our regards and sat in front of him. Neither

---

[15] In those day people who were wealthy had houses that had two sections one called Bironi (بیرونی), the outer house where the man of the house would receive people. The other called Anderoni where the family lived and it was mostly for women of the house.

of us had seen the other, and after an introduction he realized who we were and why we were there and he asked, 'What may I do for you?' " Ishagh Dardashti continued, "After explaining in detail our situation I told him that the inheritance of the Jewish Hezghia is quite considerable and his oldest son is trying to deny the fair share of it to his young sibling, his mother and the mentally mad brother. He wants to steal the whole inheritance for himself.

"After getting him prepared and changing his opinion in our favor, we offered him the plateful of gold coins that was placed in front of me for his enticement and clearly had attracted his attention as he was patiently listening to me. I pushed the plate with both hands in front of him and said, 'I hope your honor and the future Shiite Imam will accept this humble token as a small appreciation from this woman, pointing at my daughter, and honor us with your kindness. The clergyman, who inwardly was very pleased, outwardly acted as if he had no need for worldly wealth, and said he could not accept the plateful of gold coins."

Ishagh Dardashti continued, "I had well noticed the desire of this hypocrite wanting the plateful of gold coins impatiently, I insisted again (tauroof[16] تعارف) and said we are completely aware that your honor has no desire for worldly goods and how much you have washed your hands from anything that makes a man dependent on material things; however, you have a desire for helping the needy and that is why we are making this offering to be divided between the poor. His honor, who had found a pretext, agreed with me and reached to receive the plateful of gold." Then, after giving him the gold, they left his house.

Uncle Ishagh explained, "Later, I found out that this hypocrite and a wolf in sheep's clothing, accepted a bribe from the other side too, and to make all of us happy, one day he called both sides and urged them to settle their differences

---

[16]It is not culturally proper to accept an offer on the first gesture. Normally one would wait for the third or fourth gesture before accepting the offer.

between themselves. Both sides were exhausted and had spent large sums of money and had come to the conclusion that this fight has no end; they settled and sent word to the clergy that we have reached a settlement."

The purpose of writing about the above is to portray life as it was in those days and also to show the depth of corruption amongst the religious and spiritual leaders and their way of thinking and commitment to truth and good deeds. One should not be deceived by the appearance of these hypocrites and trust them. Eventually Tubai received a share of her father-in-law's inheritance and was appointed the guardian for the inheritance for her mad husband.

Ishagh Dardashti did not possess a great deal of wealth for two reasons. First, people did not trust him much because of his past dealings and the fact that he was considered a very clever man with not much influence (the perception was that in dealing with him one would always lose). Second, his household expenses and supporting four wives and their children were enough to collapse this wise and hard-working man. However, when he passed away there were only a few underage children at home, and with the help of their mothers, they managed to live comfortably.

Uncle Ishaghi's oldest son, Geula (גאולה گِئولا), went to Khuzestan, where he began working, got married and they had a son. After a few years he went bankrupt and fled from Iran to South America, leaving his wife and child in God's hands and residing in Argentina. For years no one heard from him, until one day word came that he had started working while in Argentina and had accumulated a large quantity of wealth. Geula returned to Iran and his family, and after setting up a very comfortable life for his wife and son, he returned to Argentina. He returned a few more times and purchased many pieces of real estate and had his son oversee them. He was also very generous to his siblings. Geula had also generously bought a nice house for his full brother (from the same mother),

Shokrollah (شکرالله) , and had helped him have a comfortable living. Because of many years of promiscuity during his youth with prostitutes, he had syphilis and other venereal diseases and at the age of 50 or 60 went mad and eventually was committed to an asylum in Israel. As long as Shokrollah was alive, he was visited by Geula and his family looked after him. Unfortunately, the life of this generous family man was cut short in the Americas and he passed away. Geula also married a Christian woman in Argentina and had a son by her. After his death, his wife in Argentina confiscated all of the wealth in the Americas. Once or twice, Geula's handsome eldest son in Iran traveled with one of his uncles to Argentina to claim some of the inheritance, but he returned empty-handed. However, there was plenty of real estate and other assets, so there was no need to collect anything from Argentina.

Faizollah (فیض الله) was the next son after Geula; he was a son from the fourth wife, Khorshidi (خرشیدی), of Uncle Ishagh. He also became wealthy after working very hard and he died in 1355 (the Iranian calendar or 1966) after a long illness in Khuzestan, while his family was visiting in Tehran. This Faizollah had a slight lisp in his speech and in his youth he did foolish and irrational things. In school, teachers and students alike had a difficult time with him. At times he was severely punished by teachers and beaten by his classmates and still he continued with his troublemaking. He had some friends that assisted him with his mischievous deeds. I remember one day at Alliance School (AIU) in Farsi class, the teacher, who was very unhappy with him, asked him to hold his hand out to be punished with a switch. Faizollah, who was very well aware of the pain of being struck with a switch, got off his bench and walked to the teacher and suddenly he surprised the teacher by slapping the poor teacher so hard that light flashed in his eyes. He quickly ran away from school as fast as he knew how and left the school grounds. He was absent from school for a few days until his father, Ishagh Dardashti, whom everyone in school knew, brought him back and took Faizollah to the principal and told him that this extraordinary and regrettable action of Faizollah was a reaction to an extreme foolish behavior of the teacher by causing his student to hate him and be disgusted. Ishagh Dardashti had recognized that it is wrong to punish by exerting bodily pain. He gave notice to the school that to punish an eighteen-year-old student is degrading and unbecoming. In summary, they accepted Faizollah with some conditions and after this episode no teacher punished any student by exerting severe bodily pain.

Shokrollah was the third son of Uncle Ishagh. Shokrollah was born when his father was elderly, and he had a difficult time getting attention. This resulted in him becoming wild and reckless, and he did not have much education. He lost his father in his youth and began working before he matured in order to help his mother with their everyday expenses. He and I became friends during service in the army. Our friendship became very sincere and we became very close friends. He was similar to Musa in that he was caught during a sex act with a Muslim prostitute. He was arrested and jailed. In that period, unlike the old days, the government had good control of things and no one dared to do anything unlawful. He and his friend, who was also a good friend of mine in the army, were taken to court and after a while were exonerated. Shokrollah was a very loyal and generous friend. During the service, even though he had very little money, he would always share whatever he owned. His mother, Heli, who was a heavyset woman, had her own home. That was given to Faizollah after her death. He stayed in Iran for a few years until Israel was founded, and he migrated there.

CHAPTER 5

Children of Avraham Dardashti

Avraham's sons and three grandchildren in c. 1909
Standing from left, Uncle Yehanan (یحانان) , Uncle Khodadad (the
youngest خداداد), Uncle Shimon (شمعون), my father Yaeir (یائیر)
Sitting from left, Uncle Yeshaia (یشعیا), Nemat's cousin Noorollah (نورالله),
Avraham Dardashti (اوراهام دردشتی) holding Nemat in his lap (a few months
old), Nemat's (نعمت) brother Aziz (عزیز) and Uncle Yaghub (یعقوب Jacob,
from the first wife, Sara)

As I wrote earlier, grandfather had seven sons, two of them
from the first wife Sara, and five from the second wife, Miriam.
Yaghub, grandfather's first son and the oldest child, was a short
and medium-weight man and as far as I remember he always
had a short beard and instead of wearing a hat he had an
araghchin (a small cap, عرقچین). He was a peaceful man and did
not bother anyone and minded his own business. He sold real-

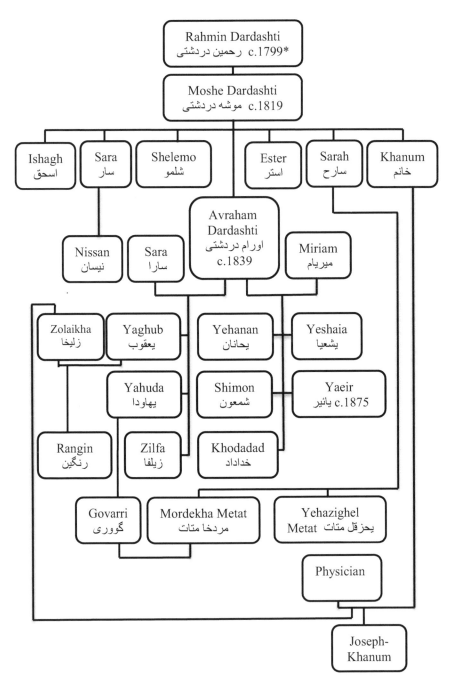

*Birth Year

estate, and sometimes he knitted socks with new machines that recently were imported from a foreign land. I remember he had bought this new and shiny machine and set it up in one of the rooms he lived in. This room was facing north (an undesirable room) and Uncle Yaghub and his wife were in that room knitting socks with every spare moment they found. After some time, they realized that this was not a moneymaking business, and gave up the knitting. The machine was stored in the corner of the room for years.

Uncle Yaghub and his wife, Zolaikha, could not have any children and because of that they adopted the eighth child, a girl, from his brother, Uncle Yahuda. It was said that Uncle Yahuda and his wife, Ester, had decided that after seven daughters if the eighth one was another daughter to kill her at childbirth. Zolaikha, after hearing about this criminal thought of her brother and sister-in-law, and the fact that she was so desperate for a child and envious of people with children, made the suggestion to her husband to kill two birds with one stone, one to prevent the killing of a human being and another to have a child that we have desired and suffered for not having for years.

She told Uncle Yaghub, "Let's go to your brother and his wife and offer to adopt their child." Uncle Yahuda and his wife of course accepted the offer, and after their daughter was born, she was given to Uncle Yaghub and his wife, who had prepared every possible comfort for her. To feed the baby they hired a surrogate mother and called the baby Rangin (رنگین , meaning colorful). Uncle Yaghub and his wife were explaining that their lives changed and took a different color and that's why the baby was called Rangin. My uncle's wife called her Rangin Nagarin (رنگین نگارین, painted or beautiful Rangin) and that became her nickname. She spoiled Rangin Nagarin and took care of her extremely well until she was married. After Uncle Yaghub died, Zolaikha sold everything she had and moved in with Rangin and was there until she passed away.

Uncle Yaghub and his wife had a relatively comfortable life. He made good money, their living conditions were formidable and enjoyed life more than his siblings because of not having many children. As I wrote before, grandfather had two houses that were divided among his children during his life. He had given one house to the two oldest sons from the first wife; the other house was given to the other five sons from the second wife. Yaghub and Yahuda, who were the recipient of a house, divided the house between them. Uncle Yaghub had a relatively large room on the north side of the house which he painted very meticulously and covered the floors with expensive carpets. There was a large walk in closet in the back of this room where he had stored all kinds of household goods and expensive items. The room also was furnished with many thick mattresses full of feathers, velvet pillows, a large table, several chairs and other pieces of furniture. The upper shelves (it was customary to have two sets of built-in shelves, upper and lower, in all the walls of the rooms) were full of fine china, crystal, and other ornamental items. There was a smaller room adjacent to this room. This room was also full of furniture and his mother, Sara, lived there. She lived with Yaghub as long as he was alive.

After Uncle Yaghub's death, she moved in with her daughter, Aunt Zilfa, and she was there until her death. I do not remember Uncle Yahuda ever talking to his mother during this period. It appeared that he was not Sara's son; it might have been because of the story that I will later write about in detail.

Zolaikha was the daughter of grandfather's sister, Khanum. Zolaikha's brother, Joseph-e-Khanum, had converted to Christianity and was smitten with Christianity. Because of this, he was appointed to run Mr. Garland's all-girl school. It was amazing how Zolaikha and her brother were educated in Farsi literature and had a very responsible job in Mr. Garland's organization. Perhaps their father was an educated and knowledgeable person or maybe Khanum, grandfather's sister, herself was interested in making sure that her children were educated. I remember when I studied at Garland school, once in a while I was required to go by the girls section, I would see my uncle's wife saying yes or no to the students. I would see her managing the school like a powerful director and ordering the teachers around. Often she would assume a teacher's position to teach embroidery and sewing "Sekmeh"[17] (سکمه) or similar things.

In those times it was very unusual for women to possess the job of directing schools. Education for the underclasses was very unusual, if not unheard of. Among Iranian Muslims, a woman's purpose was strictly for servitude; serving at home, a sex object for man's pleasure and for having children, and there was no other reason for a woman. Muslim men only allow their women to be taught the Koran by other women at home and other religious rules. This continued until some of them traveled to foreign countries in Europe and realized that women are also human beings, and like men they can be educated. However, before the doors opened up to Muslim women, Jewish women were exposed to education because of the opening of Alliance Schools (AIU) in a few important cities in Iran. Women were taught reading, writing and handmade trades. Armenians were the second group to allow girls access to schools.

Muslim women were deemed to be good for three things only, and most of them spent all their lives behind locked doors at home and had very little outside contact. Once in a while they would go out with their families. A woman usually would get permission from her husband and cover herself with a chador (چادر, burka). Her face covering was a long white cloth, knitted so she could see through. When it was necessary for a stranger to come in the house to do maintenance or some business with the man of the house, the women of the house had to be out of sight for the duration of the visit. It is astonishing how the public had not realized that these restrictions paralyzed half of the population and how a few ignorant and fanatically religious

---

[17] The art of gold thread stitching used on a traditional wedding jacket or dress.

people have kept this group of people uneducated and ineffective.

However, today women have torn up the hijab (head and face covering) and engaged in actions that surpass even those in the West. For years this country and other Muslim countries have fallen behind because of the stupidity and ignorance of backward religious thinking and people lived in misery and despair. There are still many ignorant Muslim men in Iran that would prefer to return to the hijab and are not willing to allow freedom and equality between men and women.

As I wrote before, Uncle Yaghub and Zolaikha had a comfortable and dignified life. Uncle Yaghub earned enough that could support four people well. Zolaikha's salary was saved for their old age and one could say that they had no needs and they were very fortunate and successful until destiny had a different plan for them. Uncle Yaghub became ill and had to be taken to the English Hospital. This was the only hospital in Esfahan at that time. He was hospitalized and it did not take long for the disease to progress and take the life of Uncle Yaghub, the man who thought his success would last for a long time. The disease that killed him was diarrhea. Unfortunately, because of the absence of a correct cure or carelessness or some other reason, it took the life of this young man at age 47 or 48.

The English Christian missionaries built this hospital in Esfahan and one or two English doctors managed it. In those days, nurses were not much known in Iran and a trained and educated nurse was unheard of. Necessity forced the manager of the English Christian Hospital to hire a few young men and women to be trained under the supervision of a well-educated English nurse. However, it was evident that these nurses were not educated and could not perform adequately. Because of this, doctors had a hard time doing their jobs successfully. God knows how many people died from even the most trivial diseases because of the lack of well-qualified nurses.

Uncle Yaghub died and his wife's life came apart, and her life was never good again. Her loving, happy and bright life was sad and grim after her husband's death.

Uncle Yaghub was a very peaceful, calm and unassuming man. He did not bother anyone, minded his own business and he would never stick his nose in anyone's business. He was very interested in and enamored with his family and life in general. I do not think he did not care or was not interested in others, but I also did not think he was very sensitive or compassionate with his countrymen's misfortunes and troubles. I remember during the famine in Esfahan when people were dying by the hundreds, he and his wife always had a big clay pot full of bread, and their pantry was always full of food of all kinds. Unfortunately, with callous and heartless behavior, he did not allow even a small crumb to exit their vast pantry to help someone else and a small piece of bread to feed one of his brother's children who quivered from hunger. I remember one day when I was seven years old my mother asked me to go to Uncle Yaghub. That day and all other days I was so hungry and weak that I had a hard time walking. I do not remember ever eating more than one very small meal a day because there was not enough food for me and all my siblings. I arrived at my uncle's hungry, tired and weak and met my aunt coming out of the kitchen carrying a stack of freshly baked hot bread that smelled heavenly. I almost passed out, but to save my honor in front of this heartless aunt I gathered my strength and I did not allow myself to gasp in front of this woman with a heart of stone. I relayed to her my mother's message and tried to escape, as much as my body was able to. My aunt clearly was aware of the famine and the severe hunger that had gripped people. She knew how hungry this small boy in front of her was and how much he was in the need of a piece of fresh and warm bread. She had forgotten all the laws of human decency and compassion and with extreme heartlessness ignored giving me a piece of bread. It seemed as if this woman had no heart or feeling.

His full brother, Uncle Yahuda, who with Aunt Zilfa were from the same mother, had eight daughters and one son. And as I wrote before, one was given to Uncle Yaghub. While Uncle Yahuda was alive he married off five daughters; therefore, two daughters were not married. His only son, Shokrollah, also was not married until his father was on his deathbed. Uncle Yahuda, recognizing that he had not much time to live, called his son and told him, "Marry your fiancée this very night before I pass away so I may leave this world with ease of mind." Shokrollah honored his father and gathered his mother and sisters and hurriedly arranged a wedding and as he and his bride were entering their honeymoon suite, his father passed away with a smile on his lips (this was an interesting story but sad).

Uncle Yahuda was educated and a learned man. He had a high position amongst Esfahani religious and cultured scholars. There was always a crowd of people around him seeking his advice about religion and Hebrew. In addition to his knowledge of Hebrew, the religious leaders considered him a leader among leaders and respected him. He was a strong and successful man who was respected and accepted by strong young men, Jew or Muslim, and athletes did not dare challenge him. I had heard from several people about his heroic and amazing deeds and it may be a good time to write about two of them.

On Saturdays, the day that Jews rest and do not engage in any work, the men would get up in the morning earlier than usual and would go to synagogue after washing up and putting on their best. They would pray for two hours in the synagogue and then return home and sit at a very colorful spread that was prepared specially for this day. They would discuss religious subjects and serenade happy songs for a couple of hours and finally food was served and everyone rested afterward. The Orthodox Jews spent all Saturday reading the Torah and other religious Jewish books. Jews could not start a fire and could not cook; therefore, food was cooked the day before, on Friday, and was kept warm and tasty on the cooktop until Saturday. This food was known as Shabbati food and everyone, young or old, knew what it was. At times eggs, beets and carrots were put atop the pot of Shabbati and covered with a thick cloth (called a pelass). Saturday morning the woman of the house would remove the pelass carefully, not getting close to the fire, and place the eggs, beets and carrots on a plate with the main course.

Those who have tasted Shabbati food, the eggs, the carrots and beets know how tasty and delightful they were. The Shabbati eggs were even popular among the Muslims and other enticed groups and agreed that it tasted fantastic.

Back to the subject matter at hand, the brave, heroic and strong Uncle Yahuda. One Saturday morning after finishing his meal he took a walk outside. It happened that at the same time Uncle Shimon also had gone outside for a walk and my brother, who was a child, followed him out. Uncle Shimon walked to a quarter called Saremahalle, where suddenly from nowhere Shabrang and two of his brothers jumped Uncle Shimon and began beating him up mercilessly. Shabrang had three brothers and they all were very tall with wide shoulders and strong; their jobs were manual labor and heavy work. These four brothers were loose, gambled and played around all the time. They did not hesitate to steal and often caused trouble for ordinary people until they extorted money from them. It may be that was why they attacked Uncle Shimon, and also to frighten him. My brother Aziz said, "When I saw Uncle Shimon was being beaten up I ran to Uncle Yahuda's house and found him in the yard walking. I screamed for help and said, 'They are killing Uncle Shimon, please save him.' Uncle Yahuda without hesitation joined in running with me, asking where to. I said, 'Follow me, at Saremahalle, Shabrang and his brothers are killing Uncle Shimon.' Uncle Yahuda was cursing them as he was running and he did not know what he was doing because he was so angry until we reached Saremahalle. There were wall-to-wall people around Shabrang and his brothers and there was so much chaos that no one knew what was going on. In the middle of all this chaos there were loud screams of 'kill him, kill him' and even shouts of 'he is killed, he is dead.' After hearing 'kill him,' Uncle Yahuda was enraged, he jumped in the middle of the fight like a hungry, angry and roaring lion and shouted, 'Who are you killing and why are you killing him'"?

My brother was saying, "I saw Uncle Yahuda was picking up people in his path and tossing them without knowing whether they were men, women or children. He was mad and out of control, he was throwing punches, kicks and with one deliberate, fast and hard blow would put out his opponents until Uncle Yahuda reached to the core of the fight and to the people that he really wanted to get to. Shabrang was the first person whose lights were put out with one hard blow to the head like a sledgehammer. The other two strong brothers who thought they could beat Uncle Yahuda easily were no match for punches, kicks and the strength of my uncle and were easily knocked out. Even though this whole episode did not take more than a few minutes, Uncle Shimon was bloody, bruised and crushed under Shabrang, his brothers and others that took advantage of the situation. They tried to kill a son of Avraham Dardashti, whom they hated because they thought he was a dictator.

Uncle Yahuda was angered even more seeing his brother injured and unconscious and became like a fierce tiger, attacked the crowd and knocked down whomever he could put his hands on. The crowd began fleeing and the street was emptied; Shabrang, his brothers, a few other men, women and children, injured and lifeless, were left sprawled on the ground. Uncle Yahuda started to calm down and took Uncle Shimon's hand and we walked home."

The other story that I heard about Uncle Yahuda's bravery, I will write later.

First I need to give a short explanation about the way Jews prayed in synagogue on Saturdays. They prayed according to tradition in groups that is why they gathered at synagogue to pray together. Saturday is the Jewish holy day, and the prayers of Saturday morning are different from those of other days. Men would go to synagogue early Saturday morning after putting on their best clothes and pray for approximately three hours. Every Saturday morning, the Torah, which was written on a scroll made of sheep or deerskin, was brought out of the sanctuary and it was opened and was shown to the congregation. In return, members of the congregation bowed their heads and held their hand on their face and honored and showed their respect to this heavenly and holy book. After the Torah was shown to the congregation, it was placed in front of the person at the bema to read that morning's special prayer. In the middle of reading the special verse, some people would approach and would recite a prayer to thank God for their needs and for giving the human race this most holy and valuable book. The volunteers for delivering these prayers paid a sum to the treasurer of the synagogue as an offering (these offerings were spent for upkeep of the synagogue, salaries, and other charitable deeds). Often these volunteers would try to outbid one another or to read a particular passage, and sometimes in the process of bidding they fought each other. I will write about this in more detail later.

In Esfahan, most of the Jews were afraid of my grandfather because he was the kind of a man who told it as it was and pointed out any injustice or transgression and quite frankly did not care what the consequences were. He criticized and chastised them openly and never forgave their punishment. A lot of the Esfahani Jews kept their distance and distrusted him. These distrusting people were drawn to the same lot who were hypocrites, insincere and deceiving; praising and displaying admiration for them in spite of their flaws and wrongdoing. Mr. Hezghia was very popular and loved among the Esfahani Jews because of this objectionable behavior and the fact that he never irritated anyone with the truth. For personal gain, this hypocrite did not stop at anything. Among the leaders of Esfahani Jews there were many people like Mr. Hezghia. For these reasons, grandfather did not have a large following. Even though most everyone agreed that grandfather was very wise, respectable and knowledgeable, most Esfahani Jews created problems for him and his family at every opportunity.

On one of these Saturday mornings, grandfather suggested he be allowed to read a particular prayer and that the prayer should be read solely by himself. Suddenly someone else rose and demanded the same prayer and started an argument with grandfather. This led a larger group of people to gang up against grandfather and eventually they attacked him physically. Grandfather's sons were there in the synagogue but tried to remain composed and respect the synagogue's sanctity according to grandfather's teachings and hoping for things not to get out of hand. However, the sons realized that it was not to be and it appeared that they were going to kill grandfather. Uncle Yahuda, who was there, shouted at his younger brother and said, "Shimon, why are you waiting, God make your belly swell (this was a curse word that brothers told each other), lock the door and do not let anyone leave." Uncle Shimon quickly fulfilled his brother's orders and stood at the door, not letting anyone out. Uncle Yahuda and his three brothers ran to the aid of their father, who was trying to survive under the blows and the kicks of the people. The observers who were there were explaining that Uncle Yahuda, who was very angry, would pick up anyone in his way and crash them on top of others; his punches flattened anyone in his way. Not long after, everyone started running away and rushed toward the door, where unfortunately for him or her they came across Uncle Shimon, who was young and strong. Shortly the synagogue was emptied and only the people who wanted to kill grandfather were left on the ground bloody, injured with broken bones, moaning with pain. Uncle Yahuda was still furious and was fighting and beating these people like a fierce lion and had no pity on anyone because of finding grandfather under the feet of these people being decimated. He even had no exception for women and started ripping their clothes off until grandfather screamed and ordered him to stop fighting and told him there was no reason to hurt people any more.

Thereafter, the congregation and others who heard of the fight realized that Avraham Dardashti's family was not one to manhandle. I myself had seen Uncle Yahuda and had spoken with him. In those days when I saw him, he was about seventy years old, but he still had a presence, he was handsome and his bravery was so noticeable, even though he was a calm, kind and harmless man. Unfortunately not much of his fortune was left otherwise he might not have had to work in his golden years. He was forced to accompany his only son to far off villages in Esfahan and Parse until he was completely out of energy and had to curtail all strenuous activities. Still he never would allow his son to travel to dangerous locales and tribes in the mountains by himself.

The tribes in Iran are people that until ten years ago did not live in towns and their main profession was raising sheep and goats and they roamed the mountains in search of grazing pastures. These tribes were expert marksmen and horseback riders and were extremely brave and fearless fighters. Often they attacked and ambushed caravans and stole everything, and sometimes would kill the people they robbed. This went on until Reza Shah and later his son Mohamed Reza Shah decided to end this nomadic lifestyle and settle them in one place and rid the people and government of this headache. Grandfather spent a good portion of his life among a sect of these tribes called Lors of Lorestan and Bakhtiari. Tribes of Lorestan and Lors were mainly mountain people, rebellious, brave, fearless and truthful men. The tribes also made their living by raising cattle and sheep. The Lor Tribe was composed of two families, Ilkhani Tribe and Ilbaki Tribe. The chiefs of these tribes were called Khan or Sardar, and because of their past power they had their own government and never took orders from Iran's central government. At times the Iranian government needed these fearless people to fight foreigners and appeased them by placing their leader in high places in government. Occasionally some of these leaders rose to ministerial positions or even more sensitive positions, such as Sardar Sepah and Sardar As'ad Bakhtiari (also called Hajj Ali-Gholi Khan), who became the Minister of War and I think for a short time the Prime Minister (10/6/1909 to 7/1910). These people were direct, truthful, proud and very loyal.

Grandfather's job with these people was buying and selling gold and silver jewels, termeh (clothing that had gold stitching), fine wool and silk fabric. Because of this business he dealt mainly with the upper class and leaders of these tribes. The chiefs, the influential people and women of these tribes were well acquainted with him and called him Mullah Avraham. Mullah Avraham was always welcomed with respect in these tribes because of his wisdom, fine business ethics, and trustworthiness. The above tribes honored religiously a woman's chastity and the respect for them. This feeling was so strong that if they ever had any suspicion that a man or a woman had a dishonorable intention, he or she would immediately and without any hesitation be killed, and they had no tolerance and forgiveness in this matter. To these people the innocence and purity of their women was of utmost importance, and under no circumstances would a strange man be allowed to look at any part of their women's body, not even a strand of their hair. With all that, Mullah Avraham was trusted and respected so much that he was allowed in their harems and interyards (where the women roamed without any covering on their head). He was allowed to freely walk in, speak and deal with women for selling and buying purposes. This was a very special honor that would not be extended to anyone else other than Mullah Avraham the Jew. He was respected so much that whatever he said, they would accept without question.

To prove this, it might be a good time to write about the meeting between Mullah Avraham and Samsam-OL-Sultaneh Bakhtiari (صمصام السلطنه بختیاری) at Chehel Sotun, (a palace with 40 columnsچهل ستون) in Esfahan, the seat of government.

I remember when I was ten or eleven years old one day in Esfahan there was the news that captured thieves were going to be brought to Esfahan the next day. With this news there was an unusual excitement among the people of Esfahan who were anticipating seeing the captured thieves and wondering who they were.

These thieves were people who had an uprising against the

Reza Shah Pahlavi[18]   *Mohammad Reza Shah Pahlavi[19]*

central government. The leaders were two farmers who had acquired their position by gradually becoming important

---

[18] In 1925, Reza Shah (رضا شاه پهلوی) deposed Ahmad Shah Qajar, the last Shah of the Qajar dynasty, and founded the Pahlavi dynasty. He established a constitutional monarchy that lasted until overthrown in 1979 during the Iranian Revolution. Reza Shah introduced many social, economic, and political reforms during his reign, ultimately laying the foundation of the modern Iranian state. (from Wikipedia)

[19] Mohammad Reza Shah Pahlavi (محمد رضا شاه پهلوی), 26 October 1919 – 27 July 1980. He was the Shah of Persia (Iran) from 16 September 1941 until his overthrow by the Iranian Revolution on 11 February 1979. He was the second and last monarch of the House of Pahlavi of the Iranian monarchy. (from Wikipedia)

amongst a group of farmers and people were terrified of their
fearlessness and fighting ability. These rebels had created chaos
in a large area of Iran and had robbed people of their security.
These two rebels were called Reza Khan and Jafar-Gholi
Khan (جعفرقلی خان), and they were from Joezoon (جوزون) one of
the counties in Esfahan. They began with petty robberies on
back roads and because of the weakness of local authorities they
became more brazen. These petty robbers gradually advanced to
larger and more lucrative robberies until they began robbing
caravans, and little by little more thieves and rebellious people
joined them. Gradually they attacked more important places and
at times raided and looted cities. Several times the central
government dispatched Gendarmes (French word for State
Police) to capture or kill these thieves but the government
agents would return beaten and with high casualties. The central
government even asked the occupying Russian troops in World
War I to help capture these thieves and rebels. However, even
they were defeated. The government was finally forced to ask
for help from the Bakhtiari Tribes because it had reached the
conclusion that no one else was suited for this job. Amir Jang
of Bakhtiari was given the job. He quickly assembled a group
of fighters from the Bakhtiari Tribe and armed them and he
began pursuing the rebels. Not long after, he defeated the rebels
and returned with live captured rebels. Reza Khan himself and
Ali Naghichi (علی نقی چی) too, nephew of Jafar Gholi Khan,
were amongst them; Jafar Gholi Khan was killed in the
skirmish.

Ali Naghichi was no older than 16 years old but this child
committed so many heinous crimes and killed so many people
that he had lost count. The person whose wealth was looted and
had taken his plea to Jafar Gholi Khan told me "when I walked
in the room where the rebels were, I found two people lying on
a mattress at the head of the room and in front of him there lay
two manghals (منقل, a container full of bright hot charcoals) and
opium paraphernalia put together meticulously for smoking

Reza Shah in 1936[20]

opium. There were wall to wall village chiefs and outstanding leaders of Chaharmahal (چهارمحا ل) near Esfahan. They were there to show their loyalty and obedience out of fear of being killed and looted of their wealth. There was also a manghal and opium paraphernalia in front of each one and there was a plate

---

[20] Along with the modernization of the nation, Reza Shah was the ruler during the time of the Women's Awakening (1936-1941). This movement sought the elimination of the Islamic veil from Iranian society. Supporters held that the veil impeded physical exercise and the ability of women to enter society and contribute to the progress of the nation. Women were allowed to study in the colleges of law and medicine, and in 1934 a law set heavy fines for cinemas, restaurants, and hotels that did not open doors to both sexes This move met opposition from the religious establishment. The unveiling issue and the Women's Awakening are linked to the Marriage Law of 1931 and the Second Congress of Eastern Women in Tehran in 1932. Reza Shah was the first Iranian Monarch after 1400 years who paid respect to the Jews by praying in the synagogue when visiting the Jewish community of Isfahan; an act that boosted the self-esteem of the Iranian Jews and made Reza Shah their second most respected Iranian leader after Cyrus the Great. Reza Shah's reforms opened new occupations to Jews and allowed them to leave the ghetto. He forbade photographing aspects of Iran he considered backwards such as camels. As his reign became more secure, Reza Shah clashed with Iran's clergy, as he did with all other political constituencies in the country, and he banned Islamic dress and chadors in favor of Western dress. Women who resisted this compulsory unveiling had their veils forcibly removed. (from Historical Iranian sites and people)

full of the best sticks of opium in the middle of the room. Each person was free to use as much of the opium as he wished.

Bakhtiari

When I entered the room the two rebels were already intoxicated and were in a good mood and the occasion was ripe for discussing my grievance freely. After a long greeting and many praises I asked if I might sit down. One of the two, who later I found out was Reza Khan (this Reza Khan should not be confused with Reza Khan who became king, Reza Shah), asked me what I wanted. Then I explained to him how poor and destitute I had become since his people looted all my wealth. After Reza Khan listened to me carefully, he assured me and said, 'Have no fear, all of your wealth will be returned to you.' He immediately ordered food for me and then ordered to find the people who stole all my belongings and when they were found to return all my wealth. The servants left the room with these orders and took me with them to eat. They brought me food and drink, by then I was very hungry and thirsty, so I ate and drank everything with pleasure and returned to the main room again and sat in a corner waiting to see what would happen.

A man walked into the room carrying a brand new rifle and said, 'Khan, please accept this fine Czechoslovakian rifle that has come to me as a token of my loyalty to you.' He placed the rifle in front of Jafar Gholi Khan. At this time a young man came in. He had several gun belts full of bullets and a sidearm in the hoister. He immediately noticed the rifle that was offered to Jafar Gholi Khan. He walked to the rifle, picked it up and asked permission from his maternal uncle, Jafar Gholi Khan, to test it. However, before waiting for an answer from his uncle, he loaded the rife with a bullet and pointed it toward an elderly man pedestrian in the street and pulled the trigger, killing the unsuspecting man. The man fell down, rolled over in his own blood and life fled his body. Later I found out that this mad and bloodthirsty boy was the famous Ali Naghichi. Finally, after two or three hours, the thief and my stolen goods were found and I was very surprised how quickly they located the thief and the stolen goods. At that moment I prayed to God for the Iranian government to become as efficient someday.

The famous Ali Naghichi could be seen amongst the captured rebels. The day they were brought to Esfahan I was also in Chaharbagh (چهار باق, an ancient and famous boulevard) trying to take a look at them and it was hard to get close enough because there was a very large crowd and it was hard to find an empty place. After a long wait, we could hear the sound of drums and the leader of the rebels, who was in chains, appeared. Reza Khan was in front of the pack and Ali Naghichi was right behind him; then came all the other lieutenants and others, with their names written on a white metal sheet. Bakhtiari Lors, in full colorful tribal clothing, came on foot in front of the soldiers.

For five hours people watched captured rebels and soldiers on horseback. The captured rebels were incarcerated in a prison adjacent to the seat of government in Esfahan. The captured rebels were kept in prison a few months and gradually they were all executed. For some of them, however, a hole was dug and while standing upright, plaster was poured in up to their torso or possibly up to their neck on either side of the road to Chaharmahal to set an example for others. Some were also skinned and their bodies left hanging for several days. The day that a group of these rebels were going to be hanged in the Shah Square in Esfahan, there was almost a riot, horseback soldiers had to be summoned to bring order to the crowd and keep people from entering the square. Unfortunately, my cousin Monavar's (منور) husband, Avraham, who had gone to the

square and was in front of the crowd, was kicked by a spooked
horse of one of the soldiers and his stomach was torn wide
open. He died right there.

They took Avraham to the English Hospital but to no avail,
he was already dead. His wife and two sons, two and one year
old, Aroon and Aziz, survived him. Monavar dedicated her full
time to caring for her children for four or five years and never
thought about getting married again. Then she married her
cousin, Nemat, son of her mother's sister, and her new husband
adopted her two sons. The two sons immigrated to Israel and
worked hard, married and became prosperous. A few years
later, the two sons took their mother, stepfather and other
children that her mother had with the stepfather to Israel and
helped them to prosper as well.

Because of grandfather's wisdom and know-how, he was
able to visit the tribes freely and roam with respect amongst the
Bakhtiari and Chaharmahal leaders. My oldest brother told this
story: "When I was about eight years old, grandfather took my
hand and told me, 'Come with me, I will take you to a very
interesting place.' I was always very dear to grandfather and I
was always received by him very warmly. I knew that the
reason he wanted to take me with him was his extreme love for
me. I was very excited and could not wait until I went along
with grandfather and found out where he was going to take
me."

In those days there were no cars or other vehicles easily
available for going on a trip. If one wanted to take a trip that
was farther than five or six kilometers (3-4 miles) and had the
means, he would ride in a carriage or on horseback. Otherwise
he would go on foot or ride a donkey or mule. In the cities,
people walked to work or to other places. At times you would
see someone on a donkey or a horse with a young boy or a man
walking behind or in front of the animal. These people were
mostly mullahs, religious leaders or influential people in high
positions who did this to show their importance. The rider relied

on the boy to dismount and the boy would stay back guarding the animal while the rider was conducting his business, and on his return the boy would help his boss to mount the animal again.

Grandfather, like most people, took my brother's hand and started walking, and after two or three kilometers and going through alleys, back streets, bazaars and Shah Square, they arrived at the garden of Chehel Sotun which was the seat of local government in those days. There was a long and rectangular pool in front of the building in the middle of a large garden with armed agents on either side of it. The agents stopped grandfather and asked him whom he was there to see. Reza Gholi Khan Samsam-OL-Sultaneh (رظا قليخـان صمصـام السلطنه) was recently appointed to the Governor of Providence of Esfahan and he had moved the government to historic Chehel Sotun. Grandfather had been well acquainted with Reza Gholi Khan Samsam-OL-Sultaneh and his family for a long time. Grandfather was very glad that his friend had received this honor and he was there to congratulate him. "Grandfather told the agent that they were there to see his Majesty Reza Gholi Khan Samsam-OL-Sultaneh and asked the agent to tell his majesty that Mullah Avraham has come to pay his respect," my brother said. "The doubtful agent was surprised that an elderly Jewish man expected to walk in and demand to see Reza Gholi Khan Samsam-OL-Sultaneh. Grandfather noticed the hesitation on the face of the agent and urged him to go and deliver the message to the Khan and he would see who I am. The agent reluctantly started walking toward the building and grandfather and I waited outside. "A few minutes later Reza Gholi Khan Samsam-OL-Sultaneh himself appeared coming out of the building and hurriedly walked toward us and his entourage followed behind him. Reza Gholi Khan Samsam-OL-Sultaneh entered the porch in front of the building and called grandfather loudly and said, 'Mullah Avraham, why you did not send word so we can dispatch a carriage to pick you up so you would not have to walk this long walk,' and while he was saying these

Chehel Sotun (چهل ستون 40 Column Palace)

words he started walking down the stairs in front of the porch and reached grandfather before we reached the stairs and hugged grandfather and kissed the face of this respectable and dignified man.

"Seeing the Khan, grandfather stared at Khan with his weak eyes and after a short pause he said, 'Reza Gholi Khan, is this really you?' Khan in return said, 'Yes I am the same small boy, your small Reza Gholi that you used to shower with kisses and put on your knees and caress me.' Then he saw me holding grandfather's hand and asked who I was. Grandfather replied that I am his grandchild whom I love very much. Reza Gholi Khan Samsam-OL-Sultaneh bent down and kissed me on the cheek and gently caressed me and then said, 'He looks very intelligent, please take him with you to Bibi (his wife), she will be very happy to see him.' He called one of his aides, who ran over without hesitation, and Reza Gholi Khan Samsam-OL-Sultaneh showed us to him and said, 'Take Mullah Avraham to the Anderoni (the inner yard) to Bibi Sakineh and tell her that

Mullah Avraham has walked a long way and he is tired and please make sure he is well taken care of until I return home.' "

I wrote about the above episode to give the reader an understanding of this tribe's culture and their loyalty toward their friends and their purity of origin (not marrying outside of the tribe) in Iranian history.

I myself witnessed the arrival of one of these Bakhtiari chiefs to assume his recent appointment to the government of Esfahan. I saw what kind of people Bakhtiari soldiers and Lors were, and how enemies shiver in their boots with the news of their reign in government. These soldiers were dressed in their tribal costumes of Lors and they had crisscrossed belts full of bullets and were fully armed on horseback. They resembled the ancient soldiers of the Persian Empire. People were very proud of these brave and handsome people and enjoyed watching them in parades. In front of these soldiers there was a tall and brash young man, dressed in the same uniform and fully armed. The only distinguishing difference was a white hat that he wore in a peculiar and interesting way that

Samsam-OL-Sultaneh

made him look more handsome and attractive. Later I found out that this distinguished man was the son of Amir Jang, the Governor of Esfahan, and as the representative of his father he led the parade and returned people's adulation by waving at the crowd every now and then.

These days, because of the government's hard work, these nomads and tent-dwelling rebellious tribes are establishing themselves more often as city dwellers and they are losing their tribal habits. Even though this change of lifestyle has enabled them to learn the ways of modern life, regrettably they are losing their identity and fine qualities such as being straightforward, truthful and honorable in the twentieth century's culture. The traits of self-sacrifice and being a fierce warrior that was the protector of the motherland and was the essence of stability for the country has been replaced by pathetic hypocrites who go through life with no regard for human decency.

There is a very old bronze statue of a man with one arm missing in the Museum of Ancient Persian History. This statue's clothing is very similar to the tribal clothing of these Bakhtiaris and Lors and surprisingly, over the centuries, the style has not changed.

Parthian Bronze Statue

CHAPTER 6

The Events of Aunt Zilfa, the Only Daughter of Grandfather, Avraham Dardashti

Previously I wrote that grandfather had two sons and one daughter by his first wife, Sara. The name of this daughter was Zilfa. Zilfa was married to a man called Mordekha Elyai and they had two sons and three daughters. Mordekha Elyai was a jeweler who was on the road most of the time. He had a house adjacent to grandfather's house and he would leave his wife with her mother, Sara and travel, mostly to Tehran, the capital of Iran, where most of his business was.

The father of Mordekha Elyai man was called Elyai (Elyahu) and was from a Jewish Esfahani family whose ancestors had migrated to Tehran. However, the family traveled to Esfahan regularly to visit their relatives. It has been said that Elyahu's family and the family of Moshe Rahmini, my great-grandfather, had some connection and the marriage of these two was the reason grandfather sold a parcel of the land that he worked so hard to acquire to Mordekha, his son-in-law, where he built a house adjacent to grandfather's. The house that Zilfa lived in with her mother was connected to grandfather's house, where he lived with his second wife, Miriam, through a door in a room in Aunt Zilfa's home, and that was how the occupants of the two homes visited one another.

"My husband often came home late in the evenings and I would wait at our front door for him impatiently counting the minutes," grandmother recalled. "While I was waiting I would hear voices of strange men from Zilfa's house next door and it appeared these strangers were in close proximity with the occupants of the house. I was puzzled how these strangers could

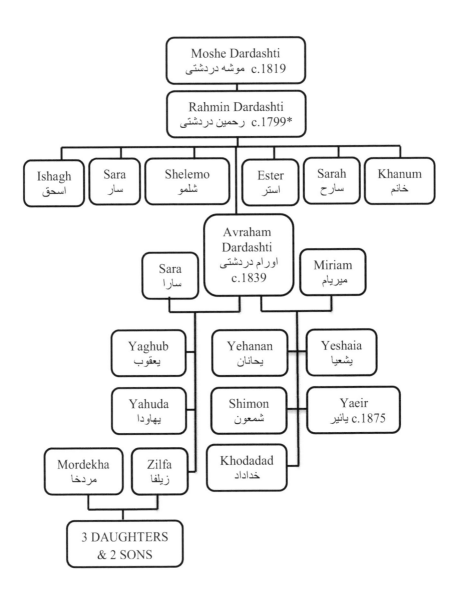

*Birth Year

be next door with these two women and they were allowed to access their home. I was too naïve to know the reason and I had a hard time unraveling this puzzle. I did not dare discuss this matter with my husband, fearing that he would be angered and this could cause a lot of trouble that might cause my husband or someone else to get killed. This went on until late one night when my husband came home and before I had a chance to usher him swiftly into our home, he noticed the singing of a strange man from one of the rooms of his daughter's home. Then he said, 'Have I gone mad or are my ears hearing by mistake, where is this singing and the sound of a Tonbak[21] (تنبک) is coming from?' " Grandmother continued, "I was very worried and fearful and tried to calm him down by trying to redirect his attention toward another subject. However, my husband was not the type of person to easily distract from such a very important subject. He went out and came back with his oldest son, Yaghub, twenty and some years old. As he was quickly and furiously going toward Zilfa's house, he was saying to his son, 'I have to find out what is going on next door.'

My husband and his son walked into Zilfa's house and noticed that there was a light in one of the bedrooms and one could hear the sound of music and singing of strange men coming out of that room. They looked inside the room and noticed that there were several men inside; it appeared they were making love to women, singing and playing the tonbak. That's when they both went mad and proceeded to break the door down without assessing the outcome of their action. With one huge rush they forced the door down and rushed in, where they found Aunt Zilfa naked, stretched on a mattress and her mother half-naked sitting at the head of the bed with a glass of

---

[21] A goblet drum from Iran. It is considered the principal percussion instrument of Persian music. The tonbak is normally positioned diagonally across the torso while the player uses one or more fingers and/or the palm(s) of the hand(s) on the drumhead, often (for a ringing timbre) near the drumhead's edge. Sometimes tonbak players wear metal finger rings for an extra-percussive "click" on the drum's shell. (from Wikipedia)

wine with three men in the room. As soon as my husband
entered the room he recognized the three men who were
hovering over the two women and were love playing with them.
Grandfather rushed toward the indecent mother, his ex-wife,
and with one blow of his cane to her face, she was unconscious.
Then he started toward his daughter to hit her with his cane but
he noticed that his son had cornered the three burly men in a
room. He quickly recognized the danger for his son from these
men and that he might be killed. Therefore he left the ex-wife
and daughter, and rushed to the aid of his son in the back room
and from there to the basement where the men had scurried to
hide. In the dark the three men assaulted grandfather and his son
and overcame them and sat on their chests trying to kill them.
Grandfather realized that he and his son were in serious trouble
and reluctantly pleaded for his son's life. The three men realized
that their enemy was beaten and desperate; they got up and
darted away into the night. My husband, however, in the
darkness during the middle of the fight grabbed one of the hats
that one of these three men was wearing. Grandfather waited in
the basement until the three men, his ex-wife and his daughter
left the house, then tired, beaten and bloody, took the hand of
his son who was also trounced pretty badly and went home.

The next day grandfather swore out a warrant for the arrest
of the three men to the local governor. He identified the men
and put into evidence the hat that he had grabbed. The
detectives began searching for the three men and after a great
deal of effort they arrested one of the three men and after a trial
and being convicted he was executed. The other two fled away
to Tehran and never returned to Esfahan. Grandfather gave up
looking for them to preserve the dignity of the family and end
the embarrassment. This subject became old news and people
forgot about it." However, the hand of revenge did not forsake
these two men and they were killed in a different fashion.

Mordekha, the husband of Zilfa, was a jeweler who was
frequently out of town. One day in Tehran a woman who was

covered from head to toe approached Mordekha and asked to
look at some jewelry, and after selecting a few pieces she asked
if they could go and show these jewels to her husband before
she bought them. The woman departed after leaving her
address. Mordekha later picked up the necessary jewels and
went to find the woman's home. After a great deal of trouble
and a long walk through back streets and allies he found the
house at the end of a deserted alley. He knocked on the door
and after a while, the woman opened the door, letting him in
and locking the door behind them. Inside, several men jumped
him and beat him to death, concealing his body by hanging it
inside the house cistern (underground water storage). They
pocketed his jewels and skipped town. The murderers, hoping
that no one will ever know about their murderous deed,
attempted to sell the jewels, unaware of the fact that detectives
and the son of the murdered man had furnished details of the
stolen jewels to most of the local jewelers. One of these
jewelers recognized the jewels and quickly sent word to the
authorities, and one of the murderers was captured, he
confessed and gave the detectives the details of the murder of
Mordekha. Detectives investigated further and sought out the
remaining two murderers but unfortunately they were not
successful in capturing anyone else.

Mordekha's son retrieved his father's body from the cistern
and buried him. He never had piece of mind until one of the
remaining men was arrested and was hanged. Later my Uncle
Yaghub and my grandmother revealed that this captured man
was the second of the three men that grandfather came to blows
with when he witnessed his daughter and ex-wife. This man was
also tried for the murder of Mordekha and was executed. Up to
now two of the butchers were killed but one was still at large
and we will see what his fate will be!

Those who have visited Esfahan know that two famous and
massive bridges were built over the Zayandeh (زاینده رود) River
during the reign of the Safavid Dynasty, when Esfahan was the

capital of Iran. One was the Allah-Verdi (الاوردی) or Si-o-se Pol
Bridge (سی و سه پل bridge of 33 arches), built by a wealthy

Allah-Verdi or Si-o-se Pol (33 Arch Bridge)

Armenian called Allah-Verdi to connect the main section of
Esfahan to the Armenian suburb, Jolfa, on the other side of the
river and extend Chaharbagh Boulevard (Four Gardens
Boulevard) to Jolfa across this bridge. That is why this bridge
was named in Allah-Verdi's honor. The other, the Khaju (خاجو)
Bridge, was built by the government to connect the highway to
Shiraz, Parse and other provinces in the south of Iran. This
bridge also extended Khaju Avenue to the other side of the
bridge. This bridge was architecturally more important and
massive than the Allah-Verdi. The bridge was built so that it is
possible to dam the river at this bridge and create a lake for
canoeing by placing specially designed gates across the pillars
of the bridge. Box-like rooms were built on the upper level of
the bridge to watch the river and the boating on the lake; the
other reason for these rooms was to increase the size of the
pillars to withstand the force of the water flow, mainly during
spring floods.

Zell-e Soltan, the son of Nasser-al-Din Shah of the Qajar Dynasty, was a very stubborn man who spent most of his life in Esfahan at the seat of the Governor for the Province of Esfahan and he was the absolute and undisputed head of state for a long time. During the spring he would order the river dammed to create a lake for boating. After the water rose enough, several boats were launched, and the public could go and watch the boats on the river. Also, the bridge boxes were opened to women and an edict was declared that no woman should cover her face and appear in front of his majesty Zell-e Soltan. The women reluctantly would sit in the boxes with uncovered faces for the governor's observation. Those who violated this order were severely punished. It was conceivable that a man who prevented his mother, sister, wife or daughter from removing their face covering was to be sentenced to death. Secret agents were dispatched to spy and apprehend violators.

Zell-e Soltan

Grandmother said, "It was the last day of Aied (the Persian New Year, it begins the first day of spring and the celebration lasts for seven days) and the news was spread that the boats were on Zayandeh River. We and other members of the family decided to go and gaze at the boats. It was the afternoon when my husband and children reached Khaju Bridge. There was a large crowd and they were jockeying around to get a better position to watch the boats on the lake. We found a small place with much difficulty where we could view the lake. Finally, after waiting a bit, the boats appeared on the lake and the crowd was deeply mesmerized in watching the boats when suddenly the news spread that a Jewish man was kicked by a mule and that he was hurt badly and he was near death. We were very frightened and rushed toward the injured man." "We reached the man when he was gasping for his last breath. At first glance I recognized him, he was the last of the three men who was at Zilfa's house and he was finally being punished for his crime." Grandmother was explaining with satisfaction, "I pushed the crowd aside and reached the injured man and bent over him and whispered in his ear and told him I am sorry that finally you have got what was coming to you for your heinous crime. God have mercy on your soul and forgive your sins. He listened to me and looked into my eyes and he passed away. The kick was so devastating, the man laid there with his internal organs exposed, blood running out of his body, and his pale lifeless form laid there for a while and the onlookers would pass by and shake their heads with sorrow".

"Grandfather, who was elderly and weak by now and had suffered for years from that infamous night that he found his ex-wife and daughter with the three men, raised his arms toward the sky and said, 'The most just and merciful God who punishes sinners and those who do wrong, now that you have taken the life of the third man, now is the time to punish my ex-wife and my daughter for bringing disgrace to our family so they may pay for their shameful actions.' "

Years later, when my father was older and heard about the details of what happened that night, he became very angry and decided to punish the people who had caused so much grief for his father. He waited for a suitable occasion until one day he heard that his sister, Zilfa, was again flirting and joking with a stranger. My father was an uncompromising supporter in the decency of family members and had no tolerance for public disgrace and did not want his sister to bring disgrace and shame to the family again. He hurried to his sister's house and found her with a strange man. He leveled the man with one blow and after he remained unconscious, he turned to his sister, clutched her firmly and cursed her. Upon hearing the commotion, other people in the house charged, they pulled my father away from his sister and prevented him from making a huge mistake.

Khaju Bridge

Zilfa, my aunt, was fairly beautiful with a nice figure, and a pleasant, attractive voice. These qualities were the reason why men were engrossed with her. She socialized with men and had no forethought as to how people perceived her actions; she was a brave and fearless woman. Back in the day that behavior was absolutely not acceptable. That way of life, to date and have suitors, was still forbidden to a young, vibrant and beautiful girl. Also, being brought up and taught by a mother that had questionable moral standards did not help the situation. To top it off, her husband was away most of the time on business trips. He would be away at times for one year, leaving her lonely. She was at home alone, with her divorced, unmarried mother and it was obvious what would be the future of that lonesomeness.

Zilfa had five children, three daughters and two sons. The sons were sent to France to continue their education and both of them returned to Iran. One of them had peculiar behavior similar to a mentally disturbed person. He could not complete his schooling in France and returned to Iran. However, the older son finished a course that allowed him to begin teaching in Alliance School (AIU) when he returned to Iran. The three daughters were married but they passed away with many deprivations. Zilfa herself lived to be eighty-five years old, alone and no one to care for her, she died in misery. I had heard that there was not a responsible person to oversee this woman and no one cleaned her for weeks at a time. It is said that when she died none of her sons were present and she was found two or three days after she was deceased. I myself often saw her and one time I went along with her to Mama Sara, the cemetery of Esfahani Jews and also a place of pilgrimage for local, devout Muslims. It was also a place for the Esfahani Jews to go for vacation and rest in autumn. I went there and I was in the care of Aunt Zilfa and her mother, Sara. They both were very kind to me and took care of me very well and I would never forget my few days with these two women. My older brother Aziz, who had taken a room on the second floor of our house and fixed it up, at times in the evenings, would give parties with his friends. They would sing and play Tar, and Aunt Zilfa, who was still full of life, would also join the young men in singing and serenading.

CHAPTER 7

Grandfather's Family from the Second Wife

As I wrote earlier, grandfather had five sons with his second wife, and the oldest was Uncle Yeshaia. He was a somewhat literate, very stubborn, hardheaded and a combative person. He was known as a bully and strict man. In his youth, Uncle Yeshaia sold his share of the house that was given to them by grandfather to his brothers. He took the money and bought two shares of a six share house, a house almost broken down, in another area of the Juybareh ghetto and began to construct a new building. As far as I know, he continued working on this house for the rest of his life and never finished it. He had designed and poured footers for a massive and impressive building in those days; however, because of the high cost of building and Uncle Yeshaia's limited earnings, he could not complete it while he was alive. This house, where Uncle Yeshaia's second son lives, probably is still not completed.

Uncle Yeshaia married his cousin Farha, the daughter of his mother's sister. This woman was also very confrontational and stubborn and she equaled her husband. Farha was the daughter of Haiem, known as Haiem Zerang (حئیم زرنگ clever Haiem) or Haiem Alafkhor (حئیم علف خور Haiem who eats grass) and the sister of Miriam, grandfather's second wife. Haiem Zerang was illiterate, argumentative and confrontational and he was vengeful. Because of these qualities, grandfather despised this stupid and argumentative man and did not want his son to marry the daughter of this man. However, Uncle Yeshaia was not a person to honor his father's wishes or listen to his advice. He

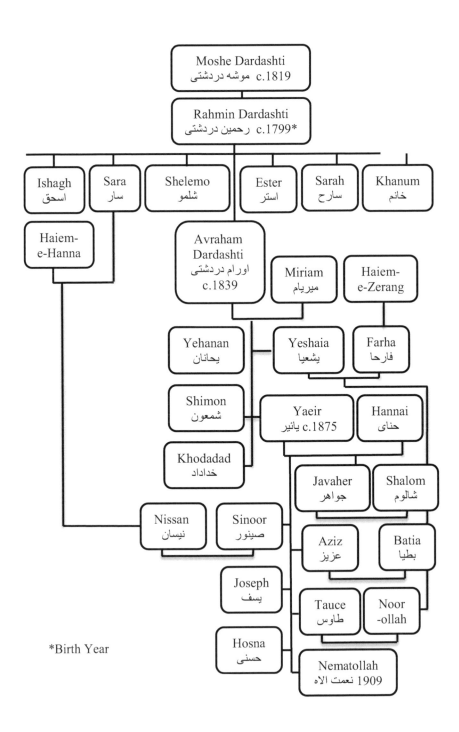

*Birth Year

became engaged to Farha in direct defiance of his father Avraham's instructions. That caused grandfather to have very little interaction with his son, and he did not care for Farha as he did for his other daughter-in-laws. Uncle Yeshaia had sensed the aloofness of grandfather and was waiting to pay back this lack of attention to him and his wife.

One day Uncle Yeshaia got into an argument with grandfather that escalated to a shouting match. Eventually Uncle Yeshaia lost all control, lifted the elderly, weak grandfather in the air and threw him on the ground, and kicked him in the head several times before finally leaving his father's home. From that day grandfather shunned him, and his son was forbidden to set foot in his home for the rest of his life.

Grandfather told a close friend, "Yeshaia will not have a happy life and will die young for disgracing his father." In actuality, that came true, and Uncle Yeshaia lived to be only forty years old and surviving him were five very young children. The oldest was sixteen years old.

I had heard that Uncle Yeshaia was elected to the Council of Esfahani Jews and he decided to improve the public conditions for Jews. He published a set of rules for small businessmen who had service related establishments and he let everyone know that the violators of those just rules would be punished severely.

One day he heard that the adacee vendor (a cereal made of lentils) at the entrance to Juybareh was charging more than the published price. Uncle Yeshaia angrily rushed to the adacee vendor and picked up the scalding pot full of adacee and hit the poor vendor on the head with it. It is so amazing how lawless and disorderly were the times that an ignorant man such as Uncle Yeshaia, could create problems for innocent people and there was no real authority, the local authorities left the ethnic groups to rule themselves. The central government was very weak and could not prevent some of these unlawful actions. People were aware of that weakness and that was why some individuals got away with encroaching on other individuals civil rights. Perhaps Uncle Yeshaia was aware that the adacee vendor knew about the disorder and chaos and thought that he could charge whatever he wanted. The adacee vendor probably was told to stop overcharging but he ignored the repeated warnings. It is hard now to judge him after so many years.

Uncle Yeshaia's house was shared with a man called Rahmin Tokhmi. Rahmin owned four shares and Uncle Yeshaia owned two shares. Rahmin Tokhmi (رحمین تخمی) was a very peaceful and unassuming man and often he had to confront his condescending neighbor and be a calm listener. This fine quality was the reason why he never allowed any discourse or misunderstanding to come between him and his combative neighbor. Rahmin had two sons and two daughters. The sons were grown and were working; the daughters had reached the age at which they were ready to be married. These two young women were very beautiful and virtuous. In those days I visited my uncle frequently and liked to gaze upon these girls and I knew that their future husbands would be very blessed.

A few years later the older daughter married a Jewish boy by the name of Khanchi (خانیچی) and they had many children. Unfortunately, the woman died while her children were very young, and this saddened the husband for the rest of his life. The other daughter also got married, and after many years of poverty and despair migrated from Iran to Israel. They became prosperous there and returned to Iran, residing in Tehran, the capital. Her husband opened a large store in the finest area of town, selling Persian rugs, and in a few years became one of the wealthiest men of the era. These two had several children, and recently I heard the man died at the age of seventy. Two sons of Rahmin Tokhmi still live in the same house, along with Shokrollah, the son of my Uncle Yeshaia.

Uncle Yeshaia did not have much wealth; his only inheritance was this house, and the investment that he had in the

bankrupt Kalimian Co. & Partners[22]   (شرکت کلیمیان و شرکاء) ,
KC&P), which was in litigation of partnership. This partnership
was with other uncles, and after the death of Uncle Yeshaia the
responsibility fell to Uncle Yehanan. Uncle Yehanan, who
himself was at a low point in his business, promised the
creditors he would pay back the loans gradually. This lasted
several years until all the loans were paid. Due to the creditors
loans, Uncle Yeshaia's wife could not collect any money from
the partnership to take care of her fatherless children. However,
this woman was so hardworking and frugal that she managed to
support the children herself.

Uncle Yeshaia had two sons and three daughters. The first
born, a son named Noorollah, married my sister Tauce. They
lived in Israel in the town of Akara with two of their children.
This Noorollah created many heartaches and trouble for his
wife, my mother, others and me. He never managed his life
intelligently or prudently in order to have a secure and
adequately comfortable life for his wife and children. Noorollah
was a generous and very warm man who would be willing to
spend all his wealth without any hesitation for his family and
friends. Unfortunately, he was not able to solve typical or
ambiguous problems. Often, because of his lack of
comprehension of problems and inability to know good from
bad, he committed mistakes that had far-reaching consequences.
During his life, he was not capable of caring for his family; he
caused insoluble problems and headaches. Finally he was
persuaded to migrate to Israel with his wife and children. In
Israel he developed mental problems and with the help of his
son Parviz and authorities, he was committed to a mental
hospital and was kept there until he was well again. Now he is
working in a business in the town he resides in, where he

---

[22] This was a company that was owned one half by my uncles Yeshaia,
Yehanan, Shimon, and Yahuda, and the other half by three brothers, Elyahu
Rahmin, Ishagh and Mayer. This was an import export company.

supports his wife and himself. He has put behind his anger and outbursts, and he lives with his wife calmly.

Shokrollah was the other son of Uncle Yeshaia. He, unlike his brother, is a very nervous, submissive and peaceful man. Shokrollah has several sons and daughters that he has reared and provided a good education without anyone's help or problem. He kept his father's house and he also bought his older brother's share and he still lives there.

Dowlat is the eldest daughter of Uncle Yeshaia. This woman had no children and was forced to adopt her younger sister's daughter after the girl's mother died. Dowlat raised this child, gave her a good life, married her off and she also raised her grandchildren with love and affection. Unfortunately, in her later years she developed mental problems and Alzheimer's disease due to the very hard life she endured. Her husband, who had similar problems, abandoned his wife and spent all his time in a corner of his home. Fortunately, Dowlat's adopted daughter took her in and cared for her.

Four years ago, while I was in Iran on a trip to Esfahan, my wife, Yafa, and I went to see my cousin, Dowlat, with my niece, Parvaneh, daughter of Noorollah and my sister Tauce, and we visited Dowlat in her daughter's home. I found her in a corner of the house withdrawn and sad, and she was not aware of anyone. I called her name and shook her and after many difficulties got her to notice us and without being happy to see us three, especially her niece whom she loved very much, she said, "You are here to take me to Tehran, I am willing to go to Israel, Shokrollah went and did not take me with him." We asked her adopted daughter what had happened and realized that when her brother Shokrollah was leaving for Israel, Dowlat begged him to take her along, but he refused to take this unfortunate woman with him. She wanted to go and see her older brother Noorollah, she was left behind disappointed. We tried hard to talk to her and divert her thoughts but we failed and it was hard to accept; this woman in normal times would be so happy to see us. If she were well, she would have showered her niece with kisses and love and would have been radiating happiness and joy to see all of us. However, now she was so quiet, out of touch with her surroundings and was swallowed in a sea of emptiness. With much sadness, we left.

Saltanat is the second daughter of Uncle Yeshaia. This woman has a heart of stone and she is a very argumentative and harsh woman. She has the ability to face the most difficult problems and not forgo her fun and pleasure for an unfortunate incident, large or small.

The oldest son of this woman is a painter. For years he had a studio on the second floor of a building on the corner of a popular square in Tehran. He painted and sold his paintings there. He also conducted art classes; my daughter, Simin, was one of his students. Simin was telling me that he had many students and most of them were young girls or married women.

One day all of a sudden it was announced that this unassuming painter had been arrested by the secret police. I was curious to know why. After some research I discovered that this man, who everyone thought was a simple and innocent man while teaching painting, was spying for an alien country. Many of his students were wives and daughters of prominent government officials and he casually collected information from them. Little by little the facts surfaced that his foolish actions were very dangerous, damaging, and important to the Iranian government. Because of the gravity of his spying, the punishment was nothing less than death.

This action was most unusual and unbelievable for an Iranian, for that matter, an Iranian Jew. The Jewish minorities did not indulge in these types of actions in the countries where they resided. This was even more difficult to accept because it happened in a Muslim country, where suspicions are high and the Jewish minority is under a microscope in search of a flaw to smear their names and condemn them.

It was a frightening and dreadful time and the Jewish community in Iran felt compelled to ensure that this young and misled man not be guilty. Therefore, all the Jewish societies, the leaders and the elders mobilized to mend the damage and prevent the further destruction of the Jewish reputation and obstruct him from being convicted and executed. The Jewish community was constantly worried and eager to know the news of his trial. However, my cousin Saltanat, the mother of this man who had a good chance of being condemned to death by hanging or firing squad, was not the least bit worried or saddened for her son.

Like others, she worked with her husband tirelessly on her son's release, but she did not forego any of her entertainment and diversions and continued as before to go to parties. One day, very distraught and very worried, I went to see if there was any news. I found my cousin all showered, very fashionably dressed and ready to go to a party I was surprised and asked her, "Do you have good news and is that why you are going to a celebration party?" She laughed and said, "No, there is no new news, why are you so surprised? I as a mother have done and I will continue to do, all I can for my son. There is nothing else I can do for him; the rest is in God's hands. My son either will be found not guilty or may be executed; I cannot allow this to ruin my precious life with these horrendously awful and sad happenings. I do not pay much attention to what people might say about me, I'll enjoy my life to the fullest and taste the pleasures of this world as much as I can." She finished saying this and continued to get ready to go to the party. Yes, this was the character and the nature of this woman.

Eventually, because of the collective efforts of influential Jewish groups and help from the merciful and kind Queen Farah and her mother, Mrs. Farideh Diba (فریـده دیبـا), this inexperienced and misguided man's life was spared and instead he was sentenced to life in prison. Then, because of good behavior, his sentence was shortened according to the law and he was freed. I did not see him after his release, but the people who were close to him would say that he had reformed and he had learned his lesson and gave up participating in politics. He had pursued his art in prison and he painted many portraits, one of which was the king. This portrait was done so well that the king was impressed; who knows, it might have been the reason for his early release.

Tuba, the third daughter and the last child of Uncle Yeshaia, married a young man from Yazd. This man had lost his father in childhood and his mother raised him. They lived in one room next door to Haim Zerang, who was Tuba's maternal grandfather. This mother and son lived in extreme poverty. Tuba was relatively old and with the help of Tuba's mother, neighbors and grandparents this young man was persuaded to marry her. Tuba's mother bought some furniture and some household essentials for her daughter. Tuba lived with her husband and mother-in-law in the most deplorable of conditions and they had a few children. Tuba was a very feisty, stubborn, rebellious, and quarreling woman. She constantly quarreled with her husband and mother-in-law about their circumstances.

This went on until both Tuba and her mother-in-law died and the children were left to their father to be raised. Unfortunately, my aunt had passed away and there was no one to take care of these children. As I mentioned before, Dowlat, who had no children of her own, adopted one of her nieces. The ailing father, who by now was completely destitute, migrated to Israel with his children. Israel had just became a nation and encouraged and assisted Jews with many children to migrate to Israel; that is why it received Tuba's ailing husband and her children with open arms. They sent all the children to school and helped each one to become a constructive citizen of Israel.

My father, Yaeir, the second son of grandfather from the second wife, was a very peaceful and kind man. He was a man who would give his life to preserve his family's honor and reputation. He always worked very hard and refused to accept

help from anyone or spoil some other person's earnings or fail
to honor their acknowledgments. Just about everyone who knew
him would vouch for this honorable man's integrity and the fact
that he never hurt any human being. Of all the sons of Avraham
Dardashti, he would always receive the kindest words and
praise. This was most evident when my father passed away; at
his funeral just about every Jewish Esfahani man and woman
was there. Everyone was grief-stricken and was shedding tears
for his death. I remember on the Saturday night that my father's
coffin was to be buried in Mama Sara (the Esfahani Jewish
cemetery); the coffin was carried on people's shoulders up to
Shah Square[23] (میدان شاه). There were at least three thousand
following the coffin. Some were shedding tears; some men and
women were mourning loudly.

Shah Square in mid-20th Century

---

[23] Shah Square originally was much smaller and was called *Naghsh-e
Jahan (the Design of the World* نقش جهان*). The square was enlarged to 163yd
x 542yd in the beginning of 17th century. My wife, our three children and I
resided half of block from this square before we left Esfahan.*

Shah Square

Ali Ghapoo

My father passed away in Morselin Hospital on Saturday morning and immediately after his death his body was taken home in a carriage. His body was kept in the basement of the room that we lived in all day Saturday because according to Jewish laws burial is forbidden on Saturday. At sundown on Saturday the body was taken to Mama Sara Cemetery, located in an isolated village about 20 miles outside Esfahan. All day

Saturday our house was full of people and wave after wave of people were coming and leaving. There were people in the yard, in all the rooms and on top of the roofs (just about all the roofs were flat in Esfahan). When the procession began in the evening and we exited our home, we noticed that the majority of people were congregating outside and had brought the traffic to a halt. People were competing with each other to be able to carry the coffin for a distance. I heard people saying, "It is a shame that this God-fearing man passed away. This man was the most peaceful and kind person amongst all of Abraham Dardashti's sons, God bless his soul."

Yes, I agreed with them, I had seen how my father during his life was the one that endured the harsh treatment, the cursing and the foul language of his brothers during any quarrel. He would go in a corner with my mother and tell her, "They are not human because they act this way toward their brother." He was very sorry and sighed heavily and exclaimed "It is sad that a person becomes so low and dirty." At times my mother would complain to my father why he endured so much grief from his brothers, and why he did not stand up for himself. My father would humor her by replying, "Woman, you do not understand, my brothers' ugly actions are deplorable and will do nothing but to embarrass our family."

To the best of my knowledge, my father was 18 years old when he married my mother, who was 12 years old. After one year they had their first child. Thereafter my mother had a child almost every year until she had 10 children. Because of having so many children, my parents were constantly under extreme pressure and they were incapable of enjoying anything. Because of these hardships, my father died at the age of 46 and left behind his painful world of hard work. My father died and left a collection of children behind for my mother to care for.

Before my father was married, he was an apprentice to many people. However, as soon as he was married he became a "pilevar," a peddler or huckster. After a short time he mastered this job to a point that he could have a relatively comfortable life for he and his wife until their first child, a daughter named Javaher (meaning jewel), was born. My parents loved each other to the point of worshipping each other and they both tried very hard to better their lives day by day. On their third year of their marriage their second child, Aziz, a son, was born. At that time boys were very important to Jewish families and it was considered a blessing from God. After the birth of a son, Jewish families would give large parties for the circumcision, a Bris or Brit Milah, where everyone would dance, drink, sing and express their thanks. My grandmother told me, "When your brother was born, everyone was very happy and immediately we began preparing for the party for family and close friends.

My grandfather was the happiest person because finally his wish of many years had come through; he did not have a grandson until then. It has been said that grandfather worshipped my brother and hovered over my brother's crib all the time. My grandfather considered my mother his favorite daughter-in-law because she gave him a grandson. After the birth of my brother, grandfather was not interested in anything else and he took my brother with him everywhere he went.

When my brother Aziz was born, my parents considered themselves very lucky and considered him a blessing that instantly improved their lives. Because of this they worked with much enthusiasm and tried very hard to better their lives to have a brighter future for their son. My mother, in addition to her housework, sewed Sekmeh, gold or silver embroidery and spun wool or cotton. This way she contributed considerably to their everyday living. My father worked very hard in Chaharmahal near Esfahan peddling secondhand goods. My father, like others, spent most of the year on the road away from his family and home. It would take months to sell all his goods to farmers and as soon as the last item would sell, he would rush home. My father's stay at home did not last long; he was home only long enough to restock his supplies and return to the location where his business was. He would leave my mother all alone again with several small children to care for.

Unfortunately, transportation in those days was at best very poor. The only means of travel was on foot or on top of four-legged animals. Travelers were forced to spend days or weeks traveling even a short distance and stop several times on the way. Today the same distance would take a few hours. Since there was no fast moving means of transportation and a lack of secure roads, thieves were constantly in pursuit of travelers. Thieves periodically attacked the passengers, their belongings were stolen and at times they were murdered. Those who ventured on a trip would put their lives and their belongings in danger.

My father, like his contemporaries, was no exception. I remember well on this occasion my father took my mother and all their children to have a sit-down[24] (بست نشستن) at the Main Stables[25] (سر طویله) of Sardar Zafr (سردار ظفر), who was the Governor of Esfahan at that time.

The reason for my father's sit-down was that the thieves stole his lifetime earnings on one of these journeys and he was frantic and very depressed. After exhausting all the usual governmental avenues and getting nowhere, as a last resort he was forced to have the sit-down.

I was no more than four years old when I saw my father, almost naked, with only a torn shirt and underpants; he walked into the house without notice. My mother and other occupants of the house, seeing my father in that unusual condition, rushed

---

[24] In the old days a sit-down was popular. When one wanted justice and a quick response, one would have a sit-down at the Main Stable of some important person. This way the owner of the Main Stable would have more pity and would be more inclined to pay attention to one's problem.

[25] Main Stable was where horses were cared for. Usually the affluent and those who could afford them would have several stables for their prize horses. In that area there was usually a platform, relatively large, that was covered with a carpet and the stable keepers spent most of their time on it. These people who took care of the horses were called mirakhor (master of horses). In these Main Stables many horses were kept; the more horses that one had in one of these stables the more influential he would be.

outside and surrounded him, asking him what had happened. My father, who was hopeless and weak and was at a point of weeping, started to explain what had happened to him. He was saying that all he had with him was stolen from him on the road and he was almost killed and a miracle happened to save his life. My mother, who noticed how tired my father was, took him in and quickly prepared a meal for him. After my father ate, rested and calmed down, he told us, "Two days ago, early in the morning we packed all our supplies and goods and started our journey with the caravan that was going to Esfahan. It was nearing the sunset and the caravan had not experienced any difficulty. The caravan bosses and I were feeling good that we had covered a good distance that day and we were nearing our destination without any danger and we were preparing to stop at the next caravansary and continue our journey immediately the next day. We were still a few miles away from our stop when we heard gunfire. Before we had a chance to gather ourselves, a few riders appeared from behind a hill and raced toward us shouting 'Stop, otherwise everyone will be shot'. The whole thing happened so fast that one did not have a chance to even think."

As my father was telling the story, the thoughts of that day made him shiver and he was visibly disturbed. After catching his breath, my father continued, "The riders came closer and ordered all the men on the caravan to assemble in one area, then they picked out two or three of the caravan bosses and took them away. The rest of us were encircled and were ordered to disrobe to our socks, and after taking all our belongings they bound our hands and ordered us to start walking in the back. We had no choice other than to obey. We walked about three hours until we approached a mountainous area and we hiked until we reached a cave where we were led. When we entered the cave we were all exhausted, thirsty and hungry and we all collapsed on the ground and waited, we were frightened and fearful about our fate. Our captors also were tired but never took their eyes off us. We sat around without a sound for a while until the thieves gathered in one corner and after a discussion and finalizing their decision, approached us and covered our eyes and made us lie down facing the interior of the cave. They also ordered us not to lift our head or move for an hour. They threatened that if anyone violated their order and looked up before they were out of sight, they would come back and kill everyone. They said after the one hour we can go where we wished to."

My father continued, "We all were on the ground face-down as we were ordered and not knowing what was going on behind us. Half an hour elapsed that appeared to me like a century passed and I thought by then the thieves were gone, I lifted my head and I tried to look behind me. All of a sudden I heard this angry voice cursing and as he approached me, he gave me a swift kick to my back and shouted 'Didn't I tell you stay down and not look behind you for a whole hour. Why did you not obey my order? Now you'll see my punishment.' He finished saying that and he sat on my chest, his hand that was clutching a knife went up in the air and my life flashed in front of my eyes. I knew that at any moment the thief's strong hand and knife would plunge in me, ending my life. My body was drenched with sweat all over and I started shivering. However, before the tip of his sharp blade penetrated me, suddenly the incensed man sneezed and the hand that was ready for killing me was all of a sudden limp and everything changed. Then he said, 'Allah be praised, today God does not want me to shed any blood.'

The man told me 'Today you should have been killed but God came to your aid. Try to follow my orders otherwise next time you would be killed for sure, go lay down on the ground like I told you and do not look behind you for an hour then you are free to go.' This time I had no choice but to follow their orders and we all stayed down motionless for the rest of the hour, counting the long minutes to go by slowly.

God only knows what I went through in that hour thinking
about losing all my fortune that I worked for and how I was
going to pay back my creditors. Even the shirt on my back was
gone; the stone-hearted thieves took everything. Now we had to
walk this long distance hungry, thirsty, empty-handed and
endure not knowing whether the distance can be covered in one
day. All of these hopeless thoughts took a frightening and
gloomy shape and its ugly face kept appearing over and over to
me. During this long hour I kept trying to figure out how am I
going to bear this heavy and awesome burden and I could not
think of a way. I was completely broken, confused and
hopeless. Several times I thought of committing suicide and
ending my misery; however, every time I would think of this,
my wife and children appeared in front of my eyes and would
reprimand me, saying, 'What should we do, what would we do
without our guardian?' I would see my children saying, 'You
are only thinking of yourself, if you kill yourself what will we
do?'

These types of thoughts quickly wiped out the idea of
suicide, and as I was busy thinking of these thoughts, my
friends shook me and made me to focus on the problem at hand.
The first thing we did, we helped each other, taking the ropes
off by using our teeth and clawing and lots of hard work."

My father continued "After untying our hands and legs, the
poor head boss, who also had lost everything, including all his
animals, stood up and said, 'Everyone follow me, I think I may
be able to find the way. I have been traveling these mountains
for years and I know every inch of it.' He was right, after a
short walk he found the road and after that he knew where to
go." My father was saying, "It was early morning and the sun
was peeking out and quickly rose. Finding the road gave us new
energy and helped us to better cope with our thirst and hunger.
We walked until noon, until we reached the first village. The
people of the village, in hearing our ordeal, led us to the village
chief and helped us in any way they could, by giving us food

and clothing. After this terrible ordeal we were all exhausted and tired, we all passed out and slept."

My father added "The next day everyone went their respective ways to their homes. It took us three days to get to Esfahan to our door. I stood at the door not knowing how I was going to face my wife and children. Finally I entered and the first person I saw was my lovely and affectionate wife, who ran to me and hugged and kissed me. All of a sudden it seemed that all the pains of the past few days left my body and felt a wonderful inner peace. I hugged and kissed her and for a while I forgot this world. It seemed that we both had grown wings and were flying in heaven without any worry or care in this world. After we were completely drunk with our love, I noticed my beautiful children who were waiting to be hugged also. I then took them in my arms and hugged them and kissed their blossom-like faces. They in return were laughing and kissing me back."

Father continued "At this time my wife finally noticed my unusual appearance and hopelessness and she was surprised that unlike other times I was without any gifts or luggage. Seeing my wife's shocked expression made me realize my sorry condition and what lay ahead for me. All of a sudden I was overwhelmed with grief and my heart felt like it was being squeezed in a vise, as if someone lowered an unbearably heavy weight on me. I felt as if I was going to come apart like a taut spring being released. With all the energy I could muster I held my composure and smiled. Then I told the children, 'Your mother and I need to talk, go and play outside until I call you later.' The children left and my wife and I went to our room. I sat my wife down and I asked her to promise not to lose her composure and be frightened. The poor woman became more worried after hearing my statement and asked me to be frank with her and tell her the whole story."

He continued, "I told her in detail what had happened to me and we both cried most of the night. My innocent children did not bother us and waited for us, but finally the two young children came in. Fortunately the children did not see our tears because we cleaned ourselves well before they had a chance to see our sad faces. I sat the children on my knees and caressed them and after that we ate. It seems the best cure for this type of misfortune is sleep, a sleep that temporarily takes away one's misery and pain."

The next day, after hearing about my father's ordeal, the family would come over trying to assure him that everything would work out and would give him hope for the future. However, my father knew it was a grave situation and how unbearable the future would be for him. After many discussions with his brothers and his friends, he decided to complain to the local government in Esfahan and asked for justice in capturing the thieves and the recovery of his goods and fortune. A very long comprehensive complaint was written and forwarded to the territory's governor, Sardar Zafr, who was one of the Bakhtiari chiefs. My father waited for weeks without hearing or seeing any response. My father realized that sitting around and waiting for some action would be the most damaging and emotionally would be more devastating. So he went back to his creditors and explained his situation and asked for their help and advice. They knew my father well and how honest he was. They told him because they trusted him, he could continue to receive merchandise on credit so he may start working again and that he could take as long as he wanted to pay back his debt. My father was happy again and felt hopeful that he could regain his economic footing.

My father was saying, "I quickly went to work with fresh energy and enthusiasm. I felt that God was with me and had blessed me with so many good things. I bought as much as I could on credit and went back to my usual territory. Luck was with me and it did not take me long to pay all my debt and I even saved some. This journey took six months and I completely sold my inventory and I returned home."

My father came home this time without any incident. He was happy, and after saving for some time to restock his inventory, he returned to his territory. Little by little his fortune increased.

My parents had ten children, but only seven survived. Their names from oldest to youngest are as follows: Javaher (daughter), Aziz (son), Hosna (a daughter who died at the age of 13 or 14), Sinoor (daughter), Tauce (a daughter who died as an infant), Tauce (daughter), Nemat (myself), Avraham (a son who died as an infant), Joseph (son), and Hosna (daughter). Before I write in detail about each one of my siblings, I would like to write about my sister Hosna, who died very young as a teenager and very much in love.

My sister Hosna, the third child of my parents, was a very pretty girl with jet-black hair and rosy cheeks; she was a very shy and innocent girl. She never revealed to anyone her deep and heavenly love for her fiancé and took this secret to her grave. Many years later I came across the man who was engaged to my sister and he told me the story of their love. When my sister reached the age of 11 or 12, she appeared physically to be 16. She was very beautiful, full of life, exuberant, with a tremendous personality and hardworking, and she was a great help to my mother in her absence.

My mother was a peddler of hand-stitched embroidery, gold stitched garments and jewelry that she would sell door to door to affluent households. That is why she seldom had much time to tend to her very young children. My mother trusted their welfare to my sister and she knew that they would be taken care of very well. The other five siblings that were born after her were all very young children and nothing but trouble. My sister had the responsibility of us from the time she rose out of bed until evening when my mother would return home. She did the laundry (of course by hand), cooked, kept all the children clean and in line and never stopped laughing and being happy. We had a neighbor next door to us that my mother had a rapport with. Their older daughter was Hosna's friend. The only son in this family was a handsome young man, hardworking and mature. He had a few pigeons and sometimes he would bring them on our roof (all roofs were flat) and fly them. This was a trend at those times that young men indulged in. Sometimes one pigeon would fly away and come back with a strange pigeon and this young man would make a profit from that. In those days, however, this was not well thought of. People considered these young men undesirable, and they were the subject of many criticisms.

This young man who for a hobby flew pigeons on the roofs had seen my sister and had fallen in love with her. Maybe in secret my sister had met with this young man and expressed her interest in him. That is why he and his mother came over to petition my parents in asking for the hand of my sister. Later we learned from this young man's sister that his parents tried to discourage him from going forward with his intentions by telling him, "Dear son, these people will never agree to let you marry their daughter because they consider themselves better than us." But the young man insisted and forced his parents to get help from some others and they jointly came forward. The first time they went home empty-handed. But because of his strong love for my sister, he never gave up and persuaded his parents to go back again for a second time until they convinced my father and received his permission with the condition that he would never indulge in flying pigeons again. He had to sell all his beloved pigeons. He did everything that he had promised to my mother and father.

After my sister was engaged she changed, she was walking on a cloud, so joyful, and she carried more responsibility with pleasure. Happiness radiated out of her, she laughed and joked with the children all the time. She would sing and dance constantly while she was diligently working. Ydidia, my sister's fiancé, also had changed and he was seen by the children on the roof hiding in a corner hoping to see my sister. Perhaps my sister also was anxious to see him but because of the culture of the time, she could not. In those times a man and a woman could not see each other without a chaperone because of some old and antiquated rules. I remember sometimes Ydidia would bring gifts and place them in front of my parents and would sit on his knees for two or three hours, very politely, and you could sense his desire to come out of his shell and talk to my sister. But he was not allowed to speak to his fiancé, my sister. This went on for a year, perhaps because my sister was too young or because my father was not completely sure about this union.

In Esfahan, to reach water, one needs to dig only about 30 feet, and because of that everyone's water needs were met by digging a shallow well. Just about all the homes had a well where a rope and a bucket were the means to draw water from the well. Those who were more sophisticated used a wooden wheel, mounted above the well, to help wrap the rope around it and to make drawing the bucket up easier. At grandfather's house where we resided, there was a well that everyone in the household used for their water source. The depth of this well was approximately 25 feet, and most of the time the water level was halfway up in the well. My grandfather had constructed this well to the latest and best architectural plans of the time. The well was bricked hexagonal from the bottom of the well to a few feet above ground level. Foot holes were constructed every so often to help descending and ascending the well for emergencies and maintenance. My grandmother, however, told me, "This well was not always constructed as well as today." Before grandfather's reconstruction, one day when one of Uncle Yahuda's daughters was drawing water from the well, the well collapsed and took her down into the well. I will provide the reader with more details about this episode shortly.

I remember it was a sunny, beautiful spring day around 10 o'clock in the morning. My sister Tauce, who was no more than 8 or 9 years old, went to the well to fetch water. She was a small girl and had a hard time reaching the edge of the well. She picked up the bucket and threw it hard in the well, not realizing that the other end of the rope was wrapped around her foot. The bucket hurtled toward the bottom of the well, unwinding the rope until it reached my sister's leg. The bucket was heavy and had enough momentum that it pulled my sister into the well. Luckily the rope was short enough and became snagged somewhere, hanging my sister upside down. Later she told us, "I realized I was hanging by the rope and I pulled myself up, pulling my head out of the water and screamed until help arrived."

We children, who were playing in the yard, heard a heavy object fall from a high point but we did not know where the sound had come from. After a few seconds we heard Tauce screaming from the well and that was when we realized what that noise was. We in turn started screaming loudly for help. My older sister Hosna leaped out of the room she was in and recognized the danger. Without hesitation she ran toward her fiancé's house, knowing that at this point the only person who could help was her beloved Ydidia. Not long after, she returned with Ydidia, who was afraid of nothing and met challenges head-on. Ydidia, realizing the grave situation my sister was in and without removing his clothes, entered the well. After a few minutes we saw him come up again, hugging my wet sister. He placed her on the ground and asked my sister if she was hurt. My sister, who was in shock and so frightened that she could not talk, shook her head indicating that she was not hurting anywhere. Ydidia asked, "Is there anything else I may do?" My sister Hosna thanked him and told him, "I will tell our parents how you bravely saved our sister from a certain death and I will never forget this incident." At this point, Ydidia, who was madly in love with Hosna, lost all control and hugged and passionately kissed her and ran off.

My grandmother explained that when this well was first dug it was left alone without bricking the sides. Two pillars were built above the well to mount a wheel. The walls of the well gradually deteriorated as water splashed on it from the drawn water. The diameter of the well gradually increased to a point that no one could descend inside the well. There was also a one-story mud hut built on top of this well. The occupants of this house had not repaired or cared for the hut or the well and had not noticed the deterioration of this old clay mud brick rubble.

No one thought that someday all of these would collapse. Until one day, when the second daughter of Uncle Yahuda, Senovey, went to the well to draw water and as she was pulling the full water bucket all hell broke loose and the clay bricks began falling on her head, collapsing everything inside the well. Poor Senovey, the wheel and the bucket all were drawn toward the bottom of the well and she was buried under the fallen clay brick rubble. The occupants of the house rushed toward the well and began digging. After hours they reached a point that they could see Senovey's fingers through the spokes of the wheel. Finally they pulled her lifeless body out of the well and placed her on the ground. Everyone was grieving her death and her parents were screaming with grief. My grandmother was saying, "I approached the girl and placed my ear at her chest and listened for any sign of life. To my surprise I heard a faint heartbeat. It seemed that I was imagining the sound. I placed my ear at her chest again and listened again. There was life in the girl's body! It was a miracle; this girl had survived being buried under all that rubble. I screamed without any control and said, 'Don't cry, she is alive.' " This young girl survived this ordeal and she grew up, married, had many children, and her children married and started their own families. Except for her oldest daughter, she had a horrible life and it was so distressing to Senovey, that finally it killed her.

Hosna was engaged to Ydidia for fourteen or fifteen months until my father backed out and dissolved the engagement because of the interference of meddlesome people, Ydidia's reputation for having pigeons and the perceived class difference. My father sent back all the gifts that Ydidia had brought and sent a message to Ydidia's parents saying it was best if their son did not marry Hosna. My father also requested that Ydidia not be seen around his daughter anymore. Ydidia honored my father's edict and was not seen again. The word got back however, that he was so affected by this decision to dissolve the relationship of Ydidia and Hosna, that he became sick and bedridden for a while mourning the loss of my sister's love. When he was somewhat better, he was urged by his parents to leave Esfahan. Thereafter, my sister lost all of her luster, her laughter, her playfulness and there was no joy in her. My sister hardly spoke to anyone, she was forever sad. A couple of months later she suddenly became ill and after a few days of a very severe headache, she left behind this mortal world and its cruel and ignorant human beings at the very prime of her life. She depart this life in her peak, just like a blossom opening, and gave up life's joys and joined the departed. After my sister's death, my parents suddenly realized the extent of their cruelty and the horrible, fatal act they committed, and the thoughtless situation they put these two innocent young lovers in by separating them. Unfortunately, it was too late. Their remorse could not reverse the happenings and bring my sister to life. My father, after a short time, recovered from the loss of his daughter (or it seemed like it) but my mother, who was in my opinion, less guilty, mourned my sister's death for years and cried over her. They buried my sister next to my grandfather and placed a fairly large stone on her grave. When my father died, his body was laid to rest next to my unfortunate sister's body.

Four years ago, I returned to Esfahan and made a trip to Mama Sara, the ancient cemetery I wrote about earlier. To my sorrow and disbelief, I found a square in close proximity to my ancestors' graves, where buses were running. Before I had a chance to build a barrier around it to protect it from the buses, I had to leave Iran for the United States. Before I die, one of my wishes is to return to Iran and go to Mama Sara and build a wall around my ancestors' graves. I have always had the wish to be buried there myself; however, I know that it is difficult to transport one's body from the United States to Iran. With God's help, maybe when I am ready to leave this world I will be in Iran and in Esfahan.

When I was in Mama Sara, I sat near the graves of my grandfather, my sister, my father and my uncles and began thinking about the past. I remembered my father holding my hand gently and stroking me with utmost love and affection and he would say, "Come here, my dear, give me your hand and let me kiss you." I heard my unfortunate sister screaming and saying, "The cruel and heartless world sent me to this grave and now I quietly rest here."

Many years later I met Ydidia in Shemiran, a suburb of Tehran. He was very happy to see me and he became very emotional and wept openly. I was surprised, and I asked him why was he crying. He composed himself, wiped his tears and said, "How is your mother, I really want to see her." I told him, "My mother is alive, let me tell you why I am here today, then I will tell you how you may see my mother." Unfortunately, I do not remember exactly when this happened; perhaps it was 1946 or 1947. My younger brother, Joseph, was ill in Tehran and I went there to help. When I arrived I found out that my brother was coughing blood, and the doctors had diagnosed his problem as tuberculosis, and everyone was very worried to be around him because TB is such a contagious disease. My brother Joseph had rented a room at the home of his cousin Faizollah, the son of my Uncle Yehanan. Faizollah had sent word that my brother had to leave his house as soon as possible because he was fearful that his children might catch the disease. My mother and I were quite desperate to find an apartment or a room for him. We both were worn out. One day my cousin Noorollah, the husband of my sister Tauce, decided to venture outside Tehran and we went to Shemiran, hoping to get lucky there.

After looking all day with no results, we were about to leave when someone told us that in a square someone was renting apartments. We walked to the square and knocked on the door and were told that there might be an apartment for rent. Fate has it that the man who opened the door happened to be none other than Ydidia. My cousin and I were shocked to find him there; it seemed as if a miracle had happened. Ydidia's surprise was no less than ours, and after we stared at each other he asked us in and asked why we were there. We told him the circumstances that brought us to Shemiran and how we were directed to his house. He called his wife in and introduced us and asked her to bring tea for us. After tea he asked me to tell my mother that we have found a place for Joseph, and Ydidia was eager to see her. He said how much he appreciated the fact that he might be a help to Hannai, my mother.

Noorollah and I had been on the verge of going back empty handed and hopeless. Now we started back to Tehran happy and energized and could not wait to give the good news to my mother. We returned and explained what had happened to us and collected my brother's belongings and went back to Shemiran. While we were gone, Ydidia and his wife had cleaned the apartment and when we returned he was ready for us. He ran to greet my mother as if he had lost his own mother for years, he hugged and kissed her while he was weeping. My mother in turn began crying, remembering what had happened to her beautiful young daughter. After both had a good cry, Ydidia helped move my brother's belongings into the apartment on the second floor. My mother felt very much at home there and was happy that she had found her lost son-in-law. We stayed there several weeks, and every day Ydidia would bring a bottle of wine to my mother and my brother Aziz. They each would have a glass of wine and reminisce about the past. That was when we found out the extent of my sister's and Ydidia's love for each other. Ydidia told us how they worshipped each other and that after my father withdrew his permission for them to get married, Ydidia became quite ill. He named his first daughter Hosna in memory of my sister.

Luckily, Joseph did not have TB; his nose would bleed and he would swallow some of the blood. Sometimes he would spit up some of that blood, giving the wrong impression, which led to the wrong diagnosis of TB.

Uncle Yehanan was the third son of my grandfather, the oldest son from the second wife. Uncle Yehanan was interesting, and the people of the time considered him a wise man. Yes, he was a bright man, but he did not have any formal education or any kind of trade. And because he always exaggerated everything he was always behind financially. He never could earn enough to match his expectations. His situation was so sad at times that my father was worried about him and would tell my mother, "My brother's situation is not good." When my uncle passed away he was so destitute that his son Faizollah had a difficult time purchasing a coffin for him to be buried in.

Three daughters and one son survived him. The oldest daughter, Monavar, was the woman whose first husband, Avraham Elyazar, died after being kicked by a horse. She had two sons with the first husband, Aaron and Aziz. These sons lived with their mother and the second husband until they were thirteen or fourteen years old; then they migrated to Israel. They went to school there and worked hard and made something out of themselves. After a few years they were well off enough that they could move the entire family — his mother, all the half brothers and sister and the second husband to Israel and watched over them until they got on their feet.

Monavar's second husband was called Nemat. He was the son of Monavar's mother's sister and was the first one to propose to her. But Monavar married Avraham. However, after Avraham's death, Nemat, who was still single, jumped at the chance and proposed again and his longtime wish was fulfilled.

Keshvar was the second daughter of Uncle Yehanan. She also married a cousin and now she resides with her grandchildren in Israel.

Faizollah, the only son of Uncle Yehanan, was brought up very spoiled, and a mommy's boy. My uncle and his wife, Sara, had raised this son with high expectations and believed their son, Faizollah was extraordinary, and this gave the impression to others that everyone should bow to this overindulged man. This man was very selfish, self-centered and ignorant. He had many sons and migrated to Israel early on. His sons all are doing well and from what I hear Faizollah has a very comfortable life.

The third daughter of Uncle Yehanan was called Saltanat. She remained unmarried and at home for many years until a tailor came along and asked for her hand in marriage. Saltanat had several sons and daughters with this man and died while the children were still very young.

Uncle Yehanan's wife was very decent, hard-working and endured many hardships without ever complaining. When Uncle Yehanan died, she moved in with her son and took care of her son's many children and household. She worked hard raising her grandchildren until she became ill and died due to neglect from her ungrateful son and daughter-in-law. God will punish those who are disloyal and ungrateful.

The fourth son of grandfather was Uncle Shimon, who was somewhat handsome, a straight shooter, very kind and warm. Uncle Shimon, like his brother Yehanan, was not an educated man and had a difficult time even writing a simple letter. Uncle Shimon was always ready for a fight and ready for a good time; however, when he died he was not as poor as his brother. Two sons and two daughters survived Uncle Shimon.

Uncle Shimon's oldest son, Habib, has very similar characteristics of his father. He is very warm, kind and has a good personality. As I write this book (Jan. 16, 1979), he is residing in Los Angeles, California, trying to get permanent residency to stay in the United States.

The second son of Uncle Shimon, Yadollah, also has his father's traits. He is a broker for imports and exports and because of his personality he is very successful. Of all my cousins I enjoy these cousins the most.

The two daughters of Uncle Shimon were Farokh and Showkat. I do not care much for Farokh because she has no respect for human decency or family, especially for her brother. Her son was married to her brother's daughter, her niece. But Farokh made her son's life a living hell until he divorced his wife. After they divorced, Farokh would never allow her grandchildren to see their mother, her niece.

The last son of grandfather is Uncle Khodadad, who I believe to be residing in Israel as I write this. If he is still alive he would probably be in his 90's. He was educated at the Alliance School (AIU), where he learned French and some English. When he graduated, even though his education was very limited, he was thought of as a learned man. After graduation he traveled to the south of Iran and began working in the Department of Customs. After two or three years, he formed a partnership to import and export. But he lost all his money and was forced to get a job with the oil company as a clerk. After a few years of working for the oil company in the South, he resigned and started a business on his own. Uncle Khodadad was a fame seeker and a playboy. That is why he left his first wife, who used to be his maid and later married her, and started living with a widowed woman who was much less attractive than his first wife. He eventually married her. Uncle Khodadad had no concept of family affection, loyalty and what love means for children. He totally overlooked his mentally ill daughter; she was left with no care or protection.

CHAPTER **8**

My Brothers and Sisters

As I mentioned before, Javaher (جواهر) was my parents' first born. She was not a pretty girl and as a child she always had problems with her eyes. My mother constantly was treating her for her eyes. Eventually, my sister lost her eyesight at age 60. She was blind for the rest of her life, which ended a few months ago at over 80 years old, in early July of 1979. Because of her looks and her eye problems, this girl had no suitors. Everyone was worried about her because she was getting up in age.

Nissan Nami Yahudi (نیسان نامی یهودی), known as Nissan Benji (نیسان بنجی), a man from Yazd, a region near Esfahan, had decided to move his family to Esfahan. Nissan Benji asked for help from my grandfather because he knew of my grandfather's fame. Grandfather helped him settle in Esfahan, start a business and took him under his wing. This man had a very nice, decent son called Shalom who was about 20 years old. Grandfather, who constantly had his granddaughter Javaher's welfare in mind, was searching for a suitable match for her. He found this young man to be very proper and shared his thoughts with Nissan Benji. Grandfather suggested to Benji that he had noticed Shalom was an outstanding young man and he would like to make him his son's son-in-law. Nissan Benji, who was elated with this opportunity, quickly accepted the offer and started formal preparation for the wedding and shortly thereafter they were married. Shalom was a very shy, honorable and proud young man. My sister, who loved him to the point of worshipping him, expected to be in in the passionate throws of love in bed all day, and never be involved in much else. Shalom could never discuss his intimate feelings openly and possibly his love play desires were not on a timely basis as his wife, Javaher. Therefore, my sister complained to my parents that

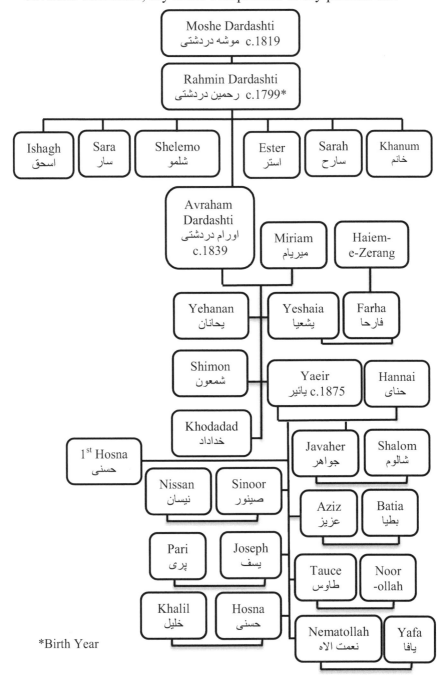

*Birth Year

Standing from left Nemat, his sister Hosna
Sitting from left his mother Hannai, his brother Aziz with his daughter
Homa, in his lap, Aziz's wife Batia, Nemat's sister Tauce on the floor from
left Nemat's grandmother Miriam and his oldest sister Javaher with her
baby in her lap (women are wearing charghat, چارقت , a triangular head
scarf, Miriam is wearing a chador as well)

Shalom was not sensitive to her needs and accused him of not being an affectionate man. My sister presented her husband to be such an uncaring and unloving man that my mother wanted to kill her son-in-law by her own hand.

The agitating and gnawing feelings of my mother continued building up until one day my father, my mother and my older brother went to my sister's house with pent up emotions of anger and found some of the relatives of Shalom at home and began scolding them. Shalom was not there because as soon as he had heard them coming he escaped and hid. I happened to be there and watched as his father and his sister were being scolded and my mother was fussing at them. But fortunately my father soon realized that this was not the proper thing to do and was very remorseful. He ordered everyone to stop and they quickly exited their house. Shalom never forgot this episode until the day of his death.

My sister and Shalom had seven children, four boys and three daughters. One of the sons, Shokrollah, while in Tehran, became ill and died due to a lack of adequate food or a decent place to live and lack of medical care. He was twenty-two years old and his death sent his mother into mourning for the rest of her life. However, the rest of the brothers and sisters were married and started families and are successful in Tehran. Alas, I spent most of my youth solving problems of this sister and her children.

This might be the right time to give you an example. A couple of years before Shalom died, he became bankrupt and because he was so proud he never mentioned that to anyone and as he deteriorated day by day. He had lost all hope; he was always very unhappy. I kept asking myself, "Why is this man in so much pain?" One Saturday my oldest brother and I went to my sister's house; Shalom was not feeling well and was in bed. He still received us with open arms. He sent one of the children to buy a watermelon and cut it for us. We sat there and talked to him and tried to get him to open up to us. Finally we found out that this man's finances were in a critical situation and we tried to find a solution to his predicament. I was in the military service and was not in a position to help him personally. My brother also was not in a position to offer any appreciable help. Unfortunately, Shalom became bedridden and was taken to the Christian Hospital of Esfahan before we had a chance to give him any effective help. He died not long after that.

The day Shalom died my mother, my brother, my sister and her last child that was still being breastfed and I were all in the hospital. That night was dark, gloomy and I thought it was the worst of times; the time seemed like an eternity to pass. He was very ill and we all expected him to die any moment. I received permission from my sergeant to be at the bedside of my brother-in-law. All night long my mother, my brother and I were outside of this sick man's room hugging and holding on to my sister and her 1½-year-old baby, Rahmatollah. The baby, who had sensed the trouble, was crying, and my sister who was scared of what lay ahead for her and her children, was shaking furiously. My sister had a difficult time making the baby be quiet. We three feverishly tried to console my sister and keep her from trembling with fear and trying to calm the baby down to stop crying; it seemed as if the baby knew that her father was dying and forever she would be an orphan.

The other patients were becoming annoyed and began to protest. Unfortunately, we could not find someone to take the baby outside and calm her. With great trouble we persuaded my sister and the baby to go home. While we were taking my sister home, the news came that Shalom had passed from this world and his suffering had come to an end. It was early morning and the sun was just peeking out when I knocked on the door of my sergeant and I tried to explain to him what had happened and begged him to give me a little more time. My brother, some of my other relatives and I initiated the arrangements for the funeral. Then we all went to my sister's house, where we found six other children hungry with no food. The next day I rushed to my unit, but the ordeal of taking care of my sister and her seven children commenced from that day forward for my mother, my brother and me. Fortunately, it all worked out and the children grew and they all took care of one another.

Nissan Benji was a strict Orthodox Jew and was deeply rooted in Jewish Yazdi tradition. I spoke to him on a few occasions. At the time of his death I was about fourteen years old. He had a Yazdi accent and he was a very interesting man when he told stories. He was explaining, "Yazdi Muslims are very religiously fanatic and are very prejudiced toward all the minorities, especially the Jews. The Muslims have very little contact with the minorities because they consider them unclean, and they expected the Jews to wear signs to clearly identify themselves. These feelings still exist and Jews are treated very harshly."

Nissan Benji continued, "I was returning home behind my donkey from one of the nearby villages. On the way I came across a Muslim mullah atop a Bandari ass (خربندرى, type of donkey) and his servant was in front of the ass. They were coming toward me from the opposite side until they reached me. When we were across from each other I greeted the mullah atop the ass and the mullah responded in return. I said my greeting and passed but shortly after I noticed the servant was running toward me saying the mullah wants to talk to you. I obeyed and started back to the mullah. The mullah was very angry and was screaming the words, 'You are a Jew.' I replied, "Yes". The mullah became angrier and shouted profanities to me, saying 'You Jud-e-Nejes (جود نجس, dirty Jew), why did you not let me know that you are a Jew before I returned your greeting?' I did not know what to do now and I was bewildered and speechless. He shouted again, asking why I was not answering him. He ordered his servant to start beating me until I find a way to undo my great error in judgement, and the servant was to continue punishing me for that mistake. The servant, who was a young and burly man was waiting for such an order, he came close to me- the unfortunate one, and slapped my face several times as hard as he could. Then he began punching me about, until I lay unconscious on the ground. As I was being beaten up I was begging for forgiveness and I promised that this will not happen again, but to no avail. Finally, the mullah ordered his servant to stop and ordered me to rub my face on the Bandari ass's ass and kiss both cheeks of the ass's behind." Poor Nissan Benji had no choice other than to follow that comical order of that savage, ignorant and nonhuman mullah.

Now that I am writing about this episode I am disturbed and saddened that there are people such as that mullah on this earth. I am also wondering how we ever survived living amongst some of these ignorant people; that man, the mullah, was supposed to be the spiritual guide for the ordinary people. It would have been much easier living in Africa among man-eating tribes than living in Iran.

For centuries the Jewish minority had to endure this hardship and humiliation, and there was no one in this wide world to answer these questions: why this minority has to be under the thumb of these heartless and cruel people, why millions of these people were massacred just because they were born Jewish, why is it that no one leaves them to be at peace in this very small homeland, Israel, where their ancestors lived after thousands of years being in exile, enduring hardship, prejudice and homelessness,, why now so many are outraged and accuse Jews for the cause of displacing and making a group of Arabs homeless , why is it that all of a sudden the world's conscience has awakened, why is it that a small country like Israel can bring in the Jews from all corners of the world and give them homes but the very wealthy countries neighboring Israel could not take care of several thousand displaced Palestinians?

Countries like Iraq killed the Jews and confiscated their wealth without raising an eyebrow; within a short time all the Jews were either killed or driven out of Iraq to other countries like Iran and other places in the world. Today it is acceptable to let Arabs occupy Jewish homes without anyone to question it. It is also ironic that the very Arab countries that fought to regain Arab land are not willing to share an inch of their land with these homeless people.

If I wanted to digress and write about the misery that Iranian Muslims brought upon the Iranian Jews it would take an inordinate amount of time. In short I could say that the Muslims consider the Jews to be infidels (one without faith), filthy, repulsive with Satan like characteristics, and finally they are primitive people. It is not difficult to imagine how dangerous it is to exist and survive amongst people with such thoughts.

I remember a few years ago, I was at my brother Aziz's house when there was a knock at the front door. I went to the door and upon opening it I found three Bazaari men (merchants from the Bazaar) asking for my brother. I called my brother to the door. He came to the door asking the three men, "May I help you"? They asked, 'Is your name Aziz Shakib?' My brother replied "yes". They said, "We have this check of yours and we want it cashed right now or we will kill you." My brother, who was surprised and confused, thought to himself how could anyone in broad daylight in the middle of Tehran, the capital of Iran, be threatened in such a manner? My brother calmly told them that they could not commit a crime in the middle of the day in Tehran. This check was a business transaction between two businessmen, the person who was supposed to receive this check reneged in his promise and that my brother was forced to put a stop to the check. The three men had thought of everything, one came forward and struck my brother and I went to help and the other two came over and a brawl started amongst us. They were three and greater in size than my brother and me. They pulled us toward a car that they had parked nearby and pushed us in the car and drove us away. Soon after we approached a police station, and we were momentarily happy. However, they had already made arrangements with the police station chief to intimidate us in paying the bogus check. What they were not aware of was my brother is not the type of person to easily be frightened. We were there in the station most of the night being cursed at and the subject of their profanity and ridicule. They were attempting to humiliate us; a disgrace to the human race and what we deserved was to be the wanderers of this planet. A heated debate ensued. Aziz and I in exasperation sought to explain to these morons that during man's history Jews have contributed to man's betterment in medicine, arts and sciences, music, and many other areas. We tried to tell them that Albert Einstein, one of the greatest physicists and mathematicians of all time, was a Jew. Unfortunately, these men were pathetical illiterates.

Finally, the police station chief apologized to us and released us because he was fearful he would be accused the next day for false arrest. Apparently the people in the house became worried when they saw us being forced into a car and driven away. They began looking for us and reported to the local police that we were missing. Later it was learned that the holder of the check was a scoundrel and a thief. He knew that the piece of land that he had sold to my brother was a wasteland and my brother would eventually wise up to it and would put a stop to

Homa, her son & husband

the check and wanted to have the money in his hand before the discovery. He had assembled the three men and the police station chief, who was his relative, to extort the money from my brother.

A few years ago, while I was in Los Angeles, California, I asked Homa, my niece, about that parcel of land. She said, "Before my father died, the government tried to locate this land but they could not find it; apparently it has always been a worthless land." These incidents are very common especially in this half-century.

Corruption has become so rampant and it has become a norm for charlatans to join corrupt governmental officials to deceive people by showing them a desirable piece of property, but in reality they were selling them a parcel in the desert. Because of the involvement of officials, the scam had become ever more convincing. These corrupt people were robbing everyone and destroying the fruits of innocent people. It seems many people recognize the problems of corruption, but they feel helpless and defenseless, therefore, it is less problematic to join the corrupt world.

In this cesspool there is a wise man, the Shah, who repeatedly attempts to protect the people of this country.

However, the people that surround him are dishonest and do not tell him truthfully what is happening around him.

Sorry, I digressed from the subject, I was writing about my older sister and her family. Shalom was a nice, hard-working and uneducated man who had learned writing and reading Farsi and some Hebrew. He was a very proud and independent man and that is why he never revealed his financial problems to anyone. My sister overall was not a fortunate person and she passed away in July.

Aziz was the second child of my parents and unfortunately he died, on April 25, 1977, about six months before I began writing this book. The lives of other members of my family and my life have been full of events and many of them were tumultuous because of the decisions and dealings of my brother. After my father died, the responsibility of all the siblings fell on his shoulders and he did not act responsibly and wisely to this obligation because he was an inexperienced young man. He wasted my father's wealth that was for taking care of his young siblings. All the heavy burden of rearing my brother, my two sisters and me was left to my mother. My mother persevered, raised us and helped us make something out of ourselves to the best of her ability. She assumed the responsibility of making sure my younger brother and I received a good education and found employment.

My mother said that when Aziz was born it was a glorious and joyous day. My brother was the first boy born to a son of my grandfather, and everyone looked at him with special affection. My grandfather loved my brother even more than my father. My grandfather at times hugged him and gave him many kisses and told him he loved him a hundred times. My brother was raised in ultimate affection and attention, which eventually led him to be very spoiled. My brother fancied having people obey him and to order others. In his youth he was penny-pinching, but in his later years he gave generous amounts to several needy people in our family.

My brother had many disappointments and bankruptcies in his businesses and he had several awful partners. But because he had patience, perseverance, ambition and competition with his well-to-do friends, he was finally successful. He used many innovative ideas and sheer hard work to become wealthy. Unfortunately, when he was independently wealthy, his health was failing and the money was not important to him anymore.

From left Aziz & Uncle Shimon

As I wrote before, my brother was very dear to me when he was quite young and he was sent to the best school the family could afford. Alliance School (AIU) was the first school that instituted modern teaching methods. It was a French Jewish institute that was established in a few cities in Iran, including Esfahan, at the turn of the twentieth century. They would teach grammar school and middle school. The students would receive a high standard of education, and after graduation the school would place the student in good governmental jobs. In those days the Swedes managed most of the Department of Customs and they needed employees with foreign language skills. Because of their knowledge of French, the students of Alliance School (AIU) were very much in demand. They were hired with decent salaries and sent to the southern ports of Iran. The majority of the teaching was in French and Farsi, but Hebrew and Jewish religious teachings were also offered. All the Jewish religious prayers were in Hebrew. My brother learned Farsi very well and could read and write French with ease.

As my brother was finishing his ninth grade during World War I, the Germans realized that the war might go the Allies way; therefore, they had opened an office in Esfahan to keep track of the opinions and attitudes of the populace. They would hire anyone with the knowledge of a foreign language. They had hired a few soldiers under the supervision of German officers and were in the process of creating disturbances and trouble for the Allies. My brother also was hired as an accountant and office manager before he had finished school. I remember suddenly one day, my brother's overall attire changed and he began wearing well-tailored suits and he was so well dressed that Muslims envied him. And he started running around with the very people that despised him. My parents often told him, "Please tone down your appearance and be careful around the Muslims." They would tell him, "Iranian Muslims do not expect to see a Jew dressed in a foreign suit and riding a bicycle through the Muslim section and Bazaar, which is the most dangerous place for a Jew because of the devout Muslims." My parents were constantly worried about that, but my brother did not pay any attention to them because he was very proud and obsessed with his looks. This went on until one day when my brother was entering the Jewish ghetto, a Muslim baker that had been waiting for him began shouting, "This bad Jew used Mohammed's name in vain, and where are the good Muslims?" Other storeowners who were waiting for this occasion began running towards him and began punching and kicking him. Fortunately for Aziz, several family and friends came to his aid and saved him by promising the Muslims that they would punish their brother severely themselves. Thereafter my brother changed his habits and the path he took home; he traveled the quiet back ways and toned down his looks.

While he was working for the Germans, he was making
good money and spent most of it on himself. He never helped
my mother, for whom money was always tight.

We lived in the house that my grandfather built, and later
this house was divided between the children and grandchildren.
This house was located in a very long and dark alley. There was
a mud brick rubble house at the end of this long dark alley. A
woman and two children (a son and a daughter) lived inside this
dilapidated home. The son's name was Mordekha and the
daughter was called Sarah. When I was 8 or 9 years old Sarah
was about 18 years old. She had big dark eyes, a beautiful face
and long, black hair. Overall she had all the features of a
gorgeous girl. Because she did not have a father and a good role
model, she was led into prostitution. The rumors were that my
oldest uncle took this naïve girl's virginity. Only God knows
the truth.

What was known for sure was that this girl lost her father
when she was young and she was left with nothing to live on.
The mother was desperate to make ends meet; therefore, out of
necessity she was forced to make use of her daughter's good
looks. Unfortunately, in those days there was not a social safety
net to save these indigent people from resorting to these acts.

So this poor girl was sucked into a whirlpool of ill repute. I
was surprised to see strange men walking towards that
dilapidated house at night and on holidays. At that age I could
not figure out why, but as I grew up I realized the reason. One
day I was playing in the yard called Big Garden[26] (Baghche
Bozorg باغچه بزرگ), when all of a sudden I saw a few men on
horseback entering this area. Ghoso-Ghazah (قوس قزح, the name
that was given to Sarah meaning Rainbow) was in the middle of
them. At this time one of the men dismounted his horse and
assisted Ghoso-Ghazah from her horse and set her on the
ground. She had a chador (چادر, a robe that women wore from

---

[26] Big Garden, the front yard of my grandfather's house, was less than
40 to 50 square yards. I am surprised that we called it the Big Garden

head to toe) on but as she was being assisted off the horse a part of her leg and her thigh were exposed and I happened to see her beautiful and sensual body.

A wealthy Zoroastrian[27] (زردشتی) businessman was among her lovers and had fallen head over heels for her to the point that he had made her his own exclusive lover. He kept her in his house and he tore down the dilapidated house and rebuilt it.

One day we saw many workers enter that old house and they stayed there for quite a long time until the house was rebuilt. Towards the end of the construction, my cousin and I dared to enter this house and we could not believe that this was the same broken-down shack. There were a few well-painted and decorated rooms, a modern kitchen and the yard was landscaped with flowers. We were surprised at the transformation in such a relatively short time.

After the house was finished, Ghoso-Ghazah and her mother and her brother returned to their newly constructed home, and thereafter furniture arrived regularly at the house. However, none of the neighbors saw the Zoroastrian businessman himself. The next time I was in that house I saw a portrait of a handsome young man and asked whose portrait that was. I was told that that this was the portrait of the man who took these people out of the cesspool.

Many years later, when my older brother and I were in Ydidia's house in Shemiran, where we had taken my sick younger brother, Ydidia told us a very interesting story about the Zoroastrian businessman.

Ydidia was saying, "When Ghoso-Ghazah began her relationship with the businessman, she was still very naïve and

[27] Zoroastrians in Iran are the oldest religious community of the nation, with a long history continuing up to the present day. Prior to the Islamization of Iran, Zoroastrianism was the primary religion of Iran. Since the Sassanid Empire was conquered by Muslims in the 7th century CE, Zoroastrians in Iran have faced much religious discrimination, including forced conversions and harassment although technically, Zoroastrians are protected as "People of the Book" in Islam.

did not know how to attract men. The businessman realized that she was clumsily peddling herself. He pitied her because he had fallen madly in love with her. He decided to protect her and her family and created a comfortable life for them. He first rebuilt the house for her mother and brother, then he relocated her in a very exclusive house in one of the best locations of Esfahan near Chahar Bagh (چهار باغ) Boulevard. He treated her just like a wife. After a while she realized the depth of his love for her and the fact that she could get away with anything. She let her family know of the deep love of the businessman and she told them that she could remove anything she desired from his house and do anything she wished.

"Sarah's mother, who lived all her life in poverty, misguided her daughter by telling her, 'This love is a short-lived love, he will not take care of you for the rest of your life and you should not fall for him. You should take advantage of the situation now and try to take some of this rich man's wealth to secure a future for you. Try to take home whatever you can from this man's house.' The naïve girl listened to her mother and brother and stole as much as she could from this man's house."

Ydidia, who himself had fallen for Sarah for a short time, was saying, "One day Ghoso-Ghazah's mother stopped by my house, saying Ghoso-Ghazah has asked for me to take my donkey and go to the businessman's house. The next day I rode my donkey to the businessman's house and met Ghoso-Ghazah. I found her waiting for me and I asked her what she needed from me. She told me she wanted me to take some things to her mother and she led me to her house, where there was a stack of very expensive rugs. She asked me to deliver them to her mother. I was very surprised and I asked what if the businessman observes me on the way, he probably will accuse me of stealing from him and report me to the police. She laughed and said to tell him that I have asked you to present these to my mother. Reluctantly I took the rugs and headed for her mother's house. As I had predicted, I saw the businessman walking home and I knew that he would catch me. Luckily, he did not notice the rugs on my donkey.

One or two years went by and Sarah lived part of the time at her house and some at her mother's until the businessman departed Esfahan and left Sarah to herself. The businessman had lost interest in her and eventually deserted her. Sarah moved back with her mother and by now she was a different person. She was hard and she took advantage of any man who crossed her; she wanted only to empty their pockets. She had come not to believe any man and she was suspicious of men. She was very cold and merciless toward all men and considered all men liars."

Just about the time that Ghoso-Ghazah left the businessman my brother Aziz was working for the German Embassy and he had money in his pockets. That is when he came across her and he fell for her also. He began seeing her and the neighbors saw my brother going to Sarah's house and reported him to my mother.

My mother was not the type of a woman to put up with that type of behavior. Therefore, she began to protect her son from the clutches of this woman. Sarah's house was adjacent to my grandfather's house and the roofs were attached and it was very easy to see the inside of either house from the roof (even inside the rooms). Mother had begun to watch my brother, and one day she noticed him entering the dark alley that led to Sarah's house. She quickly climbed the roof to watch what was going to happen next door. My mother noticed Sarah was waiting for my brother. As soon as my brother appeared they fell in each other's arms and started kissing and fondling each other all over. Just about this time a young girl appeared and asked for money to buy bread. My brother, and not Sarah, took a large amount of money out of his pocket and handed it to the girl and she exited the house. My mother quickly descended from the roof and ran to catch up with the little girl and grabbed the money away from her. Then she told the little girl to tell Sarah that Ms. Hanna was on to her. The little girl scurried back to her home. Thereafter my brother and Sarah knew that my mother was on to them and she knew everything. My brother was careful not to let my mother know about his relationship with Sarah, but mother knew that her son had natural needs and desires and that he probably was still meeting with her.

After a few months in Esfahan and creating disruption for the Allies (in World War I) in Esfahan as well as other areas in Iran, the Germans realized that they were losing the war and quickly closed up shop and departed Iran.

My brother said, "One morning when I went to work the consul met me with a box under his arm. The box seemed heavy. He opened it and showed me the gold coin content of the box. He asked me to distribute the coins among the employees and left quickly. I was given a list of names and the amount for each. I diligently followed the instructions and was nervous about coming up short. The consul came back and asked if I had enough coins and whether he should bring another box. I was surprised because the box was only half empty. It seemed that he was not worried whether I was precise or not. I told him that I had paid everyone, and the consul, without asking for any receipt, locked up the box and quickly exited. I reached over and offered the list of coins I had paid versus the list of people and told him that he could verify that everything was in order. The consul said that he did not require the list and that I should dispose of it. Then he exited the room. Half an hour later there was a general alarm in the military yard next to the consulate and very quickly 180 officers and soldiers were packed up atop horses and left Esfahan. We (the employees) were stunned at the speed at which the Germans left. One of the employees said that the consul received word that the Russians were near Esfahan and the consul had asked the Iranian soldiers to pack up and leave Esfahan but they refused. They demanded their back pay and two months' advance salary. That was why I was asked to distribute the gold coins."

After the Germans left, the Russians moved in. Everything was quiet for a few days, but then we heard that the Russians had begun to arrest the former German employees. Aziz was also arrested.

I remember well one early morning suddenly there was a lot of confusion at our home. My mother was crying and pulling her hair, saying, "My son is gone." My father was trying to put his clothes on hurriedly and left the house. The rest of us stood in the middle of the yard, puzzled at what was going on around us.

Thereafter, for one month my parents would leave the house early in the morning and would not return until late at night. At that time my father had a piece goods and cotton fabric store near our home in the ghetto. His partner, known as Shokri Ygho Sassun (شکرالله یاقوساسون), was one of my father's best friends and he and my father took turns sleeping at the store at nights because of the high rate of robbery. When Aziz was arrested my father could not sleep at the store. Shokri's sister's son, Shalom, who was my age, 6 or 7 years old and I, were asked to go to the store and stay the nights. I was very glad that I could do something to help out. I was very worried about my parents, who cried all the time, and my brother — I feared that my brother would be executed.

So Shalom and I would go to the store and lock the doors from the inside and sleep there. Even though I was very young I felt the pain of my parents. I had a very hard time sleeping all night and I tossed and turned and disturbed Shalom, who was sleeping in bed with me. I would wait with my ear to the door listening for my parents passing by. They spoke loudly and I could hear them discussing the day's happenings. I was very interested to know what was going on and I had figured out the time that they came by and impatiently waited for them. Many nights I fell asleep at the door until morning. One night, after

waiting a long time, I heard loud laughing. I pressed my ear
harder against the door and my parents and my oldest uncle,
Yeshaia, were laughing loudly. I could not believe it! Then I
heard my uncle say to my father, "Yaeir, you have a newborn
son, your son should have been hanged with some others today.
Yesterday when I was delivering a letter I knew he was
sentenced to hang. But I did not mention anything to you and
Hannai because I knew you two would have killed yourselves."
Then the voices disappeared and I could not hear anymore. I
anxiously wanted to hear the whole story and I wished I could
have been home. But I was happy that my brother was all right
and my parents were happy again.

The next morning I locked up the store and ran home. My
parents were still home and were very glad to see me. They both
hugged and showered me with kisses. My mother knew how
much I wanted to know what was going on and said, "Nemat,
your brother, Agha-Joon (آقا جون, dear sir, a nickname), has
escaped a great danger and God's willing he will be released
tonight." They said this to me and let go of me and quickly my
mother and father left the house.

That day, after a month of worry and anxiety, my younger
brother, my sisters and I were all very happy and joyful. My
older sister Sinoor, who was in safekeeping of us in my
mother's absence, assigned each of us a chore. We cleaned the
house because my mother had disclosed to Sinoor that many
people were going to be at our home that night. At around five
that afternoon my mother returned very happy with the news
that my brother was to be released soon and that he would be
home that night.

That evening my mother had cooked yakhni-adass (یحنی
عدس, lentil soup). My mother was a very good cook and I often
heard that people offered to buy her cooking. A couple of hours
into the night, my father and most of my uncles and a few
others came home happy and laughing, praising God for sparing
my brother's life. Because everyone was happy, the soup tasted

even better than ever, and everyone asked for seconds. Unfortunately, my mother had not counted on feeding so many people, especially seconds, and there was not enough lentil soup for everyone.

Days after, reading between the lines, I finally learned why my brother was released. After the Russians entered Esfahan, they decided to punish everyone that had worked for the Germans. Therefore, they began rounding up everyone who had anything to do with the Germans; they were informed that the most important person was my brother, because he was the one who handled everything for them. My brother's enemies, who despised him, had told the Russians that my brother even did their spying and all their secretive deeds. Fortunately for my brother, the Czarist regime was not like the Bolshevik regime that followed it. They believed in a fair trial and did not kill him right away.

My brother said, "As soon as I was arrested I was interrogated extensively to extract any and all important information from me, they thought I was a high level man in the Germans' operation. But after a long interrogation they did not learn much from me. I knew if they obtained the smallest bit of information from me, they would come to the conclusion that I was guilty and I would have been considered an important person in the German operation, then for sure they would have executed me. I kept repeating to them the same information over and over, that I was the person who was in charge of the kitchen purchasing and I just took care of the books for the kitchen supplies. Every day a different person with different tactics tried to deceive me to extract some important information out of me, but they all failed".

"They at times were very nice to me and at times would threaten me with death, hoping I would cave in and disclose something useful. But I stuck to the same story that I was just a clerk in the kitchen and that I just did the bookkeeping for the kitchen supplies."

After a while they reported their findings and asked for their superior's vote in the matter. In the meantime, my father and my uncles tried to find a way to release my brother Aziz. Their efforts were futile and they were losing all hope until they crossed paths with a kind man who suggested that the only person who had influence with the Russians was Mr. Sadr-Ol-Salam (صدرالاسلام), the spiritual leader of Muslims, known as Mr. Karbasi (کرباسی). He said that if you could persuade the religious leader to write a letter of recommendation, the Russians would release him for sure.

After bribing the mullah's aide, we were allowed an audience with him. They met him when he was teaching religious laws. My father clutched his robe and begged for help. The mullah stopped his teaching and asked, "Jew, what is the problem and what may I do for you?" My father and my uncles explained the predicament that my brother was in and told him that "we Esfahani Jews live under the protection of his Excellency and we expect you to protect us." My father continued, "The Russian unbelievers of Islam and God have arrested my innocent son who has not committed any crime toward Islam and his Excellency and they are trying to execute him." While my father was speaking, my Uncle Yeshaia was slipping a stack of large bills under the seat of the mullah so that the mullah could see the money. The mullah was aware of everything going on and he turned to my father and said, "Don't worry; I would not let anyone harm your son." Then he ordered one of the students to fetch some paper and a pen so he could dictate a letter of recommendation.

After the letter was finished, the mullah signed it and gave it to my father. My father and uncle quickly departed to the Russian headquarters and bribed the doorman to deliver the letter to the commander of the Russians. This was just about the time that one of the Russian soldiers had told my Uncle Yeshaia that my brother was supposed to be executed the next day. My uncle was stunned and he attempted to conceal his fears to ensure my parents would not discover this terrible news. They all stayed at the Russian Depot, very anxious that this letter might not do the job — especially my Uncle Yeshaia. They were very distraught that if this letter did not serve to perform the reversal in sparing their son's life what else could they do, this was the last ammunition they had. Luckily, the Russian commander ordered that my brother be released as soon as possible. Later it was learned that the soldier's news and the letter both were very valuable. This was a great bombshell to my father, and this was one of the contributing factors of why my father died so young.

After this episode, Aziz returned to school, which he had left prematurely. This time he finished school. After graduation, the school located a job for him at the southern ports in Khuzestan. At the same time, Uncle Shimon, who was the representative of Kalimian Co. & Partners, was on the way to Nasseri (today's Ahvaz). He agreed to take my brother with him.

In those days travel in Iran was by animals only, donkeys, horses and camels in some areas. There were no railroads or paved roads. That was why my uncle and my brother started their journey with a caravan. This journey would take 20 to 25 days — that is, if they were not prevented by thieves or faced other problems. They traveled with the caravan and left my mother at home in grief, my mother loved my brother more than any of her other children.

Two weeks later a messenger delivered a message from my brother saying that he had decided not to go to Khuzestan and that he had a job in a town called Ghahveh-Rokh (قهوه رخ), the locality where the Bakhtiari Tribe mostly lived.

What had happened was that when Uncle Shimon and my brother Aziz arrived at Ghahveh-Rokh, which was on the way to Khuzestan, Uncle Shimon decided to look up some of his and grandfather's old friends in the Bakhtiari Tribe and pay his respects. He also took my brother along with him. When the

Bakhtiaris heard that the son of Avraham Dardashti had come to visit them, all the chiefs and leaders of the tribe gathered around them and greeted them with open arms. They asked who the young man with him was. He told them that he was Mullah David's son, (my father was also called Mullah David) and that my brother had finished high school and he was on his way to Khuzestan to work in the Department of Iranian Customs. As soon as the Bakhtiaris learned that my brother was an educated man and had knowledge of French, they were very happy, because they were in search of such a man to teach their children. They made a suggestion to my uncle that they would like for my brother to stay there and they would pay him more than what he would have received at the Iranian Customs. My uncle told them the decision was my brother's and his parents', and the permission needs to come from my father. Therefore, they sent a messenger to my parents and kept my uncle and brother in that town.

My father agreed that this job was better than working for the Iranian Customs because he knew the tribes and their very good traits. He sent a message back saying, "Keep my son as a teacher and please treat him as one of your own." After the messenger brought the good news, they prepared housing for my brother and he made preparations for teaching their children.

At the time, French was very dominant and many of the surrounding countries used French as the second language. After a while, girls and women also became interested in learning French.

My brother Aziz was a good-looking and a well-dressed man who could easily attract women and girls. Wearing western-style clothing was a rarity, and people were very attracted to anyone who dressed as such. Aziz paid a lot of attention to his looks and his clothes, and because of that many women and girls in the tribe were interested in him. Little by little this became a bitter point with the men of the tribe. The tribe's men were known for their protectiveness of their women and their extreme jealousy. The men plotted a scheme to get rid of this flaunting Jew.

These tribes purposely do not interact with city people because they believe city people are contaminated and their ways are indecent, and even now they shy away from city living. Maintaining the decency and honor of one's woman or daughter is of the greatest importance to these people. They are ready to die to preserve the honor of their women. If they become suspicious of a man's intentions toward any female member of their family, it would be just cause to purge the man and the woman. In general, Iranian men that have not had contact with Westerners do not allow the female members of their family to have any contact with men at all.

My brother was well protected by the tribal leaders and no one openly tried to harm him. This did not mean that he was forgiven, and more than ever the men wanted him out of there. A group of men conspired to attack my brother at night and kill him. Fortunately for him, one of his female students discovered the plot and warned my brother. Wisely and discreetly Aziz vacated the tribal grounds one night without telling anyone. He had packed up all that he could muster and returned quietly to Esfahan.

My parents, who had no idea what was going on, were very surprised to see him one day walking back to the house in Esfahan. He kept the reason for his sudden return from my parents for some time, until some of the people who came from Ghahveh-Rokh told the story of why my brother had departed. That was when my father realized the severity of the situation and knew that his son was not out of danger, because these vengeful people do not forgive and forget so easily. That was why my father thereafter was very watchful and protective of my brother.

One day he heard that a couple of farmers were asking questions about my brother and where he lived. He knew that they had come to kill his son. He also knew that these people were very vindictive with long memories and never forgot or forgave anyone that spoke to their women. Therefore, he rushed home and sent my brother expeditiously into hiding. Soon after, there was a knock at the door, my father went to the door and found four Bakhtiari Lors. My father asked them in and asked my mother to bring them the best wine[28] we had and prepared food for them. They drank and ate late into the night. Then they hugged and thanked my parents and said, "You are very hospitable people and since we have broken bread[29] (namak gir نمک گیر) with you, we will leave in peace, it is not honorable for us to harm you and your son, from now on do not worry about us, we have forgiven your son." They said that and left. From that day on my father's mind was at ease regarding my brother and the safety of his life. Then my brother came home from the Alliance School (AIU), in the middle of the Jewish ghetto, where he had gone to hide. My mother got on her knees and thanked God for sparing her son from danger.

When my brother was teaching in Ghahveh-Rokh, he had taught one of the women of the Ilkhani[30], one of the largest families of Bakhtiari. This woman was very famous for her beauty among the tribe, and her name was Bibi Zainab Khatoon (بی بی زینب خاتون). One day mother received a large package from this woman delivered by a special courier. There was a set of the best mattresses and sheets in the package and my mother was very surprised and excited to receive this gift.

---

[28] Those days' minorities like Jews and Armenians were allowed to make liquor for their personal use. That is why there was always plenty of wine and vodka (called Aragh) at our house.

[29] Breaking bread is a very old custom in Iran and it is a custom that people follow very seriously. This meant that once one broke bread at some one's house as a guest, he could never hurt the host ever.

[30] There are two branches of Bakhtiari Tribe, Ilkhani and Ilbigi

She did not know what Bibi Zainab Khatoon's intentions were until years later — this woman was hoping that this way she could attract the attention of my brother. My mother did not know the reason for receiving this gift from such a respectable woman and she did not care. She loved the gift and used them for truly special guests for many years.

My brother stayed in Esfahan for a while, and then decided to go to the job in Khuzestan. My father, who was gone most of the time, came home immediately upon receiving word about my brother's decision. My father had become tired of working as a peddler for years because he had to be away from home often. He wished that he could spend more time at home with his family, even if it were for a short time. He was continually under the threat of being robbed or killed, and as I wrote before, he was robbed several times and on one occasion he was almost killed. My father also was aware of his brother's company Kalimian Co. & Partners (شرکت کلیمیان و شرکاء, KC&P), and the fact that they were out of the peddler business.

My father came back and had a talk with my brother. He told my brother, "Now that you have an education that is in demand, I don't think I want you to waste it in working for others, and I have plans for you and myself. Let's put together a partnership similar to my brothers' company. We could be an importer/exporter of foreign goods to Esfahan. We could take Esfahani goods to Khuzestan for export and vice versa." He also told my brother, "I have some savings that we could use and the rest I have enough credit in Esfahan that would allow us to take enough goods for our first run to Khuzestan." My brother agreed and was very happy with the decision. My father quit his peddling job and my brother took off for Khuzestan. My father promptly sent tobacco to Khuzestan in the first shipment, which made a good profit. The second shipment was also delivered and there were no incidents until the third or fourth shipment.

Each time my father shipped goods it would take about one month to reach the destination. Sometimes it would take longer than one month and at times it would be three months before my father would hear that the goods had reached the destination. The last shipment took too long and by the time it reached Khuzestan the market had crashed for tobacco and the prices had plummeted. The other merchants had shipped tobacco also and the market was saturated with tobacco. My brother, who previously had gone to India with Uncle Shimon, had shipped a large quantity of tea to Iran. Just about the time that tobacco reached him, the news came to my brother that the ship carrying the tea had been lost at sea. All this dreadful news made my brother very ill and he became bedridden.

When my brother was in India, he came across a Jewish adventurer from Tehran named David who was constantly in search of trying unusual business ventures. He attempted to deceive my brother by telling him that he had a get-rich-quick idea but no money. My brother asked him to share his idea because he might be able to help David. David told my brother that a new machine has been invented by the name of Cinematography (a movie projector) that shows pictures in motion. If we could buy one of these machines and take it to Iran, we would become rich quickly. My brother fell for the scheme and lent him the money he needed to purchase the projector. My brother gave him the money and he departed India for Iran waiting for the projector. Unfortunately, the projector was never shipped to Iran because David had not purchased the movie projector, and he spent the money for trivial things and on himself. My brother wrote many letters to David asking for the money but he never received an answer back. However, just about time when my brother heard about the tea shipment getting lost at sea he received a letter from David saying, "What we had planned did not take place and I used the money for another venture, which failed. I have no money to give back to you but I promise as soon as my situation improves I will return the money to you."

It was not hard to imagine what a damaging blow this was to my brother. This twenty-year-old man was worn out mentally and physically. My brother stayed at home all the time and did not answer any of my father's numerous letters. The creditors in Esfahan were demanding the money for the tobacco. My father had invested all his savings in this venture and had borrowed as much as his credit had allowed. My father was tight even for everyday expenses. He repeatedly sent letters and telegraphs without any reply. Every day he would come home and tell my mother that still there was no news from their son, until one day I saw my father came home distraught, depressed and exhausted. He called my mother and said, "Hannai (my mother's name was Hanna حنا, but my father liked to call her Hannai and other times Ave) come here, I need you."

My mother, realizing my father's condition, ran to him. Before she had a chance to say anything, she was ushered by father into a room. I sensed there must be unusual news; I waited by the door worried and impatient to find out what was going on. I was about ten years old but I was aware of what was going on around me. For some time I constantly had a fever of one degree above normal and I was getting thinner and thinner every day. My mother used to take me to the family doctor almost every week and his diagnosis was that I had hectic fever. He prescribed Purgative Manna[31] (شیرخشت) and Camphor.

However, my mother was told that "to cure this disease one should take medicines that are cold (all edibles were considered

---

[31] This an intensely sweet substance supplied in Iranian medical markets under two separate names of "Shahri" and "Harati". The plants producing this manna are "Cotonaster nummlaria" and "Cotonaster nummularioides" and possibly "Cotonaster Kotschyi" and "Cotonaster Oaatus" from the "Rosaceae" family. The major uses of this manna in traditional medicine are its application as laxative, tonic and anti pyrene. An anti-cancer medicine has also been recently extracted from this manna. Like Tamarisk Manifera, this substance was also used in making the famous Iranian sweet called " Gaz " . Some research scholars attribute the production of this manna to the activities of some unidentified kind of insect, while, some harvesters associate the formation of this manna to the onset of hot dry weather of mid – summer. (from Baptist Board)

cold or warm)." Therefore, my mother tried to give me
Purgative Manna (شیرخشت), Talanjebin (تلنجبین), Camphor (کافور)
, Fleawort[32](اسفرزه), the roots and bark of Kasny (endive) which
are more bitter than opium, cooked crab legs, fish, barley,
cucumber, watermelon, squash, and a variety of flowers and
vegetables whose names I cannot remember. My mother would
grind a number of these things and would put them into my
food. To make sure that I did not cause any problems for my
parents, I would eat them with no difficulty. I was always aware
that my mother had a lot to worry about and she did not need
any more difficulty from me. Now that I think back about the
ugly taste of those foods, I feel that I wanted to vomit. I had
forgotten all about my own health and I was very worried about
the bad news that was being discussed in that room.

I waited outside the door for a while until I ran out of
patience and walked in the room without permission. What I
saw was very hard for me to bear. I saw my father and mother
had their heads together sobbing and there was a letter sprawled
between them. That scene has been burned in my mind and I
will never forget that. I did not know what to do! Then I
realized that right behind me my sisters Sinoor and Tauce had
also entered the room. They were also very surprised and
puzzled to find my parents in that situation. That scene was so
heart-wrenching and unpleasant for the three of us that I am not
able to fully describe it. It took a few moments before my
parents realized that we were there, they let go of each other and
asked for us and they tried to console us and assured us that
everything was all right. They never explained what the
problem was, but days after we found out what was going on.

My father and mother were very worried that these
pressures would force their son to commit suicide or become

---

[32]Fleawort seed is the seed from either of two types of plantain known
officially as Plantago Psyllium or dark Psyllium and Plantago Indica or black
Psyllium, both belonging to the same family and both normally found
growing around the Mediterranean Sea. (from 4nature)

deathly ill. Therefore, my father decided to go to Khuzestan, but unfortunately my parents did not have the money for the trip and the food on the way. They decided to do something that my father had never done before and that was for him to go to his brothers and explain the situation to them and ask for their help. I am sorry to write that his brothers disappointed him, they made no attempt to help my father. They told him to wait a while longer until they came into some money, then they would lend him some money. The gravity of this situation was beyond his brothers' comprehension and they did not realize the problem my brother and my father were in and how important their help was to their brother and nephew. My father had no other choice than to wait for his brothers' charity. Early morning he would go to the Kalimian Co. & Partners offices and wait all day. This went on for a week with no sign of help. He finally ran out of patience and went home hopeless and frustrated, with no option left to him other than ending his own life. Luckily, my Uncle Shimon heard about the situation and ran over to my father with a gold English coin (worth about a few dollars) and gave it to my father. My father sold the coin, bought a limited amount of supplies and joined a caravan on foot to Khuzestan. My poor mother was very worried about my father and was not sure that he would have enough money to reach Khuzestan. My father and mother hugged each other endlessly and wept on each other's shoulders, and my father went on his journey. My mother impatiently counted the days waiting to hear a word from her husband and son.

Before my father departed, he told my mother, "I know what a heavy responsibility I have entrusted on your shoulders, it will be demanding and tiring to support five small children. But I am confident that you will manage this more skillfully than most men while you are being the the most loyal and tender mother. I feel confident that our children are in good hands. As I am leaving for an unknown future, I wish you much luck and success from the bottom of my heart." My father continued, "I am certain that God will reward you for your bravery, hard work, kind heart and loyalty, he will not let you down." My father was right: my mother managed to take care of us very well and lived up to all of my father's expectations.

Now when I remember that period of my life, I feel a cold chill in my spine. My mother was illiterate without any technical knowledge or knowledge of any craft or skill; she was raised in a minority group under the thumb of a majority with no social safety net. How did she manage to take care of five children without reaching for help from anyone and keeping her dignity intact? She took care of us five young children for the three and half years that my father was away without jeopardizing the family honor and respect. Unfortunately, this happened when there was a severe depression and famine. Finding food was a great problem for many, even for very able men, but my brave mother managed to find food and fed us all with tireless hard work and saved us from a sure death from hunger during the famine.

In the years 1914 to 1920 during World War I, Iran was going through the worst economic and political turmoil. There was total anarchy in Iran, and many warlords ran the country, and foreigners had a free hand in many areas of the country and competed with one another. The local government was so weak that it could not do anything. The foreign countries used Iran for their own interest and the warlords each had a foreign country as an ally. The warlords were pulling the country apart and creating havoc. The roads were not secure; therefore, no one dared to trade from one to another. Unfortunately, there was a severe drought in Esfahan Province. The city's reservoirs were being hoarded by a profit-seeking few. Therefore, it was not long before many succumbed; dying every day due to hunger.

I remember seeing many dead, decaying bodies on the public streets and there was no one to remove the bodies. People were congregating at the bakeries screaming for help and begging for a piece of bread. The lucky one that was able to buy a loaf of bread had to be very careful that someone did not strike him or her from behind to steal the loaf of bread. The people who stole bread were called ghapolam (a person who snatches something). The destitute people who had no means of feeding themselves would attack others out of desperation, knowing full well they might be beaten to death.

One gruesome spectacle that occurred in front of a bakery in the Juybareh ghetto has left an indelible mark on my mind. This episode was so disgusting that a group of us who witnessed it began crying. A woman, who had reached ahead of the crowd after many hours of waiting and with much pushing and shoving, was able to buy a loaf of oat bread. She protected the loaf of bread against her chest with all her might and tried to escape from the crowd quickly. But she was not aware that a desperate hungry man that was following her. The woman was happy that she had the loaf of bread and she would be home soon feeding her children. All of a sudden a hand reached from behind and grabbed the loaf of bread from her and without any hesitation the man shoved the bread in his mouth and started chewing as fast as he could. The woman was screaming and crying and attracting the attention of people around her. By this time all the bread was in his mouth. An angry mob quickly formed and without weighing the consequence of their action, began beating the man until he was sprawled lifeless on the ground. Then, as fast as the crowd had formed, it dissipated. I stood there watching this unbelievable scene. Some people attempted to revive the man but he could not survive the heavy blows because of many days of hunger and frailty. Yes, he was dead and gone from this cruel world and his ordeal on this earth was over. I never found out what the authorities did about the brutal beating. I believe they were preoccupied with more significant issues.

I remember my mother early in the morning would feed us either some roasted wheat or rice with a cup of tea and she would leave without eating herself. We remained in the care of my older sister, Sinoor. Sometimes we had lunch, which consisted of almonds or similar things. Many times we had nothing to eat all day, but we knew how desperate the situation was, and we would wait until my mother returned home with some food. My youngest sister, Hosna, was about 15 months old, and my mother's milk had dried up. She had become so thin that she looked like a skeleton.

This innocent, hungry child would cry all day long. We, the rest of the siblings, were very hungry and had no patience with her crying. Therefore, my younger brother Joseph and I would strike her, hoping we could stop her crying. We did not realize what an inhuman act we were committing. Now when I look back I am amazed how this frail girl survived so much difficulty. As I get older I have concluded that there is

Hosna

a hidden power and a very skilled hand guiding us and caring for us through life that protects us during these hard times.

During the famine and when I was 10 or 11 years old there were no schools open in Esfahan, so we were unsupervised at home and in the alleys. Many of the teenagers, including some of my cousins, had become street venders selling anything edible like London seed (خاکشی) or Fleawort or Jujube[33] (عناب, Annab) or similar things. In normal times these things were sold only as a medicine, but because of the famine, people ate anything that

---

[33] In Persian cuisine, the dried drupes are known as Annab, while in neighboring Azerbaijan it is commonly eaten as a snack, and are known as innab. Ziziphus jujuba grows in northern Pakistan and is known as Innab, commonly used in the Tibb Unani system of medicine. There seems to be quite a widespread confusion in the common name.

curbed their hunger. One of Uncle Yahuda's sons, Shokrollah (who is still alive), had 10 or 15 kilos of London seed that he was peddling to people. One day while I was standing near him, he told me to "come fill in for a little bit." I agreed and he left the stand to me and disappeared. I was so hungry that in his absence I shoved a handful of the seeds in my mouth and started to chew on them. As soon as I tasted the seeds I threw up the content of my mouth uncontrollably. Until today that awful taste has not left my mouth, and I will never forget those dark and miserable days.

Another day I witnessed another horrendous scene while I was near a butcher shop belonging to a man by the name of Hezghia (حزقیا) who was called Hezghi. Mullah Elyazar (I will write about him in more detail later) was making preparations to slaughter a sheep inside the butcher shop. Hezghi was holding the sheep's head steady while Elyazar was cutting the poor animal's head. As soon as the head was cut, Hezghi filled up a damaged clay pot with the warm animal's blood. Those of us who were watching all of this did not know what Hezghi was going to do with the blood. Hezghi then took the pot full of warm blood and gave it to a woman who was waiting patiently. She took the pot full of warm blood and raised it to her lips, drinking all of it to the last drop and then wiped her mouth clean and left the store. A few days later I heard that this unfortunate woman died, consuming the blood of the freshly slaughtered sheep had finally ended her excruciating hunger.

Every day during that terrible dark period one could see so many unforgettable, heart-wrenching scenes. For example, the two young Shabrang brothers (I wrote about them earlier and how they were trounced by my Uncle Yahuda), who were very athletic and burly, had a disease called dropsy. Their stomachs had swelled with water due to a lack of food. Their stomachs swelled so much it appeared that both were going to burst at any minute. They sat against a wall in the street with their legs stretched, almost naked, and panting like dogs with colorless faces looking like dead people. Their stomachs were stretched so much that they were shining like glass. This sad scene did not last long; a couple of days later I saw both of them stretched next to each other with a tattered rag draped over them just about where they had been sitting in the street.

My mother, my brothers, my sisters and I lived in grandfather's house with my paternal grandmother. My two aunts and their children also lived there. There was no man in charge in the house because they were all away on business. The wife of Uncle Yehanan, Sarah, whom we called Aunt Sarahi, was one of the aunts who lived in one section of the house with her three children, Keshvar (کشور), Faizollah(فیض اله), and Saltanat (سلطنت). The other aunt, the wife of Uncle Shimon by the name of Dowlat, whom we called Aunt Dowlati (دولتی), lived in another section of the house with her four children, Farokh (فرخ), Habib (حبیب), Showkat (شوکت), and Yadollah (یدواله). There were five of us and we lived in the north side of the house in a relatively large room, a large closet, a small room adjacent to the large room and a basement. The mothers and their children lived and slept in the same room; sometimes they all slept in the same bed (the mattress was on the floor). My mother and Aunt Sarahi both worked as peddlers and brokers and were out of the house from morning until evening. My mother's job was the reason my brother, my sisters and I survived the famine. Aunt Dowlati stayed at home and her children were not in any danger because of the protection of the partners at Kalimian & Co. (KC&P) and constant urging of my uncles to Hajj Elyahu and his brother Ishagh Rahmin (two of the partners) there was plenty of grain stored, enough that they survived very easily.

Unfortunately, my mother, because of her stubbornness and in an attempt to have my father return, did not accept the repeated offers of help from Avraham David Elyazar and Monavar's husband, the oldest child of Uncle Yehanan, who had dealings with my father. They urged my mother to accept

grain and other supplies but she told them that she did not need
any help from them or her husband. My mother would ask why
her husband had not returned home to care for his family
himself. This stubbornness was very costly and painful for my
mother and us, the children. Because of my mother's
foolishness, one or more of us could have died. Thank God
everything worked out well. I am sure a divine hand protected
us from a great disaster and avoided creating a situation my
mother would have regretted for the rest of her life.

   That same divine hand also directed my mother toward a
generous, charitable and kind lady that helped us all survive the
famine. My mother made a great deal of money during that 10
to 12 months of famine and she spent it freely. This allowed my
mother to purchase quality food for her children. The generous
lady was an elderly wealthy Muslim woman from a prominent
family; her husband was Rajabi, known as Assar. He was very
famous and respected in Esfahan. My mother sold them
expensive fabric, filigree work (silver or gold wire stitching),
termeh (similarly gold stitching), gold and silver jewelry. When
the famine came my mother pleaded to her for help and the lady
accepted her request and with open arms promised to assist my
mother any way she could. She told my mother, "Hannai, don't
worry, we will help you and your children."

   This kind lady, as she had promised my mother, gave us a
ration of two large loaves of bread a day and other foods. My
mother would come home late in the day and first caress and
hug each of us and then my oldest sister would give a report of
the day's happenings. Mostly she complained to my mother
about us not obeying her and how bad we were, expecting my
mother to punish us. She was very weary of caring for us small
children, and she would tell my mother that she wanted to
resign from having the responsibility for all of us. My mother
would listen to her and nod in agreement with her, that it was a
big job and she sympathized with her about the responsibility.
But at times mother, being so tired, she would lose it all and

scream, telling us all off. Later, I realized what my poor mother was going through and how much of a heavy weight she had on her mind, there were many looming problems coming her way. We children did not have the mental capacity to understand the gravity of the situation and how difficult it was for my mother to feed and clothe us all. All of this happened after my father left Esfahan for Khuzestan and just about the time my father and my brother were turning things around and emerging from bankruptcy.

This is a good time to explain what happened to my father after he left Esfahan and what happened to him on the way. My father said, "After twenty-two days walking across the desert, rocky and impassable, and overcoming a lot of adversities we reached Nasseri. (This was a small town at that time and it was the first stop to Khuzestan. Later, during the reign of Reza Shah[34], the name was changed to Ahvaz, and gradually it has grown to a large city and became a center of industry and commerce, an important section of Khuzestan territory). Then I proceeded to look for my son. I found him very thin and tired looking. I held him tightly in my arms and squeezed him hard as I said to him, 'Son, don't worry, I have been in this situation many times and things always have a way of working out, one should rely on God and you should not lose hope. I have always tried to work hard, to restart the business and eventually got

---

[34] In 1925 Reza Khan deposed Ahmad Mirza, the last shah of the Qajar Dynasty and was proclaimed shah of Iran. Reza Shah introduced many great reforms, reorganizing the army, government administration, and finances. He abolished all special rights granted to foreigners, thus gaining real independence for Iran.

Under Reza Shah's 16 years rule the roads and Trans-Iranian Railway were built, modern education was introduced and the University of Tehran was established, and for the first time systematically dispatch of Iranian students to Europe was started. Industrialization of country was stepped-up, and achievements were great. By the mid 1930's Reza Shah's dictatorial style of rule caused dissatisfaction in Iran. And in 1935 name changed from Persia to Iran. (from Iran Chamber Society)

back on my feet'. All night we talked, the next day Aziz (my
brother) got up with enthusiasm and a smile on his face. From
that day on we both worked very hard to earn enough money to
send back to Esfahan, for my wife and the creditors like Hajj
Hassan." My father had left Esfahan without telling anyone,
especially Hajj Hassan, who had given him the tobacco. Hajj
Hassan was very angry concerning my father's sudden
departure, and he was contemplating suing my father and swore
a warrant for my father's arrest. That's why my father and my
brother were working so diligently to earn enough money and
send it to my mother so she may deliver it to Hajj Hassan, and
convey to him that her husband had no intention of defaulting
on his debt. My mother spoke to Hajj Hassan in such a way that
he was appeased, and this deterred him from having my father
arrested in Khuzestan. That itself is an interesting story that I
have to write about later.

My father and my brother were hard-working to sell the
merchandise that remained, but the more they tried the less
successful they were. They were desperate and were losing
hope. They frequently received word from my mother that it
was becoming increasingly difficult to keep Hajj Hassan
waiting, and that made them more hopeless and frightened.
Then one day my brother received a letter from Baghdad from
David (the moving picture entrepreneur). He wrote that he had
traveled to Baghdad and was starting a new venture and that he
would soon begin sending him some money. My brother was
very tight for money; he decided to travel to Baghdad hoping to
recoup some of his money from David.

Aziz arrived in Baghdad and went looking for his evading
charlatan of a friend, David. When my brother found him, the
two old friends forgot about their differences and hugged each
other and they were happy to see each other. Then they sat
down and told each other of their misfortunes. My brother said,
"After I told him how desperate I was for money he promised
he would help me all he could, even though he himself was not

in a good shape monetary-wise." David had no money but he had an "I owe you" note from a merchant in Ahvaz. David offered that to my brother and signed it over to him. Aziz, who was anxious, quickly returned to Ahvaz, not knowing whether the note was any good. The next day he went to the man and presented the note to him. The merchant recognized the note and said, "I would like to honor the note but I have no cash, but I have plenty of merchandise and you are welcome to take merchandise for the note." My brother told him that he had to

Nemat's brother Aziz and his father sitting, Yaeir

discuss it with his father and that he would get back to him. The next day my brother took my father to the merchant's warehouse and they handpicked several rolls of sheer (a fabric or piece of clothing that is very thin and fine, almost transparent). They shipped the rolls of sheer to Esfahan to my mother, asking her to sell it in order to pay back Hajj Hassan.

One of Uncle Yahuda's son-in-laws was Mordekha (I wrote about him earlier), who at the time was called Mordekha Sarah

or Mordekha Metat (his mother's name was Sarah and his
father's name was Metat). Sarah was my great aunt, my
grandfather Avraham Dardashti's sister. She was a very able,
wise and hard-working woman and her husband, Metat, was a
very obedient man who took orders from his wife. They had
two sons and one daughter. The sons were like their mother,
very wise and skilled merchants. The daughter was no less than
the boys. This family was very well known, respected and stood
out among the Esfahani Jews.

Mordekha had married the oldest daughter of Uncle
Yahuda, whose name was Goharri. These two loved each other
like Romeo and Juliet. Mordekha also was in partnership with a
few Jews and traded between Esfahan and Khuzestan. When my
father departed for Khuzestan he asked my mother to call on
Mordekha if she ever needed any help. That's why during the
whole time that my mother was dealing with Hajj Hassan, my
mother would get advice from Mordekha. In all honesty,
Mordekha never let my mother down and was always very
helpful. When my mother received the letter from my father
about the rolls of sheer, she ran to Mordekha and asked for his
help. Mordekha, who knew the worth of the sheer, smiled and
told my mother, "Don't fear, this is very good and this will pay
for all your debt to Hajj Hassan and you should have some
money left for yourself." Mordekha accompanied my mother
and went to Hajj Hassan and worked out a very good deal for
my mother. My mother received the rolls of sheer, sold it, paid
Hajj Hassan and some of the other creditors and had some
money left over for herself.

After this episode things began to improve, my father and
brother felt better about their debts and sold all their remaining
merchandise. Now they were trying to figure out what to do for
a living.

My father, who did not have much to do during the day,
noticed that most of the oil workers at the oil company had
nowhere to have lunch or rest after work. This idea was

hounding my father until he decided to act on it and opened a small restaurant. The oil workers were very happy to have a place to go to and little by little his business took off. However, my father said, "I was not the type of man to be happy with that kind of work. My association with a group of laborers all day was not very stimulating to me. Their level of intellect was so low and boring that I was afraid that I would become like them. I would lie in bed for hours thinking about how I could get out of this territory and what I might do for a living afterward until something more satisfying happened".

Aziz was struggling to find a job in Ahvaz, but after a while he lost all hope of finding employment there. Then he heard about a labor shortage in the oil company in Masjed-Soleyman. There the British had begun to dig in search of oil. There was a lot of activity there and a great need for educated people — especially for those who knew a foreign language. These people usually came from Alliance School (AIU), Armenians from Jolfa in Esfahan, the American School in Tehran or Stuart Memorial College, which was run by the British missionaries in Esfahan.

While in Masjed-Soleyman, my brother came across one of his Armenian friends. He received my brother with open arms and offered to keep my brother at his home and promised to find him a good job. After looking for a few days, he came home one day and told my brother that an Englishman in the oil company was looking for help.

The next day, early in the morning my brother went to the Englishman's office. The Englishman asked him in and proceeded to converse with him in English. Even though my brother knew only a few words of English, he apologized and told the Englishman that he does not know English but he can speak fluent French. The Englishman was ecstatic and began interviewing my brother in French. After the Englishman thoroughly examined my brother's credentials, he was pleased with the interview and offered the position to my brother. Then he asked my brother how much he was expecting to get paid. My brother in return answered by saying "I don't know how much because I do not know what my responsibilities are and whether I am capable of performing to your satisfaction. Perhaps it might be best if I work some, then you pay me what I am worth." The Englishman agreed and my brother was put to work immediately.

The place where Aziz began working was an office where one had to work accordingly in a very particular manner. Until that time no individual had been able to satisfy the Englishman's work ethics to a point that he considered hiring someone from overseas. Even when he gave the job to my brother, he was not hopeful that he could fulfill the task either. After a few days, to the Englishman's surprise, my brother understood the requirements and performed well. After one month, the Englishman shook my brother's hand and congratulated him on a job well done and told him, "Contrary to my belief, you performed very well and you went beyond my expectations and I do not need to further consider anyone else at this time. Now we need to determine your salary. Tell me what do you expect?"

My brother explained later, "I was hoping to make a good salary of 150 to 200 rials per month. I knew this amount was too high and I did not expect that amount. In response to the generous Englishman's question I said, 'I still do not know how much I am worth to you. I would like to leave it to you to give me whatever you think I should earn.' He shyly and apologetically, with a lot of hesitation and bestowing me with compliments, said, 'I have tried very hard to get you the most that is befitting to you. But I am sorry I could not get any more than what the guidelines allow, even though this amount is the maximum, and for you the best employee, it is too low. But I promise I will work to get you more money and promote you as soon as possible.' During this whole time I was thinking to myself the amount is probably about 100 rials and I was not unhappy. The words of this Englishman were very comforting and assuring."

"The Englishman took a typewritten letter out of the pocket of his jacket; he put it in front of me and asked, 'Please do not be too disappointed, I promise I will make it up to you.' I read the letter and I was stunned to see the amount in the letter. The following was written in the letter: 'Due to the local situations and other company regulations and restrictions I cannot pay you more than 350 rials per month. I am hoping that in the near future I will increase your salary. The higher management is aware of your qualities and your performance and that is why in the near future we will remedy the situation.'

"The letter was written with a lot of praises and compliments. I left the letter on the desk and turned to the Englishman and told him that I'll try to not only satisfy the upper management but that I would try to make him, my immediate manager, pleased ."

My brother and his friend happily began looking for a room and some furniture. After getting settled in a few days, my brother sent word to my father that he had a job and that he was planning to rent one of the oil company stores for my father. He also asked my father to close the restaurant and move to Masjed-Soleyman.

A couple of months later, my brother, with the help of the Englishman, rented one of the oil company stores. The oil company had built these stores to attract businessmen to stock them with goods for the benefit of the oil workers. (similar to a commissary) The stores were rented only to people who would sign a contract promising that the store would be stocked with oil workers' essentials, and that was why my brother had to sign a contract for my father. After my father heard from his son, he sold the restaurant and went to Masjed-Soleyman without any hesitation. Then he spent a few days studying the situation and assessed what he might need to stock the store with, and then he left for Nasseri. He had very little money and no credit;

therefore, he could buy only a minimum amount of merchandise and went back to Masjed-Soleyman. The next day they opened up the store after stocking it with whatever goods he had at hand.

My father started this business with enthusiasm and finally luck was with him, his business took off so nicely that he had to hire help. He sent word to my mother that he needed help and asked if my Uncle Elyahu, my mother's brother, who had been out of work for a few months, would like to have a job in his store. Elyahu was glad to have a job and quickly packed up and left for Masjed-Soleyman.

I wrote earlier about Nissan Benji from Yazd, whose son Shalom married my sister Javaher. Nissan had three daughters and one son. When he came to Esfahan from Yazd, he brought two of his daughters and his son with him. The one sister who was left behind was married and had a daughter, but shortly after, her husband died and she had to leave Yazd and go to Esfahan to live with her parents. The name of this woman who lost her husband in her youth was Golabi (گلابی). She lived in Esfahan until her daughter was thirteen or fourteen years old and the daughter was wed to a much older man from Yazd.

When her daughter was married off, she traveled to Khuzestan and got a job with a young Esfahani Jew by the name of Mr. Moise, who had a very sensitive job at the Iranian Customs Office. After working closely with this man for several years, Golabi became pregnant and had a son. She then sued Mr. Moise and claimed that the newborn was his son, but Mr. Moise denied it and they had to go to court. Unfortunately, Golabi had no real proof and could not obtain a judgment in her favor with Mr. Moise. Distraught and desperate, Golabi took the child and went to Esfahan. Out of desperation, she appealed to the Anglican Church of Esfahan. This boy was raised in the church with a lot of help from Jalinus Hakeem (جالینوس حکیم), God bless his soul. He finished high school in Esfahan, and then he continued his education at the University of Tehran in medicine. By then his mother, who was elderly, had died, and he decided to go to the United States to complete his doctorate. To raise enough money for his trip to the U.S., he worked for the oil company in Khuzestan. Now he is a prominent doctor in New York City. The name of this man is Aziz, and in his youth he often visited us. He always took care of his half-sister, Sarai (سارائی), as long as she was alive.

Bibi, Shalom's other sister, stayed in Yazd with her husband. Bibi had two sons, Raphael and Aver. When the sons were fifteen and thirteen, their father died. Their mother became penniless and asked for help from her father. Her father asked her to move to Esfahan and gave her a room in his house.

I remember their situation became so grave it was hopeless beyond one's imagination. The elder son, Raphael, worked until he was twenty years old when he wed his cousin (his mother's sister's daughter). He had a son and I remember they all lived in this very small room (five people). Even though these destitute people lived in this small and dark room and they never complained, my sister constantly fought with them and wanted them to move out. These people's misfortune had no end. When Raphael heard that my Uncle Elyahu was on his way to Masjed-Soleyman, he went to my mother pleading for help and explained their plight to my mother. He asked my mother if he also could go to Masjed-Soleyman and work for my father. Because my mother had experienced hardship herself, she had pity on him and told him that he could also go to Masjed-Soleyman and she gave him some travel money.

Uncle Elyahu and Raphael took off for Masjed-Soleyman to work for my father. My father was very confident of making sure they would both earn enough money to end their family's misery when they got back to Esfahan. I remember Raphael always praised my father and was very thankful to him. My father and my brother were in Masjed-Soleyman for two-and-a-half years. My brother had moved up a great deal in the oil company. I do not know why my brother decided to stop working there or why he was asked to leave. Father and son went back home to Esfahan after being away for years. My mother was extremely happy to finally see her beloved husband and son and she shouted with joy and began sobbing uncontrollably. This news was as if someone had bestowed a new life on my mother, and her frail and tired body was rejuvenated.

From that moment everything changed in our lives. My mother brought painters in to paint the room that we lived in, she bought a few pieces of new furniture, and she bought new clothes for us children. It took about one-and-a-half months from the day we heard that my father and brother were in the process of returning home until we would see them in the village of Sarvarvparizon, about 20 miles from Esfahan.

I will never forget the day that I rode with Shalom, my sister's husband, on a donkey back to Sarvarvparizon (سورو پریزون). That was one of the most memorable and happiest days of my life.

A few days before my father and brother were to arrive; my mother was planning to send me with Shalom for a reception party. She also sent my younger brother, Joseph, my cousin Noorollah, my sister Tauce's fiancé, and a few of our close friends in a carriage as the rest of the reception party. From the minute I heard that I was going to meet my father and brother I was very excited, and I counted the minutes until the day came. I got up early, washed my face, put my clothes on and hurried to my sister's house, where I found Shalom waiting for me at the front door. When I got on top of the donkey it was a very early summer morning and the sun had just peeked out.

Shalom had arranged to stop at the fish market and have breakfast there. Breakfast was soup consisting of the sheep's intestines, stomach, lungs, feet and a few other parts. These parts were put in a large boiling pot of water and cooked all night. This was a very tasty soup with a fabulous aroma. Many people had lined up to have some of this soup, called avashi

(آواشی), for breakfast. We began our journey after we indulged in the avashi and one hour after sunrise we arrived at the village of Dastgard Khiar (دستکرخیار) which was about eight miles from Esfahan. From there we proceeded to Sarvarvparizon and after passing through the center of the village of Dastjerd (دستجرد), we noticed a carriage on the side of the road on the outskirts of the village. Passengers had spread a carpet next to a stream and on it had placed a concoction for smoking opium. These were my parents' friends, who had arrived to join us for a reception in honor of my father and brother. It was a gloriously beautiful day and the air was fresh, it was truly a magnificent day. The passengers of the carriage invited us to have breakfast with them. We cordially explained that we already had partaken of breakfast and we had to be on our way. After an hour we arrived at a very beautiful wooded area on the side of Zayandeh-Rood in the vicinity of Sarvarvparizon.

We were ready to continue our journey when we heard the voice of my father. Apparently the caravan that my father and brother were traveling with had also camped in this picturesque and scenic area. My father and brother, who had heard that some people might be attending their reception, also had a spread prepared for breakfast. My father caught sight of us and quickly dashed to us and gave me a hug and a kiss on the cheek with much enthusiasm. He also hugged and kissed Shalom and inquired about his family. Then I noticed my brother, Aziz, who was walking toward us. His attire and his demeanor was strange and foreign to me. He was wearing a pair of riding pants and a jacket similar to the European Chevaliers; the legs of the pants were narrow and tight against his skin where there was leg rapping up to his knees. He had on a very chic pair of riding boots, a fashionable fedora with sun glasses. After bestowing much attention on me with many hugs he greeted Shalom and asked about his family. Then we all sat and had breakfast. By this time the first carriage of greeters arrived where my younger brother Joseph was amongst them. Shortly thereafter, my father thought it might be best if Shalom and I would return since the people returning in the carriage would proceed faster than the two of us on the donkey. I had hoped that on the return trip I would ride in one of the carriages but my father convinced me that since I am older I should return on the donkey.

Shalom and I departed this pleasant and scenic location and arrived at Baghche-Bozorg, our home, after four hours; we were exhausted and depleted. There were many people at our home to greet my father and my brother. In the one room that my family lived in, my father was sitting on a mound of fluffy hand stuffed

Sinoor

mattresses, his back leaning against overstuffed pillows and beaming with happiness and contentment. My mother had a broad smile and was tending to her guests with great satisfaction and joy. It was a glorious day for her family after several years of separation from her husband, the sacrifices and the misery. She was tasting the sweetness of her success and the fruit of her hard labor to a point that she felt drunk and giddy with happiness. She repeatedly thanked God for allowing her to reach this eventful moment in her life. We children were drenched in our father's love and attention, his gentle caresses and his prolonged happiness. The enjoyment of that day has been etched in my memory for all these years.

Man has sweet days like this only a few times in his life and by far they are a fraction of the countless cruel and miserable days. People come to this world without a choice and they are drawn in mistakenly, and positively bound to this world. Life is too short and it is full of pain and misery. Luckily these attractive and deceiving moments are so delightful and pleasant that it does not allow anyone to think of their meaningless future and absorb the bitter taste of reality. Man hangs on to the very few good days and struggles all his life to find a few more good days. But he does not know that life is full of disappointments, emptiness and there is nothing but hardship in this life.

I have overlooked writing about my sister, Sinoor (صینور), becoming engaged to be married to Nissan during the time my father was gone. Nissan loved my sister very much the first few years they were married and provided for her very well, and there were no complaints. But a few years later after the first child Nejat (نجات), a son, was born, the situation changed and a period of misery and poverty began until Nejat and his six brothers grew up and went to work.

Nissan, my sister's husband, like thousands of other illiterate Jews, had no skill or education, and the only thing that he could do was to become a peddler or a seller of clothing and clothing material. At first he was trading between Esfahan and Shiraz. This man not only did not possess a skill or education, but in my opinion he could not manage his business and household affairs. When he and my sister were married he had a small nest egg that he used to manage his small business. After the first child was born they had no home, so my sister convinced him that they should take this money and buy a lot and build a house on it. My sister had not given any thought that her husband had absolutely no skill other than being a peddler and using the small nest egg to make a living.

Before the house was finished, they ran out of money and Nissan completely stopped working. He did not have enough common sense to borrow the amount needed to finish the house. In all probability he might have sold the house with a good profit and he consequently would have built another house, and this way he could have had some income. Not only did his family have nowhere to live, but he did not have a job and had nothing to live on. He committed my sister and his children to a life of impoverishment and adversity. If not for the hard work of his wife and the help of her brothers, his family would have perished.

Shalom, my oldest sister's husband was also an uneducated man without any skill, and the only thing he could do was to go to the nearby villages around Esfahan and be a peddler. Shalom was a very proud and honorable man and until his death no one knew how desperate his situation was. After he died, my parents and I realized the severity of his problems and why he suddenly died. It was realized that what he left behind were countless debts, and as we scoured around to locate something that we could sell and collect some cash for his family, we found nothing. My mother, my brother and I were faced with an impossible task. My sister and her seven young children (the oldest one was 14) were destitute and we three had to take care of them. We three were not in better shape ourselves. The situation was very grim and it seemed that there was no means in which we could care for them, but by the grace of God, things worked out and they survived. The Creator of the Children watched over them and did not forsake them. The children grew to have families and good homes. Unfortunately, Shokrollah, one of the sons, died at the age of 21 in Tehran and my sister mourned his death until her own mortality.

People who are under the impression that they should resolve problems by themselves, often become anxious, frightened and withdrawn and feel they are inept. Unknown to them, there is always someone or some natural force in the universe that directs these problems to resolution. I am sure that one should attempt his or her best and leave no stone unturned, but one should also know that a greater and mysterious entity is with us all the way, and he also intervenes in our affairs. Many times to our surprise, the

Sinoor & a few of her children

very dreadful end that we predict turns out to be working well to our benefit.

When my father and my brother returned from Esfahan, my brother and Mirza Ayube Hakeem, son of Mirza Joseph-Khanum, whom I wrote about earlier, and Aziz Ishagh Yaeir (this person was a close relative of Mirza Joseph) were partners and started up an import/export business between England, Europe and Iran. My brother used the savings that he and my father had accumulated while in Khuzestan and Aziz used this money as his share in this partnership. He would not allow my father to have any influence in the matter.

One day I witnessed my father and Aziz having a heated discussion which resulted in Aziz leaving the house angrily and my father began crying. My father was very disappointed in Aziz, to whom he had given and sacrificed so much. Even though I was very young, I could feel my father's pain as he was saying to himself "I trusted my son with my savings that I worked so hard for and he lost it all due to his inexperience" such as trusting a shady character the likes of Mr. David. My father's outrage was for traveling long distances on foot to rescue Aziz and working at jobs he despised —becoming a short-order cook and other similar undesirable jobs. He lived away from his wife and his young children for years and worked in the mountains of Masjed-Soleyman and endured hardship. Now that things were improved, he expected his son to be thankful and appreciate him for all of his hard work. Even now when I look back it saddens me and I am sorry for witnessing my father's disappointment in my brother Aziz. My father was depressed because my brother was not appreciating the sacrifices my father had made on Aziz's behalf. It especially grieves me to have seen the devastation in my father's face for being accused of not contributing any toward the savings that was brought back from Masjed-Soleyman.

My father did not have a gratifying day from that moment on. He followed my mother aimlessly; my mother, who was an uneducated woman, reasoned, now that her husband was without work and shadowed her throughout the day, he deserved to be ordered around. My father was obligated to obey her demands without any question. She did not realize how drastically her actions were breaking this very proud man. At times when my father and mother fought, she belittled him and spoke to him in a manner that was not worthy of my father. My father did not expect this kind of treatment after many years of arduous work and many sacrifices; he expected now to have a respectable and comfortable life. Instead he felt the humiliation of his wife and son. He became bitter toward the world and everything in it. My father did not complain outwardly; however, internally it was devastating him and he had a volcano inside him. These thoughts were gnawing at him and made him increasingly hopeless until one day he coughed up blood and a few days later died in the hospital, leaving this unjust and cruel world for the next life.

During the two and a half years after my father's return from Khuzestan and after being confronted with the disrespectful treatment of his wife and son, my aunt, the wife of my Uncle Yeshaia, visited my father frequently and they discussed their problems. My father felt obligated toward his brother's widow and their children and wanted to help them in any way he could. The oldest son of Uncle Yeshaia was about twenty and he had abandoned his schooling and was trying to support his mother and his siblings, but he instead was constantly creating problems for his mother due to his lack of experience. My aunt sought help from my father to direct and advise her unruly son. She was also pressuring my father to keep this boy under his wing and maybe make him his son-in-law. She persisted with this pressure until she first swayed my father and then she got an agreement from my mother, who was not too fond of this union. One day they arrived with several relatives and close friends to ask for the hand of my sister, Tauce. From that day on, Noorollah, Uncle Yeshaia's oldest son, was officially engaged to my sister. Tauce, who is two years older than I am, was very unhappy with this union. She repeatedly protested that she had no desire for this arranged union to continue with her cousin. In those days it was not proper for a decent girl to question her parents' arrangement of her impending nuptials and no one listened to her, Tauce was wed to her cousin Noorollah.

Noorollah was a conscientious hard worker and a flamboyant spender; he was very affectionate to the family but his decisions are without basis and merit, not well thought out and not wise. Until today, January 9, 1977, while he is living in Israel, this man has not been able to have even one year of secure life for his wife and children. During the forty-five years that he and my sister have been married, they are incapable of living together in peace and my sister frequently has tears because of his foolish and disastrous actions. When I claim that these two have spoiled a good portion of my youth it would not be an exaggeration. When I write about this man's unwise actions and how he disturbed my mind for so many years, it would require a separate book and it would be a distressing and dismal story.

The wedding of Tauce and Noorollah did not take place during my father's lifetime. Their marriage took place the same night as the wedding of my brother Aziz and Batia. God willing and if I live long enough, I will write about these two weddings later.

Previously I wrote that we took my father to British Morselin Hospital in Esfahan for examination and diagnosis of his ailment. At that time penicillin had not been invented, and the only treatment that was administered to him to clear his lungs was drinking warm water and cough medicine. That was why several times every day he was given steam to inhale for his lungs. This seemed to help him breathe better. This treatment continued for ten days, and on a Thursday afternoon my father said, "I am hoping that in a couple of days they would release me from the hospital and I can come home." My mother, my grandmother and I along with several other people who were there were excited and began to collect my father's belongings and prepare to go home, unaware of what fate had in store for us. That night and the next day until dusk time passed

uneventfully. Unfortunately, about seven o'clock in the evening
my father coughed an inordinate amount of blood again and all
of a sudden his breathing became very problematic. That night
my mother, my grandmother and her sister and I were with my
father until the next morning. He had a hard time breathing and
he was in great pain. That night we were all hopelessly praying
for him and were begging God to heal him and make him well.
But nothing helped and his condition worsened with each
passing hour. My mother took me to a corner and quietly told
me, "Hurry home and get your brother and tell him he needs to
come to the hospital immediately." I hurried home as fast as I
could. When I got home my brother was eating and with his
insistence I ate also. Then all my brothers and sisters and I
rushed to the hospital.

In my long life I have come across many dreadful
happenings, but that moment when we all gathered at the
hospital was the saddest and the most unforgettable day. We
saw a crowd near the hospital, and as we approached we saw
my mother, my grandmother and her sister in the street gullies
in the back of the hospital, putting lajan (mud لجن) on their
heads, wailing and sobbing hysterically. We realized what had
happened, my father was dead, and he had left this world of
pain, hard work and disappointments. Yes, my young,
affectionate and loving father had passed away at the age of
forty-seven, he had finally ended his struggle in this world and
he had departed to the next world.

I remember well when my mother saw my brother Aziz; she
screamed and said, "Now all of you are orphans." My mother
pulled aside my younger brother Joseph, who was not more
than eight, and told him, "Run home and tell everyone that your
father is dead. My brother was crying and in a daze as he ran
home and told the family and friends that our father was dead.
That day was Saturday, and according to the Jewish laws the
dead cannot be buried on Saturday. That was why we had to
wait until the sun had set to start preparing my father's body for

burial. We took my father's body home and put him in the cellar because it was a warm day. There were so many people at our house that there was not even standing room. At six in the afternoon his body was put in a coffin and was carried atop people's hands for several miles to Maidon-e-Shah (Shah Square), and then he was placed in a horse drawn hearse with an entourage of carriages following behind, slowly and sorrowfully making their way to Mama Sara, the ancient public Jewish cemetery.

When they transferred my father's coffin to the hearse, the wailing and crying commenced uncontrollably and my mother, my brothers, my sisters and I attempted to journey along with the hearse to Mama Sara, but we were not allowed. Instead we were all taken home. From that day on, several times a day my mother would gather my father's clothes to a corner of our room and as she clutched my late father's clothing, my mother would quietly sob into them. My grandmother, who by now had lost two sons, would also cry over her latest loss and would only eat one meal a day, without anyone concerned for her.

Little by little my father's death became outdated news and my mother realized that she had the responsibility of caring for her young children. My older brother Aziz also knew that the situation as it was, had changed and he realized that now he had undeniable responsibilities toward his brothers and sisters that, right or wrong, had been bestowed upon him. The first thing he did was take me out of school, and he told me, "Now you can come work for me and I will teach you myself." Now that I look back I realize that decision was unwise and how detrimental this decision was for my education. At that time I was in the upper classes of Alliance School (AIU), if I had not been taken out of school, there is no doubt in my mind that I would have finished Alliance. If the circumstance of my father's untimely death had not occurred I might have continued my education and possibly have received higher degrees with honors.

For one or two months Aziz taught me for two or three hours a day, then he became tiresome of the routine and he quit. Thereafter, Aziz made me and Tauce to be his loyal houseboy and cook My sister took care of chores and errands at home for him and I took care of chores outside the home, we did all this work with no benefits. Because of my mother's superior managerial aptitude and capabilities, she financially supported seven or eight people well, and she also paid for some of my brother's expenses. We were acquainted with the store owners and they allowed us to purchase on credit the supplies we needed. My mother would reimburse them later. This went on until Aziz was married and finally assumed responsibility for his life.

My mother thought her eldest son was a philosopher and void of any faults. All she knew was hard work; she would leave our home early in the morning and would return home late in the evening. She knew the household chores were taken care of well, first by my sister Tauce and next by me. My mother, having confidence that everything was stable and secure at home, earned decent money as a highly successful broker for exotic fabrics, Termeh (Cashmere), jewelry, gold stitched clothing, and similar items. She had several years of experience and had developed an expertise that was unmatched. She was very pleasant in her approach and customers trusted her and enjoyed having her in their home, where women gossiped and shared their secrets. Some men even bought jewelry from my mother. She was so well thought of that she was able to enter anyone's home unannounced and make her way in their rooms. The merchants gave her supplies as much as she requested without any collateral or contract because they trusted her fully.

During the twenty years that she was in business, she never had a dispute with any of the merchants. At times she had more than one hundred customers and mostly she sold to them on credit. Even though she was illiterate, she knew to the penny each customer's account — she stored all that in her memory. If by chance someone questioned her knowledge about their personal account, she assured them with calmness and logic and fully disclosed the details of their accounts. That is why anyone who knew her for some time never questioned her, and whatever she told them, they believed.

My mother devoutly continued with the Jewish traditions following my father's death and every month she performed the Jewish religious rituals. My mother obliged her sons' participation in the rituals and I bore the entire burden myself. My mother supported my resolve in attending synagogue and praying for my for father's soul three times a week on Monday, Thursday and Saturday. This was in addition to all Jewish holidays such as Yom Kippur, Rosh Hashanah and other special services in the synagogue and where it was necessary for me to be there. My mother also encouraged me to participate in reading the Torah at the bema (alter). This was difficult for me at my age. Before my father died, my father and I would attend the synagogue and he would instruct me on the proper way to

Kenisa-e Mullah Rabbi (Mullah Rabbi Synagogue)

he died, I was dutifully prepared and knew what to do (תפילה). worship and pray for a couple of hours. This explains that when

However, I had never stepped up to the bema (מיעז), to read the Torah and I was overcome with anxiety when I went up for the first time. I was fearful that I might not be able to perform exactly and properly. In any case, my mother had the opinion that it was necessary for me to go to the bema and pray for my father's soul.

My mother's belief finally gave me enough strength and courage that one Saturday morning I stepped up to the bema scared and trembling, and I began reciting the prayer. I read the first part of the prayer with all the energy I could muster, which took about 30 minutes, and then I stepped down. I might have to explain that in the Jewish religion, reciting the Torah and prayers are read in Hebrew, which is considered the proper holy language. This was the official language during the triumphant days of Jews in the Holy Land, when Jews were their own masters. This language is a branch of the Aramaic language, which is similar to Hebrew.

But after the destruction of the Holy Land during Nebuchadnezzar II[35] and the migration of a large number of Jews to Babylon and banning of sacrifices in the temples, the

---

[35] Nebuchadnezzar was the oldest son and successor of Nabopolassar, who delivered Babylon from its dependence on Assyria and laid Nineveh in ruins. According to Berossus, some years before he became king of Babylon, Babylonian dynasties were united. There are conflicting accounts of Nitocris of Babylon either being his wife or daughter. Nabopolassar was intent on annexing the western provinces of Syria from Necho II (who was still hoping to restore Assyrian power), and to this end dispatched his son westward with a large army. In the ensuing Battle of Carchemish in 605 BCE, the Egyptian army was defeated and driven back, and Syria and Phoenicia were brought under the control of Babylon. Nabopolassar died in August that year, and Nebuchadnezzar returned to Babylon to ascend to the throne. Nebuchadnezzar engaged in several military campaigns designed to increase Babylonian influence in Syria and Judah. An attempted invasion of Egypt in 601 BCE was met with setbacks, however, leading to numerous rebellions among the states of the Levant, including Judah. Nebuchadnezzar soon dealt with these rebellions, capturing Jerusalem in 597 BCE and deposing King Jehoiakim, then in 587 BCE due to rebellion, destroying both the city and the temple, and deporting many of the prominent citizens along with a sizable portion of the Jewish population of Judea to Babylon.[6] These events are described in the Prophets (Nevi'im) and Writings (Ketuvim), sections of the Hebrew Bible (in the books 2 Kings and Jeremiah, and 2 Chronicles, respectively. (from Wikipedia)

religious leaders felt it was necessary to pray instead of sacrifice. Therefore, they wrote a book with some instruction for prayer. There was also a hidden reason for the book: the Jews were scattered in many distant lands and in order to keep unity this book would assist them in utilizing the same set of rules. This book gradually grew and many new laws and instructions were added for all occasions and all the festivities. This book eventually was accepted by all Jews of all lands and became the second Jewish Holy Book, The Talmud. Since every Jewish man had to pray several times a day, most elderly men were able to recite the prayers by heart. They all sought to finish the prayer in short order so they could return to their business. This nimble recitation became customary, and some thought that reading fast was advantageous.

When I began reciting the first prayer I could not read as fast as the older men who had recited these prayers for years. I aspired to read the prayer slowly but clearly. However, the devoutly religious Jews did not agree. When I was on the bema I could ascertain with certainty the impatience and fidgeting by some of the men. At that time I thought their method was desirable and I was concerned that I was squandering their time; I was nervous and began making many errors.

Today in hindsight, when I examine the actions of a few ill-informed men I regret there was no one to enlighten these men that "when someone wants to pray to God he should pray with respect and with clear words." When one reads a prayer in haste and concludes the reading as quickly as possible, it shows disrespect with no sincerity.

With my mother's insistence and encouragement, I accomplished what was expected of me and completed this period of my life. After my father's death my sole responsibility was to obey my brother. My mother was remiss to include me in any decision making. My mother spoke with my Uncle Yehanan in secrecy and persuaded my brother to create a plan to lay the foundation for the inheritance, and my brother would manage it exclusively. Several years after my father's death, as I was sorting through my mother's clothes I came across a bundle of letters bound by a string. This peaked my curiosity and I opened the package. On one piece of paper I found a couple of sentences in Hebrew and Farsi, my brother Aziz's signature and my Uncle Yehanan's signature as witness (I don't recall the date on the documents).

"We three, Yehanan the brother, Hanna the spouse, and Aziz the son of the late Yaeir, met in the back room of Uncle Shimon and decided how to divide the inheritance left by, God bless his soul, Yaeir. Two thousand tomans to remain in control of Aziz, the oldest son, until the remainders of the siblings are grown." I took this document and kept it for later. Unfortunately, I do not know what happened to it; maybe someone stole it from me. Only God knows what happened to the document and who took it from me.

After my father's death, our daily life was returning to normal. We, the living, were becoming accustomed to my father's absence, and began planning for the future. Often my uncles and my brother would get together and discuss the day's business news. They would discuss real estate property investments and invariably they would discuss what to do with grandfather's house. It was very constricting for everyone. There were discussions about selling it and everyone buying their own house after collecting the money from the sale of grandfather's house.

CHAPTER **9**

Sale and Disbursement of Grandfather's House

The decision to sell Avraham Dardashti's house and its disbursement was shocking news to friends and relatives alike. This news was so unanticipated and surprising that it became gossip and drew protests. The response was that this action was heartless and contrary to tradition; God forbids strangers to occupy or to modify the house of Dardashti. The Jewish community declared that this home was the embodiment of Avraham Dardashti's family and it was the embodiment of an heirloom; it had a history and it was similarly a museum. However, these arguments did not sway my uncles or my brother because they were all in dire need of money from the impending sale of this house, and day by day their feelings toward selling the house grew deeper.

Although there was extraordinarily hard work that the family valued in this house, there was no offer made to buy the house. The reason was everyone assumed the price would be so prohibitive and no one would be able to afford it. This went on until my father's cousin, Mordekha, came forward and made an offer. Until then my brother and my uncles had not put a price on the house, so they all huddled for hours discussing the price. Some thought that the price should not exceed 800 tomans per four-fifths of six shares. Some thought that was too low, but all agreed that they would price it 1,500 tomans to gauge the response from a prospective buyer. Then if the buyer balked at the price, the price could be lowered. When the buyer, father's cousin Mordekha, heard the price he was very happy and accepted the purchase price, and they all arranged a time for the next day to close the deal and the buyer would have his money present. I remember the next day Mordekha arrived at the house atop a donkey. The donkey's saddlebags were full of silver coins for the purchase of the house. My brother and my uncles expected either paper money or a bank note and they all were dumbfounded. No one could imagine that Mordekha had saved all these coins over the years and kept them at home. Yes, there were still people like Mordekha that did not trust unfamiliar financial institutions referred to as "banks" to handle their money and instead they hid their money at home until a need like the purchase of a house arose.

All of the 1,500 tomans arrived in the saddlebags of the donkey in silver coins in burlap sacks. The coins were minted in pure silver in one, two, and five rial denominations (one toman is 10 rials). Today these coins would be worth at least 150,000 tomans (worth $25,000 in 1977).

The four-fifths of six shares was supposed to be divided among my grandmother, Uncle Yehanan, Uncle Shimon and the children of my father. However, my brother and my uncles decided to withhold my grandmother's share and no one bothered to discuss this with grandmother. It is astounding how these covetous men were full of themselves, that they did not even contemplate disclosing to her that her share was divided amongst the two uncles and the surviving children. In reality they should have acquired her permission to sell the house. In any case, these selfish men collected their share of the sale and promised to vacate the premises in a few months after locating other housing.

From that day on, every member of the household was in search of a parcel of land to start building a home. Uncle Yehanan bought an old dilapidated two-bedroom near Monar –e Sareban (Sareban Minaret) of Esfahan, at a bargain price. He immediately began remodeling and with extreme hardship made the house habitable. Uncle Shimon and my brother Aziz bought two pieces of land adjacent to each other, not far from Uncle

Yehanan, near Monar-e Sareban[36] and also began building. Uncle Shimon's parcel was not as large as ours; it was about three hundred square meters (about thirty-three hundred square feet). Our lot was full of trees and my mother called it Baghi Chi (small wooded garden). Uncle Shimon started building a two-story house. But before he had a chance to complete the house he depleted his funds, and with much difficulty he finished one or two rooms in order to move in.

Aziz picked a relatively elaborate design for a house and started construction without estimating what it might cost to complete the construction. I was designated the foreman at age 14. At first Aziz examined the construction daily with enthusiasm but soon he lost interest. The only person who intently remained with the construction was my mother, who also was diligently working to earn money to pay the workers. I also stayed with the construction during the first and second months and in my opinion, performed admirably — this was not an exaggeration, it was what everyone was stating.

Due to my brother's inexperience in building homes he had made many errors. These errors and miscalculations were passed along to bricklayers. The humble bricklayer would lay brick all day and create a beautiful arch but by afternoon the arch would collapse, due to the legs of the arch could not support the weight.

---

[36] There are two minarets near each other at the northern edge of Juybareh. [36] The Sareban Minaret, also known as the minaret of the camel driver, is a perfect example of a free-standing brick minaret from the twelfth century Seljuk period of central Iran. The minaret is 48 meters high, and was built between CE 1130 to CE 1155. The minaret was probably part of a mosque complex, now gone. Over time the minaret has acquired a visible tilt to the west. (from kufic.info)

The other minaret, Monar-e-Chehel Dokhtaran (The Minaret of 40 Virgins) stands in a small alleyway leading south from Khiaban-e-Sorush. This minaret stands some 21 meters high. The local people also call the minaret "Gar Lang" according to Honarfar, and he tells the story of the derivation of this name from that of an English missionary, Father Garland, who had moved into the area at the start of the twentieth century with the express aim of converting the local Jewish population. (from Isfahan.org)

There were many do overs and head scratches. The bricklayer's desire was to ensure a high quality brick job; therefore he would stay late rebuilding. A top-notch bricklayer would make two-and-a-half rials a day and a hard- working mud packer made as much as one-and-half rials. Every day there were two bricklayers and five or six mud packers. Due to a shortage of work, everyone struggled to keep their job and would bend over backward to please us. At that age I thought that no one should even take a cigarette break. I myself worked like a dog every day and by afternoon I was totally exhausted. Some days, to entice a few of the workers to work even harder, they were promised one Shahi (a fraction of a rial) more.

Unfortunately, by the end of the day when my mother arrived to compensate everyone, she would not honor my promise and she and I had many discussions concerning this matter, she would leave me embarrassed in front of the bricklayers and workers. This continued for two or and a half months until I was totally depleted because of the aggravation with my mother and the disinterest and apathy of my brother not fulfilling his responsibilities to compensate the

Monar-e-Sareban or the Minaret of the Camel Driver (منار ساربان)

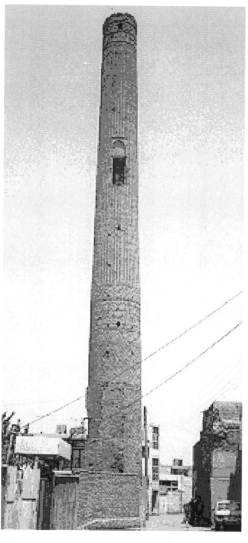

Monar-e-Chehel Dokhtaran (منار چهل دختران)

workers. All of these pressures made me despise construction. I remember one day my mother and I were having one of our regular discussions. My mother was under extreme pressure herself—she not only had to earn money for us, she had to in addition earn enough to pay the workers. She was doing her routine work as well as my brother's. My mother, without giving much thought, expressed a complaint in regard to me, to my brother. My self-absorbed brother, the without weighing gravity of the situation, gave me the beating of my life and locked me in the woodshed. This was his way of modifying my behavior and putting some sense in my head. He was supposed to be my example, my role model and my teacher. At that age I had full comprehension and was aware of my surroundings and I knew the difference between right and wrong. I knew that no one purposely wanted to hurt me; I knew this was my brother's way of educating me. He was wrong; this was not the method to make me an obedient person; he should have been a better example for my siblings and me.

My mother loved her children to the extreme, and I am certain when I was being admonished by my uncle, she must have been mortified. My mother was not at fault and I do not want to vilify her, she was under extreme pressure. I surmised my mother's accountability that required her to work relentlessly or the construction would come to a halt and there being no one to complete or fund it.

My mother would leave early in the morning and return home late in the afternoon depleted, she understood the enormous burden of supporting five children and the cost of the construction. She knew she was not receiving help from Aziz. When she arrived at the building site she did not need any difficulty from me. In her exhausted condition, if I dared to open my mouth I would face her wrath. I know that if we, my siblings and I, had a decent role model and guardian who encouraged us to go to school and to be compassionate to my mother, that my mother could have been more at ease. We should have been more obedient and better-behaved children.

In any case, after my beating and being imprisoned in the woodshed, I decided to go on a hunger strike and kill myself to end my misery. However, my mother's cries and begging made me change my mind and I decided to eat. My mother had gone to Uncle Yehanan to convince me to eat. I decided from that night on, to refuse managing the construction even though I knew my weary, devoted mother would have to pick up the loose ends. I was very tired of building!

The first-floor skeleton that was made with sun-dried mud bricks was completed when my mother and brother, who also were drained from building, halted the construction. By now we had to relocate from grandfather's house because it was sold. Therefore, my mother and my brother decided to complete a couple of the rooms and make it habitable to move in. When we moved in, the porch in front of the rooms was not paved. As one stepped out of a room the floor was dirt and a much of it was dragged inside to the adjoining rooms. I reasoned that I could pave it with the leftover stone. Therefore every day, every chance I had, I forced my brother Joseph to assist me in making mud and move heavy stones to pave the porch. A few years ago Joseph disclosed to me that "when we were paving the porch, I worked beyond my capabilities." I asked him why and he said, "At that time I was eight or nine years old and you would order me to carry heavy buckets of mud and stone that were more than one hundred pounds to deliver them where you needed." Yes, he was right; I too, was so ignorant that I would force this child to do things beyond his capabilities. Now that I look back I am ashamed of and remorseful for my actions.

Center sitting Nemat's youngest brother Joseph, interpreter for the British Army during WWII

Joseph and I paved the porch, the area in front of it and some areas on either side of it with leftover stone and brick. This helped stop the flow of dirt and mud inside the rooms. I should remind the readers that this lot was one thousand square meters (less than a quarter-acre). Half of it was left for the house and the yard and the other half was planted with grapevines. The grapes were seedless and were the highest quality. The first couple of years the vines produced a bumper crop of excellent grapes due to constant care. This half was leased to the Department of Revenue, where they constructed a building. Due to a lack of care the grapevines dried up and died. The Baghi Chi (small wooded garden where we lived) had two water sources, one cow well (water was drawn by a cow) and another by a public stream.

I should digress and explain how the farmers irrigate their fields in Iran. Iran is a very mountainous country with very little rain fall. A great deal of the land is barren due to a lack of water. The little water that the farmers use derives from one of two sources: ghanot or river water. Because of this water shortage the farmers frequently skirmish with each other and at times it leads to a farmer's fatality. The way a ghanot is constructed is as follows: a specialist would find a reservoir of water underground at a bank of a mountain, and then he would recommend digging a well. After the well is dug and it is determined that in fact the reservoir is large, the decision would be made to take the water to the farmlands. Then a tunnel would be constructed underground that would eventually surface some miles downstream where the farming would start.

The surface water that flowed in small streams was the result of the melting snow and the rainwater in the mountains, where it would begin in small streams. Then small streams would join to form a river. Farmers would direct the river water into canals that led to farms. To protect oneself from floods and wasteful runoff of water, people constructed dams to store the water for summer and dry periods. Many dams were constructed in Iran in the first half of the twentieth century, especially during Reza Shah's time, and it alleviated some of the country's thirst for water.

Baghi Chi (small wooded garden, باغی چی) had the privilege to use the water out of one of these surface water streams. There were times that I asked the water manager to kindly direct some water towards us. This water had to pass through a lot above us, across an alley, under our house to finally reach our vineyard. The gardener in the lot above us, however, occasionally would block the water and not allow a drop to reach us. We constantly had to bicker with him concerning this matter, until one day I reached the end of my patience and picked a fight with him. I pinned the obstinate gardener on the ground and he begged for mercy and promised he would never block the water again. Thereafter, we had no problem with the surface water.

CHAPTER 10

I Started School Again

After the construction concluded I started thinking about my future. I observed that my classmates from Alliance School (AIU) had continued their education at the English College. Within a short time they had acquired some English and they were able to locate decent jobs in Khuzestan at the oil company or in the oil fields of Masjed-Soleyman with relatively good salaries. I was quite sad that I had missed that opportunity and I was determined to find a solution to my problem. After studying my situation carefully, I realized that it was not too late and all was not lost. So I joined forces with two dear friends of mine, Shimon Manzoorollah (شـمـعون منظورالـه) and Sassoon (ساسون), who were in the same situation. I suggested to them that the three of us apply to go to school at the English College (it was actually a high school) to continue our studies. This suggestion was met with enthusiasm and it was decided to proceed to the school the next day.

The three of us arrived at the English College and met with the principal, Mr. Thompson. I will never forget that day. I got dressed early in the morning and carried a cane and put on my father's light robe. I looked like a middle-aged man who was attempting to look distinguished. I thought I could attract the attention of Mr. Thompson who was a very intelligent person! I did indeed make an impression. When we arrived at his office, we stood in front of the principal's desk and introduced ourselves and explained our intentions to register at the English College. Mr. Thompson, who was no more than thirty-five years old, eyeballed us up and down for some time, while we three did not move a muscle and stood in front of him waiting for his reaction. Mr. Thompson then studied us carefully, especially myself, and inquired from each of us many questions

From left Nemat, Joseph Ausher (يوسف آشر)

concerning our level of education and our family situation until he became comfortably familiar. At that time I was about 16 years old and my two dear friends were about the same age.

Mr. Thompson requested that one of the teachers, Mr. Harris, an Englishman, would study our cases with Mr. Thompson and decide if they would accept us. My friends were placed in the sixth grade and I was placed in the seventh grade. Mr. Harris, the English teacher at Stuart Memorial College in Esfahan, was different from other teachers. He was very interested in learning the Farsi language. He would venture to villages around Esfahan on horseback and occasionally he would travel as far as the mountains to the Bakhtiari Tribes and Chaharmahal and socialize with them. Later, during World War II, as soon as the war began the other English teachers departed for England. Mr. Harris, however, journeyed towards the Bakhtiari Tribes and Chaharmahal and then on to Khuzestan, where he then departed for England. There was no news from Mr. Harris until the Allies occupied Iran.

The reason the Allies attacked and occupied Iran was that the Iranian government had allowed German agents to penetrate Iran and that threatened the security of the region. The factual reason was the Allies desired a path for ships in the Persian Gulf to supply Russia with war materials, and this was the most beneficial route for the Allies.

At this time, unexpectedly Mr. Harris surfaced again and became the Deputy British Counsel. Mr. Harris' actions during the war were complex and interesting. For example, he had hired some of his former students to spread rumors or news, or at times report the pulse of the people and their thoughts. He was especially interested in any information one could gather about secret German agents. This Mr. Harris was in the business of apprehending German spies and he arrested many that were troublesome for the British and the Allies. On one occasion he had traveled to the Bakhtiari Tribes and invited a doctor friend named Griffith to join him and conveyed to him that it would be a pleasant and relaxing outing. Dr. Griffith accepted Harris' offer and brought his young son along. Several servants and cooks accompanied Harris and Dr. Griffith so their excursion would be enjoyable and comfortable

They mounted horses and mules and departed Esfahan. Early that morning as they traversed their way to the mountains, Harris, Dr. Griffith and his son, who were riding at the head of the caravan, entered the Chaharmahal and Bakhtiari land. Suddenly, gunfire was heard. Before anyone had a chance to discover the direction of the gunfire, Mr. Harris was shot and was killed instantly. Dr. Griffith jumped off his horse immediately and yanked his son off his frightened horse and they swiftly ran toward an enormous boulder, to be safe from the aim of gunfire. The gunfire continued and Dr. Griffith returned gunfire, but unbeknownst to him and his son, there was little to no chance of surviving this ambush. Dr. Griffith and his young son were both killed. The servants and the cooks made an attempt to conceal themselves behind other rocks and boulders wondering what their fate would be. After the three were killed, the gunfire ceased. A member from the attacking tribe signaled to the servants and conveyed to them that since they were native to Iran they were spared and could return home. The servants and the cooks returned to Esfahan and went to Iranian authorities and the British Embassy to explain what had happened to the Englishmen and his guests. Later we learned that the Iranian government captured the assassins and they were transferred to the British. The bodies of the three were located and they were shipped to England and Australia respectively.

The very first day that I attended school I decided to complete one or two grades as quickly as possible and begin my pursuit of employment . So for one and half years I worked diligently at my schooling, and I was prepared to embark on the mystery that lay ahead of me.

My education in totality was not more than five or six years. My elementary years were interrupted at Alliance School (AIU) and I never received a certificate of completion. I was out of school for four or five years, patiently waiting for my schooling to get under way again at English College. After completing the eighth grade I ended my schooling again to look for employment. Unfortunately, I could not bank on my high aptitude because I did not possess a wise, caring, and sincere guardian. I especially excelled in math and my perception after the fact being I could have marveled at a potential contribution in this field. Sadly, the time passed and it was not retrievable.

Today at educational institutions, people of this talent are sought out.

I had to abandon English College because there were no funds for me to continue. My two dear friends and I decided to apply at the English Oil Company office in Esfahan (in those days, a large portion of Iranian oil was in Bakhtiari, Masjed-Soleyman and the southern part of Iran, and they had several oil wells that had just been drilled into a major oil field and the company now needed many employees). The name of this company was Anglo-Iranian Oil Company (AIOC). We three filled in the necessary forms and one day walked to the oil company. We found the placement clerk by the name of Ammanollah Khan Daragahi (امان اله خان درآگاهی), who was about thirty or thirty-two years old at the time. I had met him before at Morselin Hospital, later called the Christian Hospital. Amman-Khan

Mr. Ammanollah Khan was a Baha'i[37] (بهائی) and he was a faithful spokesman for this religion. This man was very religious, truthful and had a pleasant disposition; one of his noble qualities was that he never dismissed anyone that reached out to him for help. He had a very good sense of humor and likewise, he made everyone laugh that came in contact with him, he was very likeable fellow. Unfortunately, there were some that had taken advantage of his good nature and had made life miserable for him. However, his good friends aided him in his time of need and assisted him to get back on track. Later I will write more about him.

Mr. Ammanollah Khan met us with enthusiasm and received our applications and promised that he would mail the applications to Masjed-Soleyman as soon as possible. He also

[37] Founded a century and a half ago, the Baha'i Faith is today among the fastest-growing of the world's religions. With more than five million followers, who reside in virtually every nation on earth, it is the second-most widespread faith, surpassing every religion but Christianity in its geographic reach. Baha'is reside in more than 100,000 localities around the world, an expansion that reflects their dedication to the ideal of world citizenship. (from Baha'is, Baha'i International Community)

snapped our photos to include with our applications. One of us was small framed and had a frail body. He was my best friend, Shimon Manzoorollah. We three put our applications in and waited, it seemed like an eternity before we received a reply from them.

After two weeks had passed, we were informed that our applications had been reviewed with their responses. We rushed to the oil company offices and met with Amman-Khan. However, the news for me was disappointing and unexpected. The letter had indicated that Shimon Manzoorollah and Sassoon had been accepted and offered a job in Masjed-Soleyman, and included was their sincerest apologies that there was no opening for Nematollah Shakib. Ammanollah Khan recognized my disappointment and tried to comfort me, but to no avail. I returned home sad and dejected, but to my dismay, it was fate unknowingly, had something much better in store for me.

My friends borrowed some money for their journey to Masjed-Soleyman and departed within a few days. I was left behind, feeling humiliated and hopeless. I went to Mr. Thompson, dejected, and explained my plight; he too was surprised and could not determine why I was rejected. He comforted me and said, "Do not worry; I have some other job in mind for you." Anxiously I asked him what he had in mind. He said, "There is a new doctor from England who has just arrived in Esfahan and he is traveling on to Kerman, but he does not know Farsi and I was planning to hire a student from our school to accompany him as a translator. I will choose you for this job and if you are willing, I will introduce you to him today, right now." I quickly accepted the offer and we went to meet the doctor.

This young English doctor, named Dr. Melanie, had just graduated from medical school. Dr. Melanie was about 27 years old, a tall, handsome man and he was so kind that I became one of his disciples right away. Dr. Melanie accepted me only after a thorough interview, where he inquired about my background and my temperament. He promised he would educate me about health care so I could quickly acquire some needed experience and he would be my guardian. Dr. Melanie was a deeply

From left sitting Avram (Avrami, husband of Showkat Moradzadeh), Shimon Manzoorollah, Noorollah Monavar, & Nemat. Standing from left Yahuda Avram & Ribbi

religious Christian and sincerely man who wanted to help me. Unfortunately, he was not long for this world; he died in Kerman after two months due to the exposure of typhoid fever and rendered this world sad and in mourning. Now I will recount to you the details of my journey and employment in Kerman.

I received an offer to work in the hospital in Kerman. It included three free meals in the hospital's kitchen and housing was provided in the hospital. My salary was seventy rials a month. For that time period, the offer was very generous; it was especially appealing to me because I received individual attention from the young doctor. I was elated to learn I would have some degree of knowledge and skill to perform as a nurse or a medical person, and I felt that this job was no less than that of my two dear friends in the oil company.

I packed up and prepared myself for the journey to Kerman with an elderly English woman who was also traveling to Kerman. Unfortunately, I do not remember the name of that kind and sweet English lady. We began our journey in two Dodge station wagon caravans. The walls of the cabin were made out of chicken wire and we sat next to the luggage. We were the sole passengers in each of the Dodge station wagons, and each of us was seated next to the drivers. The drivers had agreed not to separate from one another and the English lady wanted every now and then to stop, she was concerned with my well-being. With each pause in our journey, the English lady would rush over to me and offer me nuts and candy from a bag and insisted for me to fill up my pockets so I would have something to eat between stops. This continued until we reached Kerman. I received so much kindness from that lady that I have never forgotten her. Now it is March 28, 1979, about fifty years later and that kind woman I believe is still alive. If she has passed away, God bless her soul, and if she is living I pray that God grants her good health.

Our journey from Esfahan took five days. We left Esfahan on December 23 and arrived at Yazd the next evening. Usually this time of year the weather is severely cold, especially in the mountain passes. The car I was in had some problem climbing the mountain passes; its radiator would boil. We had to stop every now and then and let the car cool down. In order for the car to not roll backwards, the driver had instructed me to put a heavy log behind the rear wheel. Even though the weather was extremely cold, I was sweating because I had to move fast and carry that heavy log, so I did not feel the cold at all. This went on for half an hour until we reached the highest point of the mountain pass. That was when I got in the car and I realized how exhausted I was. After that we were ascending downhill and there were no problems until we reached a café. The English lady, who was in the other Dodge station wagon, was anxiously waiting for us at the cafe, wondering what might have happened to us. I explained the ordeal that we had to deal with and this put her mind at ease, she was very concerned for my safety.

When we arrived at Yazd it was Christmas Eve. The English lady was planning to spend Christmas with her good friend Miss Aiding, who was the principal of the girls' school in Yazd. The English lady took me also to Miss Aiding, a very religious Christian and kind lady. Miss Aiding took us in with open arms and took care of us warmly. Miss Aiding previously had received word that we would be arriving; therefore, she made every attempt in our comfort and made us feel at home. We spent that evening amongst the many Yazd Christians and the next day (Christmas Day) we participated in Christmas ceremonies and I received a very attractive English wool sweater and a long wool shawl, a product of Yazd. These two items were very useful for me in that miserable cold on the way to Kerman.

I do not know whether Miss Aiding is still living; according to my niece, Heshmat, who visited the United States last year and decided during her visit to permanently relocate, to the United States. Heshmat said that Miss Aiding was very old and frail. If she is still alive she could be more than ninety years old. This lady, who remained single all her life, adopted a son and a daughter, and cared for them and gave them a good education and tried to find them good jobs after they finished school. Both are married and as far as I know they are happily living with their families. Unfortunately, Miss Aiding was abandoned in her mature days, when she could have used some comfort from her two children. She was left behind and forgotten about, this mother who gave up everything in life to take care of them.

They behaved as if she did not exist. She was lonely and most of the time she was in bed and no one to look after her.

The next day the English lady and I resumed our journey to Kerman. The weather improved and we did not experience any of the problems that we encountered on the way to Yazd. After we arrived at Kerman, we went directly to the Morselin Hospital. The young doctor, Dr. Melanie, had arrived ahead of us and had ordered a room and some essentials for me. As soon as I arrived they directed me to my room and after cleaning up and resting, I went to see the doctor. The young doctor received me with enthusiasm and warmth and promised all kinds of help and a bright future. Every day he would call me in and as he was diagnosing the ailments of patients and he would explain to me his procedures. Unfortunately this did not last long and after two months of working with Dr. Melanie, he caught typhoid and after 10 days he died, leaving me bewildered. God bless his soul.

During these two months everyone around the doctor was jealous of me, and at times for no reason at all, some mean spirited individuals would pick a fight with me. The more they were malicious to me the more the doctor would ask them to be kind to me. No one would listen to me and I was shunned and ignored. With the doctor gone I was left with many enemies in a hostile environment.

After the English doctor passed away, the hospital came to a near standstill. The only medical care came from a male nurse who was in the process of obtaining his medical license. This man had very little experience and at times he had to meet with the female doctor in the female section of the hospital for consultation. This female doctor was a young Australian who had just completed her medical work in England and was hired by the English missionaries to work in Kerman. It was not long after her arrival that she met a young Englishman who was the assistant to the English Consul in Kerman and they were engaged. These two were deeply in love and spent a lot of time together. The young man would arrive and abscond with his lover, the doctor, without anyone knowing when she would return. She was responsible for two hospitals and more than forty patients. There were also about ten more patients that would walk in. All their lives were dependent on her care, but the doctor was unfazed — she was madly in love. She did not realize the awesome responsibility that was bestowed upon her and how she was affecting their well-being.

The following story is about two young people who died because of this doctor's neglect. One afternoon a young man about twenty-five years old was brought in. His nose was bleeding severely. The young man was from Tehran working in one of the governmental offices. I was the nurse on duty and tried frantically to locate the female doctor or the head male nurse. Unfortunately for the poor young man, neither was anywhere to be found. Another nurse who had just a bit more experience than I, struggled with much difficulty to stop this young man's bleeding, but we failed at our attempts. Eventually he lost most of his blood and in front of our eyes, his lantern of life dimmed. On that horrid night, the sad events of that young man terrified me, his anxiety of waiting for the doctor, his disappointment of not seeing the doctor, his tears and distress due to the absence of his parents were making me very frightened and I almost had a nervous breakdown. I tried in vain to give him hope by repeatedly telling him that the doctor is on her way and that she will stop his nose bleed soon, but he could see the fright in my wide open eyes, and he did not believe me. From that moment I decided to leave this dreadful environment and never speak of the medical field.

The other young man who lost his life because the young female doctor was absent from the hospital was a very well built young farmer. One morning he was brought in from a nearby farm with severe abdominal pain. The head nurse diagnosed his problem as appendicitis after an examination, declared this patient was in need of surgery as soon as possible. However, the head nurse did not have his certificate and he could not perform the surgery. He tried to locate the female doctor, but again, she was found after five hours of searching. The patient's appendix burst, and everyone knew that this was an avoidable death. If there was any justice in this world, this doctor would be charged with the demise of these two young men.

It was just about the time that Reza Shah had gained control of the country and he was frantically trying to improve social conditions. But the conditions were so deplorable that it might have been the worst time in the entire history of Iran. For example, in the territory of Kerman, a relatively important and large area of Iran, this small understaffed hospital was the only place for the infirmed to go and the female foreign doctor was the only doctor on duty. This doctor understood how grave the situation was and she also comprehended that there were no consequences to her actions. Therefore, she would ignore the awesome responsibility that was bestowed upon her and the dependency of other people's lives on her, to pursue stolen moments with her lover.

During this period of chaos and confusion almost everything came to a halt. The only hope was a nurse who was about forty or forty-five years old, he took charge and tried in every conceivable way to assist the patients in being comfortable. He had begun work in the hospital at a very young age; he worked tirelessly all day and loved his work. I worked under his directive and I made every attempt to please him and I obeyed every order he gave me without any question. The total time that I had spent in this hospital was five months, two months of which was with Dr. Melanie, the doctor who died of typhoid. All this time, I was paid only three hundred fifty rials and I had tried not to spend it at all to have enough for my departure from Kerman and my return trip to Esfahan. I had saved about three hundred rials and I had hid it in a small box out of sight until the following happened.

Before explaining what happened, I will digress to my religious beliefs at that time. When I was at the English College, I had converted my religion because of the repeated Christian indoctrination by the English missionaries; I had become a devout Christian. I said my prayers every morning and read a few verses from the Bible, and then in the evening before retiring to bed. I never missed my prayers. In Kerman I participated in every religious meeting and followed all the Christian indoctrination. I was known as a very faithful Christian.

Because of my religious beliefs, I tried dutifully to help anyone, without question. One day a young man was sitting on a patient's bed and was singing. I quietly approached, sat and listened to him. He was a handsome and attractive person and his songs were sad and had a profound effect on the listeners' inner soul. He had attracted everyone to his corner and each person was listening to him quietly and intently. I was homesick and his singing had affected me and I enjoyed it. When he finished singing I approached him and after exchanging greetings, I inquired which patient had he come to visit. He replied "No one in particular. I am here to help uplift the patients' spirits and be a help to them". I was very taken by this young man and his actions. It was late in the afternoon and time to go have something eat. As a polite gesture I asked him if he would join me for supper and he accepted without any hesitation and he sat at my table. I ordered an extra meal for my guest. We spoke until midnight and the time arrived to turn down the bed, and I noticed he wanted to stay. I was placed in a predicament; I did not know what to do other than offer him my bed and I explained to him that I would spend the night in one of the empty beds in the hospital. Before I left him, he wanted me to show him everything in the room, including my small box of money that I hid carefully. I was so taken by his profound words that I never gave any thought to not trusting him.

The next morning I got up early, I had breakfast by myself and started my work. I had informed the cook that when my guest arrives in the kitchen to please feed him breakfast and convey to him I was sorry that I could not join him for breakfast. At 10 o'clock I found a moment and I hurried to see my guest, who I thought would be waiting for me. I went to the dining hall, but he was not there. I ran to my room and gently knocked on the door and after not hearing a response, I opened the door but he was not in bed. Then I ran back to the dining hall and asked the cook if he had seen my guest. He said no, perhaps he is still in bed. I ran back to my room and began looking around and I found a note from him saying, "I had to run, thanks for everything."

Things seemed very normal on the surface and I had no reason to have any suspicion. I thought perhaps he did not want to trouble me anymore. At noon I went to my small savings box and naturally I reached for the leather bag that my savings were placed in. I opened it and to my misfortune I could not find my savings! I looked in every layer in the bag and there was no sign of my savings. I realized that my savings had been stolen, the money that I needed to return home to Esfahan, the money that I had built up all my hopes upon, the money that I made so many sacrifices to save. All of a sudden my eyes opened wide and everything became clear. I then understood why that young man was so interested in knowing everything about my room.

I was about 16 years old, I was very naïve and inexperienced and I saw the world through rose colored glasses. I was not aware that there is more to a person than what appears on the surface, and there are situations that will be puzzling. Losing my savings was a severe blow to my spirit. Sadly, I told the story to co-workers and the hospital workers and asked for help. Unfortunately, they knew very little about the young man, and on the surface they expressed their sympathy to me. However, in private they accused me of a very disagreeable behavior that in the following I will disclose and write about.

A few days passed and then one day I was told that Miss Petley had requested to see me (Miss Petley was a 65-year-old English lady who was the director of the hospital). I hurried and when I entered her office I noticed that this lady that was always very kind to me was now ignoring me. Then she said, "We have decided to return you to Esfahan." Inwardly, this news made me happy, but I was perplexed. I told her that I had no money for my return expenses to Esfahan. She replied, "I know everything, I know the reason for the disappearance of your savings and I have a return ticket for you." Then she said, "Collect all your belongings and be ready to leave by tomorrow morning." I replied "Fine, and might I please have a letter of recommendation". She turned her back to me and as she was walking away, she said, "On this matter I cannot do anything for you; when you return to Esfahan, Mr. Thompson, the principal of English College, will explain everything to you." I asked if there was anything that I needed to be told and why she could not give me a letter of recommendation. I noticed she was not prepared to discuss anything further with me and helplessly I left.

I happily began packing, unaware that there was a conspiracy by the hospital workers who did not want an outsider amongst them. They had made up a set of lies that I had spent all my money on whores, gambling and having a good time and that I had fabricated the story about the disappearance of my savings. This story had been told to everyone, especially the English lady, Mrs. Petley. The lady had believed them and considered me an undesirable person. Unfortunately, no matter how much I insisted, she never would tell me the reason for my release.

A few days after returning to Esfahan, I went to the English College to hopefully find out the reason for my dismissal and perhaps get a recommendation for my next job. By now Mr.

Harris had replaced Mr. Thompson and I tried to talk to him, but he was also very cold and drove me away. I returned home very disappointed, but I was more determined than ever to find the reason for their cold shoulder. After I discovered the reason, I was angry why all of these self-proclaimed honest people did not speak to me and give me a chance to defend myself before judging me. My "faith" which was very resilient before this event, became very fragile, and I lost faith in this Christian group. This incident drove me away from these people.

CHAPTER **11**

Weddings of My Brother Aziz and My Sister Tauce

I will now return to when my grandfather's house was sold and we moved to a new house that we named "Baghi Chi" (باغیی چی, small garden with trees). After a couple of months, my mother and brother Aziz decided to have my sister's wedding at the same time as Aziz's wedding. Tauce was to wed Noorollah, the son of my Uncle Yeshaia. I have to admit that it had taken so long for these weddings to happen because the responsibilities for both weddings had been placed on my brother Aziz. He had postponed the weddings for various reasons until he could raise enough money. His fiancée's family (Batia's family) and Noorollah's mother constantly badgered him. My mother, who had wished for years to see her son's wedding, could not wait anymore and announced to everyone that she would bankroll both weddings herself and promised my brother that she would give a very decent wedding.

My mother who was quite a businesswoman managed to provide both of them with very elaborate weddings. I have to admit that my brother at this time was very tight; he had a difficult time managing the expenses of his new wife and himself. My mother, who was supporting three children at home, took on helping my brother and his new wife. That had forced us to cook and eat together, and my mother had to endure her new daughter-in-law's verbal abuses. They would go at it to a point that they would curse each other and scream at each other.

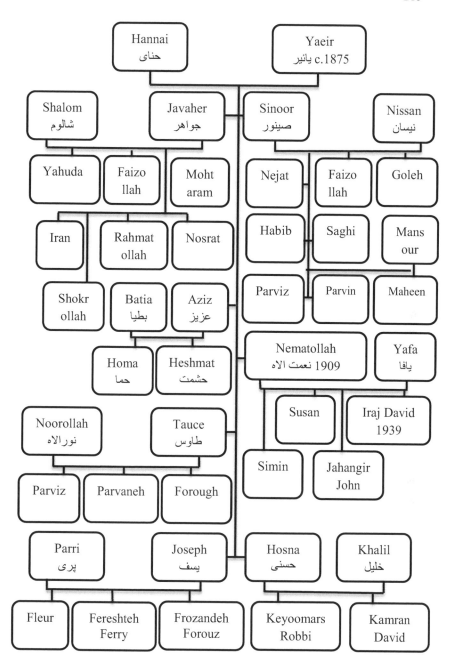

My mother knew the reason for Batia's unhappiness but she could not tell her that the problem was her husband; he was the one who had the financial problems. My mother kept everything in and was seething, and it appeared that any moment she would explode. My brother, rather than thanking my mother following the death of my father, incessantly accused my mother of not being amiable with her daughter-in-law and this was the main cause of the turmoil. Aziz would say this while I was present. I was well aware of what was going on — my mother was completely innocent.

Nemat in his early 20's and his family, c. 1933
Standing from left, Nemat and his brother Joseph
Sitting from left his sister Hosna, his sister Sinoor, his mother Hanna
holding her granddaughter, Homa, from her oldest son Aziz, his sister Tauce
and Aziz's wife Batia

Finally, my mother, in order to have peace with Batia, was forced to ask Aziz and his wife to separate from the remainder of us, and for him to assume the responsibilities for his own family's welfare. After that, Batia and mother did not have much contact and the fights ceased. Batia was raised without the proper discipline and she had inherited her father's gruff and abrasive behavior. In addition, my brother overlooked many things because he always set the highest priority on the happiness of his wife and children no matter what.

My mother loved Aziz and had tremendous respect for his intellect; she had high expectations from Aziz. Therefore, she overlooked many unreasonable demands that were placed upon her. Her adulations for Aziz diverted some of my mother's attention from the young children.

As I mentioned before, Aziz was very stretched for money and was forced to rent out the building that had been built and leased to the Department of Revenue and move the family into an apartment belonging to an Esfahani Jew. When I returned to Esfahan my family was living in that apartment.

For several months I was unemployed and I was uncertain of my future. My mother noticed how unhappy I was, and unbeknownst to me she began scouting out jobs for me. Out of desperation she contacted Mr. Garland (the same Christian man who deserted his comfortable life in London, England, and

*From left Batia's nephew Iraj, Aziz's youngest daughter Heshmat,
Aziz's wife Batia, Nemat's youngest son Jahangir (John), Nemat's oldest
brother Aziz, Aziz's oldest daughter Homa
(Iraj converted to Christianity and became a clergyman in the Anglican
Church)*

came to Esfahan to save the souls of the ghetto residents) for help for her son. My mother never had a conversation face to face with him. However, he knew much about our family, possibly because of the interaction with my brother and many hours of debate with him. Mr. Garland might have attempted to sway him toward Christianity. Anyway, my mother went to him one day to solicit help finding a job for her son Nemat.

She explained to Mr. Garland what had happened to me. Mr. Garland, after much pondering, told my mother, "I am sorry, I cannot help your son but I have heard that the oil company in Esfahan has opened an office and they are looking for employees." God bless his soul, he noticed that my mother was bewildered and did not know where to apply. He told my mother, "My dear lady, do not worry, I will research this and notify you when I find out where to apply."

Mr. Garland, as he had promised, sent word to my mother along with an address of where to apply. When I returned home that evening I found my mother at the door waiting for me impatient and very happy. She told me the news and asked me to apply early the next morning.

CHAPTER 12

My Employment with the Oil Company

That night I wrote a letter to the oil company requesting a job. Early the next morning, I dressed very neatly, took the letter I had written and went to the address my mother had obtained for me. The oil company had rented a temporary storefront in a shopping area on Khosh Street in Esfahan. The office was closed when arrived there and I waited about half an hour before the doors were opened and the janitor washed and swept the storefront. To my surprise, I found the same Ammanollah Khan, who was the recruiter for the oil company in the south of Iran, behind the desk. As soon as he recognized me, he received me warmly, and asked me "What can I do for you?" I gave him the letter without any preliminaries and hesitation. He opened the envelope, examined the job request and began reading it. I was nervous that I could be rejected and remained quiet, watching for any kind of expression on his face. After reading the request a smile appeared at his lips and my worries subsided somewhat. Ammanollah Khan, who was a kind man and enjoyed helping others, recognized my nervousness and quickly said, "You are in luck and you have come here at the most opportune time, we have still one more opening!" Then he said, "I will process your request immediately and I will let you know the day after tomorrow. Come back about noon time the day after tomorrow, I hope I will have good news for you."

I went home and returned after two days to Ammanollah Khan's office. Ammanollah Khan's face was very jolly and he received me warmly and started teasing me and kidded with me and then he said, "Dear boy, your request has been accepted and you may start work tomorrow." Hearing this news was like someone opening a door to all the opportunities of the world after many months of unemployment and despair. I thanked Ammanollah Khan many times and after receiving my orders and the location of my work I ran home. The letter written to me said, "Your salary will be 180 rials per month, and if after three months your performance is satisfactory your salary will be increased." At that time 180 rials was plenty for one person. Even though this was a fraction of what the salaries (about 350 rials per month) were in the south of Iran, I had many benefits. Life was more pleasant and less expensive in Esfahan, I was with my family and I could save more than half of my salary. Early the next day I reported to work. My home was about four miles away from where my work was and I walked this distance on foot every day. Even though this was a long distance it did not tire me because I was so excited about my job. My three months of training ended and my manager, Mr. Sadri (known as Safe-Ol-Mamolek), one day asked me to his office and thanked me for the good work I have accomplished and showed me a letter praising me for my performance and indicating a salary increase from 180 rials to 250 rials. Now my salary was very respectable and was the source of envy for others.

More than ever, now I knew how much being rejected by the oil company in the south of Iran was to my benefit. When I was rejected I was very disappointed and hopeless and considered myself to be one of the most unfortunate people on earth, not knowing that someone above had a much better future planned for me. From that time on, I believed that one should not be disturbed quickly at the sign of trouble; one should have faith and patience and wait for the results before judging. I experienced this several times in my life, and every time it was for my best.

I started work with the Anglo-Iranian Oil Company on May 21, 1929, at age twenty and worked with them continuously until 1969. During this forty year period I have encountered many bitter and sweet events but no matter what, I completed this long career without any interruptions. Even though my education was very minimal, I managed to rub shoulders with many college graduates and excel to unexpectedly high positions. Because of my hard work, perseverance and personal innovations, I managed to educate myself about my job and remain in step with my college graduate contemporaries. My superiors were always very complimentary of my work and assigned me to greater, more challenging and difficult jobs. I started on my career path as the assistant to the warehouse manager in the oil company. Then gradually I moved to the following ranks: warehouse manager, salesman, manager of a gas station, accountant, recruiter, purchaser of foreign supplies and overseas contracts, comptroller of technical accounts and the manager of cash and loans in the oil company, auditor of all contracts and many other positions. When I decided to retire I was offered many well paid post-retirement positions. But I refused all of them because I was tiresome and I decided to enjoy my remaining years. During these forty years (other than the two years in the military service) many things happened that I will write about if I have time in my remaining years.

I wrote before that not finding employment in the south of Iran, where the weather is harsh and hot, was to my benefit. I realized this when I came across an old folder in the oil company storage while I was searching for something entirely different. The tag on the folder said, "HIRINGS FOR THE OIL FIELDS IN THE SOUTH OF IRAN." I took the folder and opened it and began flipping through the pages when I noticed the picture of Shimon Manzoorollah (منظورآله), one of my dear friends that was accepted to work in the south of Iran. The picture was attached to a letter that said, "Reject Nematollah Shakib because he is too small and weak to be able to work in the harsh weather of the oil fields." Now I realized that the small stature of my friend was mistaken for me, and no one paid any attention to the mistake, and I was dejected and it made me sad and depressed! I was unaware that destiny had other good things in store for me!

One day thirty years later, when my friend Manzoorollah was retired, I met him and reminisced about the old days. That was when I told him about the mix-up. He told me that he was always envious of me because I stayed in Esfahan, which had wonderful weather, and even though he earned more, he had less than I did. He also explained how grueling it was working in the oil fields. I tried to explain to him that we both were at the mercy of destiny and neither one of us had a chance to do anything about it. We should accept it and do not question it.

I told him, "If you do not agree with my explanation, try to listen to this story." After I had worked with the oil company for two or three years, I was working under Ammanollah Khan. The oil company was located in the Hezar Jerib. This was located on the road to Shiraz, on a large parcel of land that included some farmland and was managed by an Englishman called Hickok. The bare land was used to store oil products and the old house and the green area around it were used for the manager and his assistants. In one corner of this land there was a two-story building that had several rooms and a kitchen on the second floor and could house a family of four to five people. The first floor was used as a warehouse. The oil company had fixed this broken-down building and housed the warehouse manager. Ammanollah Khan, who was a renter himself, packed up his semi-engaged wife (engaged to be married) and his two sisters and moved into this building. This faithful man had allowed the warehouse workers to come into his house without permission and take whatever they needed. Ammanollah Khan spent every dime he earned and did not worry about the future. Often I advised him and would tell him, "My dear friend, think about your future and your old age and do not spend all your income." In return he would say, "Don't worry, the one that I have put my faith in will watch over me and will protect me and take care of my needs." Unfortunately, this honorable man and these fine characteristics fell prey to a few rare and despicable friends. He gambled and lost everything to them and he was left in a miserable state.

Anyone who lives in Iran knows that many Muslims gamble all night during the holy month of Ramadan (the month of fasting). Most of the working populations slow down during this month and they try to remain home and sleep. This is so they can cope with the hunger. Most people knew that the people who sleep all day probably have been gambling all night; gambling makes time pass. Gradually gambling had become so popular that even those who did not fast gambled during Ramadan and there were many gambling parties during this holy month. Ammanollah Khan regularly joined these gambling parties. He first came to gambling as entertainment but gradually it became an obsession with him. This very naïve and sincere man, who looked at everything positively and with a good heart, did not recognize the underhandedness of these close friends and did not recognize that their main purpose was to acquire all he had. By the time he wised up to the events and proceedings that was taking place, all his money including some of the oil company's money that he managed, was gone.

In those days there was fierce competition between Anglo-Iranian Oil Co. and the Russian Oil Franchise in Esfahan, and each tried to position themselves to be the dominant distributor of petroleum products. Due to this, the Anglo-Iranian Oil Co encouraged employees to sell their products at all cost to prohibit the expansion of the Russian petroleum distributorship. Therefore, Ammanollah Khan and I were allowed to hold in safe keeping overnight the proceeds of petroleum sales for one day and deliver it to accounting the next day. This explains why we had a large sum of money was pending the following morning, before our normal duties we would deliver the

previous day's cash and receive our receipt. After 10 days into
Ramadan, that procedure was altered and Ammanollah Khan
was nowhere to be found in the morning to deliver his previous
day's sale. I had observed him and I discovered that his
morning deliveries had not been dropped off to the central
office. I became suspicious and in addition I noticed that
Ammanollah Khan, who was eternally jolly and had a smile on
his face, was very subdued, depressed, and his jovial demeanor
had vanquished. He began avoiding most everyone and he did
not show up at the office as often as he should. Therefore, I
decided to get to the bottom of this problem and one day I
confronted him. Initially he was reluctant to disclose
everything, but I was persistent with him, he divulged all the
details to me and what had happened and how he had lost all of
his and the oil company's money.

That was when I fully comprehended the problem. I was
quite dismayed and disappointed; I attempted to resolve his
difficulties. First I made an honest attempt to help him replace
the oil company's money without involving the company in
hopes that they would not learn about this predicament. I had
him promise that from then on he would not associate himself
with gambling parties and those friends that enjoyed that type of
activity. I told him that it was imperative to make and uphold
this promise to me before I could help him by lending him the
amount he had pocketed from the oil company. But
unfortunately I was not successful in this endeavor, he was not
capable of controlling himself, he was beyond hope. He would
say, "I need to go back to win back the money and then, I will
promise that I will never gamble anymore." Finally I gave up
and let the events take their course. I promised myself to protect
him as much as I could and try to hide the fact that some of the
oil company's money was gone. The amount was negligible
enough, that I myself could replace it. I decided to collect all I
had plus some that I borrowed to replace the money the first
opportunity that came along. But Ammanollah Khan was not

satisfied with these initial losses and continued to attend these nightly parties and continued losing. The loans from the oil company grew larger and I witnessed him removing mostly all of the day's proceeds for the evening game. I begged and pleaded with him, but to no avail, he had a closed ear to me. I knew if the oil company discovered the money was gone, we both would be arrested and charged with embezzlement and that would have terminated our careers at the oil company. At this point my unquestionable duty was to report the missing funds to my superiors to vindicate myself and keep my job. However, it was not in me, I felt tremendous loyalty toward this man who had done so much for me and I tried, in vain, to protect him as much as I could.

My thoughts concerning this matter were not as clear cut, until the twenty fifth of the month. As usual I arrived at work early in the morning and I found out that Ammanollah Khan had requested that I assume his responsibilities because he could not come to work. I knew what transpired and thought he must have had a quite a wicked night. I began feeling sick to my stomach and I felt so bad that I passed out in my office. The workers had found me on the floor and called an ambulance to take me to the hospital.

I spent two weeks in the hospital, and when I returned to work I found out that Ammanollah Khan had been found and arrested. There was a new manager in place and no one questioned me or charged me with any crime. At the time that I became ill, I thought to myself this is a terrible setback. But in reality my illness helped me to be out of sight.

When Manzoorollah heard this story he was shocked, and thought to himself one should not be unhappy with one's destiny. He turned to me and said, "Nemat, who knows, maybe it was not in my best interest that I was sent to the oil fields."

During my forty years of service in the oil company, there were many ups and downs, there were happy times and bitter times and through all these moments I learned a lot. I was transferred to Kerman to be the warehouse manager after three years of service. The day after I arrived and settled in a hotel, I met a local man who was very outspoken and had a striking disposition. He approached me and sat at the table where I was sitting and asked how I was doing. Then he said "It seems that you have just arrived in town and you do not know anyone in town". In return I told him that I had just arrived in town to work for the oil company and that I was looking for a place to rent.

He asked if he could be of assistance to me and I said, "I would be very grateful for your kind help". Hearing this, he smiled and said, "Let's get to know each other first. Of course I will help you, there is no hurry." I ordered a cup of tea for him and we started a long conversation. This young man was from a very prominent family and lived alone in a very large stately house with many rooms, basements and inner and outer yards. He was working for the Department of Revenue and he was on vacation. He wanted to find someone to stay in this large house so he could visit a resort village where his mother and sister were temporarily residing. We spoke about our lives and our families and we became better acquainted with each other. Then he turned to me and said, "Now that I know you work for the oil company I know you are not a drifter and I can trust you. You are very welcome to stay in my house and you may occupy two or three rooms as you wish until I return from my vacation."

He continued, "I am single and lonely and the house is too vast, so you may live there, I could use a real friend." I was very pleased and quickly accepted his offer and gathered my few possessions from the hotel and loaded a carriage to his house. This was a very distinguished old house in Kerman and it was located on the outskirts of town and was built to a lofty standard of luxury and grandeur. It had a large exterior yard for conducting business and a large interior yard for everyday living.

The Muslim men housed their women in a yard adjacent to their own yard to protect them from strangers. Of course, these yards had high walls. Some devoted Muslims still maintain this tradition. However, now in the late 1970s, twenty-five or thirty years later, the women are so carefree and expose themselves in front of men, especially while at the seaside and swimming pools. They have no scruples in lounging on the beaches with the skimpiest bathing suits. The young man showed me every corner of the house and asked me to select an area of the house I that I would prefer.

I chose a room from the interior yard, which was the larger of the two, and I moved my belongings into the room. The next day the young man departed on his journey and I had begun to develop my daily routine, I would go to my bedroom room late in the evening and then straight to bed. The next morning, after eating my simple breakfast, I would leave for work straight away. This went on until one early morning, something unusual happened.

Behind this large house there was a small house. Between these two houses there was a set of steps that would go down deep, approximately 15 meters, called a ghanot. The steps were shallow and one easily could go down the steps and access water.

Iran is a very arid and mountainous country. Water is at a premium and every drop is cherished. Most of the farms are irrigated either by water from ghanots or from waterways or canals that divert melted snow water from mountains. The Kerman area is even more arid. The government has tried with much difficulty to harness every drop of water and create as many dams as possible to help this parched area.

The fact that this house had this ghanot was very important. It showed the affluence and importance of the owners.

Every day I would descend the stairs to the water to wash my face and my dishes until that morning.

The sun was just peeking out when I knelt down to the water level, and I had just splashed water on my face when I noticed a man downstream, moving around. The water passage was just large enough to allow a slim person to pass through. It was so unusual for me to find someone in this body of water so early in the morning. As he was crawling through, he was grunting and was trying to see who was out there.

I was so absorbed with what was going on that I forgot where I was and what I was doing, I was very anxious to know what I was confronted with. After 15 minutes of this cat and mouse game suddenly a muddy man emerged from the water passage and stood in front of me. The fright almost made me fall backward, but I overcame my fear and waited for his reaction. Eventually he exposed all of his muddy body. After further examination he appeared familiar and I could see that he too recognized me. The more I stared at him, the more familiar he looked. All of a sudden I recognized him; not only was he an old friend but he was a distant relative. I was so surprised — how could it be that hundreds of miles away from my hometown I found a relative inside a ghanot in this manner? He was no less surprised to find me there. Then I turned to him and called him by his name and asked him, "What in the world are you doing here, in the ghanot, this early in the morning?" He calmly and simply said, "This is the best time of the day to fish in this ghanot. I had heard that there were many fish in this ghanot. So, I entered this particular ghanot from outside streams and swam to this point." Then he said, "Unfortunately, the passage is so narrow that I could not carry anything to store the fish in and that is why you see me with no fish." I asked him what he was doing in Kerman. He said that he and his father's job was to go to distant places to find antiques and historical items and ship them to Tehran, and that it was a very profitable business. Then he wanted to know about me and what was I doing in Kerman. I explained to him that I was here on oil company business.

I did not see him again until I changed my housing to a Jewish family's home. That is where they told me more about him and how popular he was with the Muslims. Apparently he had fallen in love with a Muslim girl and in order to win her heart he had converted to Islam in the Bazaar. I forgot about Dawud (David) until I returned to Esfahan and one day I saw him at his cousin's house, Shokrollah Haizadeh (he is Batia's brother, Aziz's brother in law). He told me that his work was finished in Kerman and he had not had time to call on me before he went back to Esfahan.

Because the large stately house was out of town, I made an effort to find housing in town. My brother, Aziz, wrote to me about a Jewish business client, named Rahim, in Kerman and asked me to seek help from him. But before I had a chance to contact this family, the elder son of Rahim came looking for me and offered to rent me a room in their home. Rahim told me, "We have a very clean and nice room in our home for you that you could live there comfortably." God bless this man's soul, he persuaded me to move in with them with a special kindness and gentleness. The next day I moved my belongings to their home.

The elder of this family was a simple and very ordinary man; his wife was very kind and interesting. The two were elderly and frail. They had eight children, seven sons and one daughter. The eldest son was married and had his own home where he lived with his wife and children. The fourth son, at the age of 15, had run away from home and after many years, he wrote to his parents that he was in the United States. He said that he was married with many children. The only daughter was married with two children. She had abandoned her children and husband and moved in with her parents because she did not love her husband. The parents, the sons and the daughter lived in three rooms. The parents and three sons occupied the largest room, which had a large closet. The room that they gave me was freshly painted and used to be their living room. Because Rahim was tight for money he was forced to rent this room to me. This family was very proud and tried to live a dignified life—they were very frugal. This family was not able to have three mails a day on a regular basis. Even though they were destitute, they were very happy. As soon arrived home from work they were jovial, happy and playful until such time they went to bed. With all the recreation available to us today such as radio, TV, clubs, and restaurants, it seems that people are not as happy as they were in those days. It appears that the simple things in life were more meaningful and pleasurable.

Every morning Rahim would bring me my breakfast and in the evenings as soon as I arrived home they shared their supper with me. After a few days I decided to have my own separate life. I asked their daughter, Kokhob, if she would be willing to cook for me and keep my room clean. In return I offered her enough money to provide for three meals, in addition to a cash amount. She accepted as if she had already thought about it. I gave her some money and she went to work. When I returned I found my room very meticulous, a delicious meal was prepared and the table was set. It was then that I realized how much this unfortunate dear woman craved having a normal life and how unfortunate it was that she was married to an unworthy vile man.

Later, Kokhob told me, "My parents could not wait to get rid of me; they forced me to marry this uneducated, cruel and abusive man whom I did not love." She continued, "At first I fought my husband and did not go to bed with him. But my parents, my brothers and the rest of the family pressured me and I finally gave in and with much disgust I went to bed with him and now I have two children.

"Now I have brought to this world two innocent people and because of them I have to endure this despicable man and live with a man whom I hate. He is the lowest of all men because he would beat us several times a day. The abuse became so bad that I had to leave my children whom I love more than life itself and come to live with my elderly parents." She continued,

"Because my parents financially are not in a position to support my children also, I cry every day and night and do not know where to get some help to have my innocent children back with me."

The pitiful woman was saying, "You are God-sent. Now I can help my children with some food and clothing. They seem somewhat happier now."

For one year this woman took care of me very well, with considerable kindness. She was so warm and kind to me that I had considered if she could divorce this hideous man, I would marry her! I was so taken by this woman's devotion that I was prepared to forget about my own feelings. At that time I was about 20 years old. Kokhob was 24 years old and I knew that if I married her I would have the responsibility of raising her two children. However, because of her kindness and her ordeal I wanted to protect her and give her sanctuary by marrying her and saving her. Fortuitously, something happened and I could not do that.

I had worked with the oil company in Kerman about one year. My mother sent word that the armed forces were looking for me to induct me into the army and that if I did not report in they would arrest me. To prevent any trouble for my mother, I made preparations to leave Kerman for Esfahan. Kokhob was very disheartened and was weeping when she sent me off.

Leaving this kind and devoted woman was difficult. I had no choice — I had to leave, but I promised that I would help her anyway I could. My destiny had other plans for me and circumstances came up that took away any kind of help I could offer her. For a while I wrote to her but this also came to an end and I lost track of her. I saw her once again when I was traveling to Israel and by then I could not do anything for her, the circumstances being I was married to Yafa, and it was too late. After that I never heard from her.

CHAPTER **13**

My Service in the Army

While I was in Kerman I was drafted. My mother, who at any cost, did not want me to enter into the army, considered finding a way to keep me out. She had dealings with the wife of the draft board director and my mother had asked her for help. The director was pressured by his wife to find a way to obtain a deferment for me. He had informed my mother that if she could bring a letter indicating that she had only one son and this letter was witnessed by several people; in all likelihood he could obtain a deferment. My mother, with the help of some family members and the persuasion of some friends, prepared the necessary papers. She delivered the papers to the draft board and for a while she did not receive news from them — thinking everything was in order and I was spared from serving in the army. But a disgruntled person who disliked my mother had reported that my mother had purposely lied and that she indeed had two more sons. Suddenly, without notice, the director changed and the new director studied my dossier and determined that it was a misleading document; that my mother had two more sons and a warrant was issued for my arrest. That is when my mother summoned me to hurry back to Esfahan.

I arrived in Esfahan after a couple of days and I immediately reported to the draft board. I was informed that you must first begin your service, and then we will determine what the punishment will be for lying. I told them I was ready for service and after a few days I was officially enlisted and they shipped me to Tehran. For two weeks, every day I would go and wait all day for a hearing. Finally I was sent back to Esfahan, where I persuaded the officers to accept me as a student in the corporal school and I started my service.

If I desire to write about the nature of the armed forces of Iran in that period, that itself will become a book. The situation was horrific and it would be quite unsettling to the reader. Bribing and thievery were rampant, confusion and mismanagement were the norm and as a whole, the vast majority would sell their mother, country and souls for money. The best proof I have is that when the Allies entered Iran in World War II, after several days all but a handful of officers deserted and the government of Iran fell quickly. I am going to describe in short order of how things were.

Nemat in the Army, c.1929

When I was accepted into the corporal school, initially for the first three months we had no uniforms. There were about 175 of us and we were forced to serve in our civilian clothing. Every day we were promised that tomorrow we would receive our uniforms. After three months, it was announced that today is the day for our uniforms.

It was about noon when the sergeant summoned us to roll call, and while standing in line at attention, the commander of the group who was a very serious and strict officer, gave us a lengthy speech. He began, "From this point on as you wear this sacred uniform you will have a special responsibility and loyalty to our country and his majesty the king. Now more than ever you will be asked to sacrifice and be willing to give your life for your country and the king. While wearing this sacred uniform that will embellish your body, you must guard it with reverence and do whatever you must to be worthy of wearing it. Until today, no one knew that you were soldiers, but as of today, after wearing this sacred uniform it is assumed that your duty will be to protect Iran, its safety and security, and the people of Iran expect you to be worthy of wearing it."

The commander was so persuasive in his remarks that he had all of us excited and we completely believed in what he preached to us. But after the delivery of the old, tattered and filthy pile of uniforms that looked like anything but uniforms, we quickly realized that the commander's speech was disingenuous and nothing more than hypocritical words to excite us. As one touched the uniforms, a cloud of dust emanated from them and made one hate to touch them, much less wear them. We were ordered to select a pair of trousers and a jacket. We reluctantly approached the pile of dirty uniforms and with disgust rummaged through the pile; I chose a pair of pants and a jacket and quickly returned to the line, leaving the tattered uniforms strewn on the ground in front of us. To my dismay, of the jacket and trousers that I selected the trousers were one leg shorter than the other and I moved back into the line. Both the jacket and the trousers had so many patches that one could not recognize the original cloth. When I brought the uniform home my mother would not allow even the thought of that tattered uniform in the house and I had to leave it in our storage area. It was emphasized that we should take care of this uniform because after the completion of our service the uniform had to be returned to the army, and failure to follow this order would bring a severe punishment. I surmised that our sergeant understood the events of the day were damaging, and how the belief in our country and the king had eroded, and how much our trust in Iran and the defense of it were diminished. Our commander made us aware of the thievery that occurs and how profound the corruption was. The commander was not a person that could be undoubtedly accused of these crimes. We noticed that he too was disgusted with what was transpiring and he was unable to do anything about it. Therefore, because of his frustration of not being able to locate anyone in the higher command to hear his grievances, he overdid his speech about how magnificent the uniform was, and this made us infuriated.

From the lowest rank of corporal to the highest-ranking officer, all tried to steal from the soldiers and anyone else associated with soldiers. Most of the soldiers were from the lower classes, indigents and farmers of Iran and they were forced to join the army with little or no assistance from their families to supplement them with food for their empty stomachs. Those in charge stole from the soldiers' supply of food, clothing and other necessities that were earmarked for the soldier. That's why most of the soldiers had torn uniforms, empty stomachs and were dirty.

I was one of the fortunate ones. I had additional money for food, and there were always a few that were continually hungry, I tried to help them.

I was born in Iran and consider it to be my country, and it does not give me any pleasure to belittle and show the true nature of corruption in this society. Unfortunately, I have to write the truth: corruption has penetrated this society like termites, deep and throughout. Thievery and bribery have affected most everyone and it is boundless, no matter how determined they are and how hard they try to eradicate it.

For centuries Iran did not have a leader as conscientious and able as today's king, Mohammad Reza Shah. This man was struggling to take this backward country to a progressive and tolerant stage. Even though the internal corruption of Iran was overwhelming, it was anticipated that with his efforts gradually the behavior of people would change, which could have led to the betterment of Iran. The relentless efforts of this able leader started showing much promise, and if the revolution of 1977 and 1978 had not come about, this country would have completely changed. Unfortunately, the Iranian students within Iran and abroad painted him as a stubborn dictator, corrupt, merciless and a traitor due to their naiveté and influence of mozer (مضر, damaging) propaganda. They eventually deposed this heroic man who had no other desire than to make Iran great again. The traitors who had no other reason other than personal gain forced the king to involuntarily relinquish his command of the country. It is too soon to see the results of these divisive acts, these traitors to Iran. The world will see in its entirety the extent of their damage to Iran.

The founder of this dynasty, Reza Shah Pahlavi, the father of this king, was also a patriot and a valiant soldier. Unfortunately his education was limited. By sheer determination and fearlessness he was the impetus that set Iran in motion toward the 20th century. He attempted to change the culture of accepting daily insecurity and the feudal and Mongolian kingship traditions (molookolkalam ملوک الكلام, khankhani خان خانی). Unfortunately, World War II began and because of his leanings toward the Germans, the Russians from the north and the Americans and the British from the south squeezed him out of office. His reforms abruptly were halted and his capable but very young and inexperienced son,

Mohammad Reza, replaced him. He was exiled to Morris Island near Africa. Mohammad Reza initially did not have much influence, but with patience and quiet diplomacy overcame the complexities of the time and gained control of the country. There was a momentary setback during the time that Mossadegh (مصدق) was the prime minister, when the king almost lost his monarchy. He was forced to leave the country for Italy. He stayed in Rome until one of his generals, Zahedi (زاهدی), overthrew Mossadegh and urged the king to come back to Iran as soon as possible. The king journeyed back to Tehran immediately and secured the reign of the country. Mossadegh's cronies were rounded up and deposed, but Mossadegh himself was spared. He was placed under house arrest at his home in a village called Mohammad Abad. Little by little the king strengthened his power base until he was the supreme leader.

Once again I have deviated from the main story, now I will return to the corporal school in Esfahan. For four months I was sent to Farah Abad base in Esfahan, where I received my corporal rank. I spent the rest of my two-year service at the same base. As soon as I was discharged I was notified that the defense department, Harb (the military court), had asked for me to select a lawyer. I chose my commander (Saied Javad Khan Malik Khosrovi) in school, who was fair, honest, and capable. I was sure that this commander knew me well and was completely aware of my fine service and I was also certain that he would do his best for me. Fortunately, I was right and he was able to obtain an acquittal for me.

After those two years, the only other time I had to return for duty was for a one-month period. That was during World War II, when it seemed the entire world was burning from the ravages of war. Most countries were fearful that they would be dragged into this war. Therefore, all countries were preparing themselves and had maneuvers.

During these maneuvers I saw shocking incidents that were beyond belief. Here is an example of one incident that showcases the incompetency of the officers in the Iranian Army.

The day I arrived at the base I was ordered to buy my uniform and have it altered on the base using the tailors who were stationed there. I had no choice but to pay and get my uniform. After dressing in my uniform I was ordered to join a battalion in a small village. We started early in the evening and walked until past midnight. We had only one meal. There were about 170 of us and when we camped, the others slaughtered a very puny goat. After skinning it they put the whole goat inside a large pot and poured water they fetched from a nearby stream over the goat. The logs and branches that were brought by the soldiers heated the pot. They also added some beans, chickpeas, turmeric and salt to the pot. The cook began cooking this soup while we were camped in the desert and after the meat was done the goat was transferred to another pot where it was divided into smaller portions. The officers were fed first. The dishes were undersized and dirty. By the time the officers were fed there was very little meat left, and it was divided among the sergeants. Colored water, beans and chickpeas were left for the 170 soldiers. They were very careful to make sure that no one received more than a small ladle of the soup. Almost every soldier that received his soup poured the soup portion on the ground and ate just the beans and the chickpeas. Half of the soldiers received their ration of the soup and the pot was almost empty. The remaining soldiers were wondering how they would be fed. The head cook had a plan: he quickly ordered one of the cooks to fetch water from the nearby stream and poured it in the pot. The dispensing of soup continued as the cold water was being added to the content of the pot. Eventually everyone received a portion of the soup. As the soldiers received their soup, they walked away cursing. After dinner we started walking again until we reached a camp where we were housed in tents that were already erected.

We were housed in those tents for one month while we were going through military training. During the day we had desert exercises and hiking, which was supposed to ready us for military maneuvers. I myself, was the commander of a few soldiers and I was somewhat familiar with what a military maneuver was. The commanders studied the terrain, located the fields and the hills for their machineguns and the artillery, picked their targets and after much discussion separated the men into two camps, an offensive group and a defensive group. They reviewed the plans over and over again and finally decided on a time and date for the maneuvers. We went through dry runs several times a few days before the actual date to ensure a smooth operation. Finally the designated night came and the two groups (offense and defense) departed for their destinations. The night was very dark, and finding one's path was difficult. My subordinate and I were assigned to the offensive group and according to our commander's order we initiated the attack. We walked in the dark for a while and I noticed that our direction had changed and we were ordered to continue our progress. We walked back and forth for several kilometers in the desert until dawn and we did not know whether we were ever going to reach our destination. The sun began to rise, but we had not encountered any defensive forces. We were all fatigued and there was no one to tell us what was going on. After the sun rose, suddenly we were ordered to make an about-face and return. Later we learned that the commander had become disoriented. The commander did not know how to return until an experienced sergeant requested for permission to take the lead. It was four o'clock in the afternoon before we finally returned; tired, hungry and thirsty, to our original departure point. We were ill and exhausted for several days.

We eventually found out that the defensive forces were also lost and had gone the wrong way and had to return to base without any encounter. I hope that by now the reader realizes the incompetency of the Iranian forces in that time and period. From what I heard, however, under the leadership of Mohammad Reza Shah, the Iranian forces were well trained using the latest military tactics and there was no comparison between these two periods of time. The modern Iranian defense forces are under the command of highly educated officers.

We spent the remainder of the month learning trivial tactics and we then returned to Esfahan. As I wrote earlier, this was during World War II when the Germans had occupied most of Europe and were pummeling the Russians. The Americans had clearly entered the war and were fighting the Japanese in the Pacific and were attempting to help the English and the Russians. To send arms and supplies to the Russians, the United States had traveled long distances. The Allies searched for a trouble-free path and Iran was chosen in order to hasten the support for Russia. The United States had to occupy Iran to ensure a secure path for the multitude of arms and supplies that were to be shipped to Russia.

The Allie's spies reported that the German forces were throughout Iran posing as engineers, technicians and teachers and at any time would be capable of causing disruptions in the shipments to Russia. The Allies knew that with Reza Shah in power they could not easily create a secure path. They also wanted to eliminate the threat of terrorism by German spies by expelling all fraudulent Germans posing as technicians, engineers etc. Subsequently, they deposed the king and arrested all the German spies. The way this happened was on the evening of September 11, 1941; the Allies suddenly attacked Iran from land, sea and air and overcame the Iranian forces, which were very weak with respect to the Allied forces. In one day the Iranian army surrendered and the soldiers deserted their positions.

This happened exactly a month after I was released from maneuvers and it was about the time the Iranian government had just summoned the reservists to service. Reza Shah was deposed and he traveled via Esfahan en route to the southern part of Iran. Then he was put on a ship and sent to the island of Morris, where he remained until his death. The Allies entered Iran and confiscated everything and remained until the end of the war.

Earlier I promised that I would write more about Mr. Harris, the schoolteacher in the English College in Esfahan. Stuart Memorial College had a few English teachers, and there were two by the name of Harris. One of them was a religious man who had profound Christian convictions who eventually gave his life for his faith. This young man would spend all his weekends and holidays traveling on foot or other means of transportation to small villages to preach the gospel and attempt to convert the local inhabitants to Christianity. This faithful man did not hesitate to participate in the everyday activity of the farmers. He ate what they ate, and he slept under the same korsi (a low, square table covered with a thick comforter, containing red hot charcoals in a metal receptacle under the table, and four mattresses on four sides with many pillows as a back rest) as they did. In doing this he caught typhoid, which most Iranians were afflicted with. In his case he did not have immunities as the local populace did, and he died.

The other teacher named Harris was a very energetic and intelligent man who was indifferent toward religion. This young man also traveled to different areas of Iran and mingled with ordinary people. But after England entered the war with Germany he resigned his job and joined the British Armed Forces by way of Bakhtiari to Khuzestan where he went to England. After the Allies occupied Iran, the Russians dominated the north and the British and Americans controlled the south. The British sent several infiltrators, including Harris to southern Iran. He was appointed as the Deputy of the British Counsel in Esfahan, a very dangerous and sensitive area in Iran. The reason he was selected for this position was that he was fluent in Farsi and he knew the Iranian culture very well. He also had a very close relationship with Bakhtiari tribal chiefs. His job was to seek and rout out the Germans wherever he could uncover them. He also had the task of befriending the Bakhtiari tribal lords to ensure that there would not be any difficulty transporting the war material through their territory. This young man did a superb job and he was successful in capturing many German spies. Unfortunately, on one of his many trips to the Bakhtiari region he was killed by fanatic and misguided tribesmen. Dr. Griffith, an Australian, who accompanied Harris, was slain along with his son.

CHAPTER 14

My Marriage to Yafa, My Wife

One year before World War II, with the urging from my mother and my sisters, I decided to get married. However, each young woman they introduced me to did not suit me as my life partner. My bachelorhood continued until I was twenty-eight years old, when one day my sister Tauce returned from the Jewish Women's Public Bathhouse and excitedly informed my mother she met a young attractive woman with a shapely figure

Standing from right Yafa's youngest brother Ruben, Yafa at 18, front right Sonia (Sara's sister & later she became Ruben's wife), Joseph's wife Sara, Yafa's 2nd youngest brother Joseph, Yafa's Mother Zolaikha, Yafa's Father Hezghia, c. 1937

and inquired about her from the other women. Tauce found out that she and her family escaped from Soviet Russia and fled to Iran and they currently reside in Tehran. She was in Esfahan visiting her sister Tamara who was married to Monsieur Gabbay

(گبای). My sister was insistent that my mother and I call on
Monsieur Gabbay so we might catch a glimpse of this unknown
young woman. My mother, now aware of whom to speak to and
where to go, discussed this with me and asked for my approval.
Collectively we decided to visit with Monsieur Gabbay to
explain our intentions for meeting with him and if all goes as
plans to ask him, "Would this girl agree to marry and reside in
Esfahan?"

A few days later I alone, paid a visit to the Gabbay's house
and met with Monsieur Gabbay and Yafa. This was my first
encounter with Yafa, I felt a strange and satisfying feeling
occupying my body and soul and I knew this young woman was
my life partner. I sat directly facing Monsieur Gabbay and as

was his nature, he joked with me and
playfully mocked me, he then inquired
as to the purpose of my visit to his
home. I was frank with him and
explained my purpose and requested
his help. Monsieur Gabbay, God bless
his soul, promised his full cooperation
since he knew our family and my
grandfather Avraham Dardashti very
well. He said "I have no problem with
this union because I know your father,
your mother and all the Esfahani Jews

Monsieur Gabbay

know that your family is among the most respected Jews in
Esfahan. Therefore, I will make an effort to speak with her
father, mother, brothers and her sister, who is my wife".

Monsieur Gabbay requested Tamara, his wife, to join us,
and after introductions, he gave Tamara a recitation on how
outstanding my family was. I was served tea and traditional
cookies and discussed various subjects and I departed Monsieur
Gabbay's house patiently waiting for a message to arrive. Two
or three weeks later, after many visits to and from the Gabbay
residence and after Yafa's sister completed a background check

of me and my family, they gave their blessing. To formalize their acceptance of this union we set a date for an engagement party and my family and I were busily preparing for the formal announcement. I bought a ring, many packages of nuts and sweets, crystal sugar candies, and several other sweets that were popular in Esfahan. We invited a few prominent Jewish families from the Jewish ghetto to the bride's sister's home. That evening, Monsieur Gabbay was not in town. My eldest brother Aziz, representing my family, was also out of town.

The engagement party concluded and I dated Yafa for that one month almost every day while she remained in Esfahan. We

Monsieur Gabbay & Tamara & their family at Lisa's Wedding
2ⁿᵈ from left Liza, Zolaikha, Gabbay, Khalehjan (Tamara), Turan, Essie,
kneeling from left Bahman, Enayat & Jojo

went on outings and had a delightful time together — those were one of the most memorable and enjoyable times of my entire marriage. I do not think that today's society (second half of the 20th century) young men and women could have the same heightened feelings towards each other as it was. Today's young people to that extent, have considerable access to each other, they mingle with the opposite sex so frequently that the oddity of a man and a woman encountering each other has lost its excitement; the relationships are informal and effortless. In my opinion in a contemporary engagement setting, there is little delight and not much mystery. In the past, because of the many social restrictions on young people, the engagement period was one of the most exciting times of their lives.

After I was engaged and knew that Yafa and I would be married I felt a great responsibility to act decisively and soon. Early in life I understood I could not rely on anyone and to never expect anything from anyone. Never did I ask for anything from my mother. Therefore, immediately after my engagement with Yafa I began looking for a house to purchase and putting together a nest egg. From the time I began working I regularly saved a portion of my salary.

Fortunately I found a house not too far from my brother's residence and I bought it. Without hesitation I moved my mother, my brother, my sister and myself to the new house. Then I purchased a few pieces of furniture. A month after buying the house I prepared for my departure to Tehran to marry Yafa. As I journeyed to Tehran I encountered many problems, which is a long story, and I will not bore the readers with it. I will, however, write a short story about a notable problem I faced after I was married and the way Muslims treat the minorities.

Earlier I wrote about Yafa's family and how they became destitute and lost all of their wealth when the Communists took possession of the Soviet Union and they were forced to escape on foot and seek asylum in Iran. When I went to Tehran to get married, the family's status was unchanged. Two days after our marriage I began filing papers on Yafa's behalf to obtain a birth certificate. For several days I went to a government office, where my case was referred to an army officer. Every day I reasoned with this army officer to issue Yafa a birth certificate. Initially he was very polite and would even order tea for me and we had become good friends. Then one day he asked for my own birth certificate in order to prepare a birth certificate for Yafa. With no hesitation I handed him my birth certificate and upon opening and reading it his face became red and the veins in his neck became large and he became extremely agitated and he asked, "You are a Jew?" I replied, "Yes, sir, I am a Jew." Then he said, "Why didn't you disclose to me at our first meeting that you are a Jew, I would not have shown you so much respect and have been courteous to you?" Upon hearing these words, I felt the world crashing on me and I was nauseated. The only thought that came to mind regarding this ignorant and ridiculous man was to answer his question with a question,   I told him, "What is wrong in being a Jew?" With that I took my birth certificate in disgust and left. On the way out I informed him, "If you decide to issue a birth certificate to my wife it can be mailed to me in Esfahan".

This revolting and hideous treatment was a testament to the degree of hatred and repulsion the vast number of Muslims felt toward the Jewish minority. At that time a very able man, the late great Reza Shah, was leading Iran. He strove to educate an enormously illiterate population and he was desperate to sway people away from fanatic religious beliefs and place them on the path to progress and to create a secular society. I am sure the king would have been disgusted with such behavior and would have been completely critical of such blatant discrimination.   I am certain if the higher governmental authorities were cognizant of this foolish man's behavior, they would have disciplined him severely. There is no doubt in my mind the reason I received Yafa's birth certificate was the fear of the king. For fear that I might appeal to the Shah's court; the army officer had ordered the birth certificate to be issued to Yafa because she was married to an Iranian.

This was a small sample of how the Muslims treated the Jewish minority in Iran then and now. I doubt it will ever change. I believe one of the main reasons for the revolution of

1978 and the ousting of the Shah, Mohammad Reza, was he befriended the Jewish populace and gave them a great deal of latitude. This hatred of the Jews became obvious after the revolution, when the Ambassador of Israel was deposed and Yasser Arafat was embraced in his place. The love and affection bestowed on Arafat was the greatest testament to the Iranians' hatred and animosity toward the Jews.

When I went to Tehran to get married, the only person who accompanied me was my cousin who was my sister Tauce's husband, Noorollah. Friends and family are crucial to Noorollah, more than money. When he heard that I needed help, he quickly stepped forward and offered his assistance and with no hesitation he accompanied me to Tehran. When we departed Esfahan we had no knowledge of where to stay. Upon our arrival in Tehran we went directly to our Uncle Yehanan's house. In retrospect, we should have made other arrangements, and the reason is as follows.

Uncle Yehanan at this time was quite impoverished and without a decent job. His situation appeared hopeless and with no possibility of relief. His greatest problem was he had a daughter at home who was nervous, volatile and in those days considered an old maid. No matter how much he tried, he was unsuccessful to find a husband for his daughter. She was not educated nor did she possess any known talent or skill. She was a great burden every day and every minute of the day for her mother and father and a source of worry. Unfortunately, she was not pretty either. My aunt and uncle expected that I ought to have considered their daughter first and there was no reason for me to marry an outsider. In Uncle Yehanan's mind I was duty-bound to ask for the hand of their daughter. He and his wife did not consider love and mutual attraction to each other to have a priority in a marriage. The fact is, if two people did not like or love one another, so-be-it, what was important was that the couple spend the rest of their lives together. Unfortunately, I was an uninvited guest at my aunt and uncle's home, and unbeknownst to me I had no prior knowledge of their lack of money, no consideration in marrying their daughter and I was further insulting them by desiring to espouse an outsider. They had all the reasons in the world to be very annoyed by my stopover at their home.

When Noorollah and I arrived at their house the evening sun was setting and it was time for our uncle to return home from his mediocre job. Noorollah and I had scarcely moved our suitcases into a room when my uncle entered in, and upon discovering why we were visiting he lost all control and blurted, "My house is not a caravanserai (a desert inn for traveling caravans) that you may barge in at any time. What right do you have to come to my house unannounced and without my permission?" I was devastated. I quickly grabbed my suitcases and exited my uncle's house and never again set foot in his house. Even now, when I reminisce about this event it sends shivers up my spine; it has left such an impression on me that I have not forgotten the episode.

Before the wedding preparations commenced, the bride's family informed me they were not able to spend even a penny for the wedding. However, it was not acceptable for their daughter not have a wedding ceremony. Therefore, I gave all of the monetary means which I possessed, 2000 rials, to my bride's brothers for a small wedding.

Yafa and I returned to Esfahan a couple of days after the wedding. My financial situation was not on firm footing. I was not able to purchase even two tickets because I had exhausted all of my money for our nuptials. I was obliged to borrow money from my school friend, he lent me 150 rials in order to return to Esfahan after we were married in Tehran. On returning to Esfahan I developed a severe case of diarrhea and I became so gravely ill that I was passing blood. Upon arrival in Esfahan I visited with a doctor and he prescribed for me to remain in bed several days, but I could not follow his orders since I was worried I would lose my job if my illness lagged on. My choices were to walk the ten or twelve kilometers to work or to ride my bike. At that time I had no fear of death, all that concerned me was to provide for my young bride and to fail at this task disturbed me terribly.

Yafa in her wedding dress, Oct. 1938

In Esfahan the people who gave us wedding gifts were my late sister Javaher and my Uncle Yeshaia's wife, Farha. Thank God, Yafa and I managed to live through these arduous times, and day by day, our situation improved. We ultimately sold the small house and in time purchased a significantly larger home.

Yafa became pregnant and we saved every penny to prepare our lives for our baby, until one afternoon she developed pains and I took her to the Christian Hospital. The doctor on call announced that Yafa was ready to deliver her baby and we checked her into the hospital. I had to return to work, I was leaving Yafa at the hospital with my mother and sister Sinoor. When I returned to the oil company my manager instructed me to go to Yazd and prepare to transport a company car that had been in an accident, then return to Esfahan. My manager insisted that I remain with the car until it was on its way to Esfahan otherwise there was a good chance the car could be stolen. At that time I was so terrified of losing my job that I did not utter a word, even to convey that my wife was in the hospital having a baby. I thought that if I did not submit to my manager's order I might have been fired. I was not too mistaken, at that time there was no one to defend the rights of workers. Fortunately, years later, with the help of Mohammad Reza Shah, many legislative bills were passed to provide workers more rights.

So without hesitation I boarded a car and drove to Yazd. Approximately 80 kilometers outside Esfahan, between Nain and Koohpayeh, we arrived at the location where the car had run off the road. At first glance it was obvious that the brand new car was traveling at an excessively high speed and the driver's mistake or over correction had caused the car to run off the road. The car was about 40 meters away from the road, in the middle of the desert and appeared that it had overturned several times, finally landing on its top with its tires up in the air. We looked for the driver but found no sign of him. Luckily, there was no sign that anyone perished; the driver must have walked away from the scene. Later we learned that the driver had obtained a ride to Yazd in order to rest.

As I had been instructed, I remained with the damaged vehicle and sent my driver to town to fetch a tow truck for the damaged vehicle. Thankfully, the temperature was not too frigid in the desert night and I endured being wide-awake all night. Early the next morning, the driver returned with a crane and a tow truck. The vehicle was turned on its wheels and towed to Esfahan.

God is my witness how much I agonized about my wife that night. I arrived at the hospital early in the morning just as the sun was lighting up the sky. I found my sister Sinoor all smiles and ecstatically telling me "go and buy some candy and sweets." I repeatedly asked about my wife's condition and Sinoor just as insistent, repeated to me that I ought to purchase some candy. I finally forced her to tell me what happened the night before. The first thing she said was, "Nemat, you are the father of a son. Don't worry thank God, Yafa is doing well and everything went well last night." Then we entered the hospital and we went directly to my wife's room where I saw my first child sleeping. I had many mixed emotions, I do not recall exactly how I felt but I know I was in high spirits. My mother and my wife's sister

Iraj David

Tamara were there and congratulations were in order for me, for having a son. My mother and Tamara wished my son a long and happy life.

After a few days in the hospital and after Yafa had been well rested, I took her and my son, Iraj, home. Everything was proceeding well until Yafa became pregnant again after barely six months and our second son, Jahangir, was born. Having two sons was not an extraordinary phenomenon, but it was perceived by my family and friends to have high importance. Everyone considered Yafa and me very fortunate to be blessed with such an honor. My mother was the happiest, and she worshipped her two grandsons. To have a grandson from a son was very important, and Iraj was the first grandson in her family — she adored Iraj. At all times she was very protective of him and her desire that no one should do harm to him. On occasion if I attempted to punish Iraj by striking him on his legs or arms, my mother would throw herself upon him for protection.

She loved Jahangir as well; when he was ill with typhoid, she settled in by his bed and was hardly able to sleep until he was well enough and could walk again. I remembered that one day Iraj did something naughty and I was very angry with him. I began to run after him so I could administer his punishment, when my mother realized what was happening. She threw herself in front of me to prevent me from reaching Iraj. I accidentally collided into her and we both tumbled to the ground. In the process she sprained her shoulder, however, she hung onto my legs even though she was in great pain and I was never able to reach Iraj— she was afraid I would harm him.

Yafa and I decided to not have more children; we already had two healthy boys, so we planned to be very careful. We were successful for six years when one day Yafa was being examined by a female doctor at the Christian Hospital, she was told that she was not able to have more children. When she returned home and conveyed the news I was very happy; this was something we had hoped for, for some time. Thereafter we let our guard down and did not continue with our vigilance any further, unaware that the doctor had misdiagnosed. When Jahangir was five and a half years old, Susan was born, and six and a half years later Simin was born.

Iraj, Jahangir and Susan were born in Esfahan, but Simin was born in Arak (formerly called Sultanabad), which is 340 kilometers (about 210 miles) from Tehran.

Iraj was born in a hospital under the care of an educated physician, but a midwife named Morvarichie (مرواریچی) delivered Jahangir and Susan. Delivery in the hospital cost about 120 rials, our midwife charged anywhere from twenty to forty rials per child. Thank God, the two that were delivered by midwife were healthy and without complications. An educated gynecologist delivered Simin at home. The delivery cost was approximately 2,500 rials. One can see the inflation in 14 years and see how the cost of living had increased. Today the cost of a delivery in the United States is about $500 to $600.

My four children developed the usual sicknesses, including two dangerous types, typhoid and chronic fever that went through their cycles. Luckily they survived without any complications and disfigurements and I am very thankful to God that he looked after them.

Iraj was nine or ten when he contracted typhoid and was bedridden for a month at the Morselin Hospital (the same Christian Hospital) in Esfahan until he was well and came home. However, when Jahangir became infected with typhoid, his condition was much worse with added complications and his recovery took longer. He was sent home two

Nemat as he was rushing home to care for Yafa & Susan during lunch

weeks after his fever broke. However, shortly thereafter his fever returned. My mother was very perturbed and sought out help from some of her friends. They suggested giving him shirkhesht (a gum-like looking substance similar to tree or maple syrup, sweet. Doctors prescribed this to their patients to counteract a "warm nature." According to them, everyone at times is either warm-natured or cold-natured. Shirkhesht has a cold-natured property and would make the patient weak). My mother acted under pressure from other women and gave Jahangir shirkhesht without weighing the consequences. She did not know this would further weaken Jahangir's condition and this substance must not be administered to a child who was recently hospitalized. The result was this innocent child went into convulsions and began shaking profusely. It was unbearable for his mother and me to watch him in this condition. We rushed him back to the hospital and tried as much as we could to stop his shaking. Jahangir returned home with us again and we asked one of our friends, Moshe Heim, who had some education in medicine and was a nurse in Ahamadieh Hospital, to help us and he came to my son's bedside. He prescribed several medicines and waited by my son's bed for the results. However, up to midnight there was no result and we were losing hope until Moshe Heim ordered us to bring him cognac and a piece of well soaked Nan-E-Khoshgeh (a flat bread that has been dried in an oven and is crispy like crackers,نان خشگه) which we quickly did. He put several drops of the cognac on the bread and fed it to Jahangir and it was not long before he showed signs of improvement and his shaking began to subside and his color came back. This event will always stay with me, and I have concluded that doctors cannot rely solely on the books he/she has read and at times he/she should employ innovative ideas to aid a patient in order to save him from dying.

Susan was about two years old when she too became ill with typhoid. This happened a few days after Yafa was bedridden with high fever. Their situation deteriorated day by day and their fevers became dangerously elevated. Unfortunately, at that time neither my mother nor any of my siblings were in Esfahan and there was not a soul to look after my wife and my daughter when it was time for me to leave and bicycle to work. Every morning before leaving for work I would place food, medicine and other necessities that I thought they might need near Yafa and leave them in God's hand as I went to work. At noon I would hurry home on my bicycle to assess their situation and help them with anything they required until I returned home in the evening. Iraj and Jahangir, even though very young, had realized the severity of the situation and tried to help as much as they could. I had guessed that both Yafa and Susan contracted typhoid and I knew that it was nearly impossible for them to have an appetite to eat; therefore, I tried to feed them mostly soup. I brought home a lady physician from the Christian Hospital but she was not able to clearly diagnose their infirmity and did not prescribe any medicine.

At that period of time antibiotic medicines were not readily available and penicillin was the only drug of choice. Previously I wrote that this disease was very common and the experienced, mature physicians understood how to successfully treat it. I myself knew adequately about this disease and I also recognized that there is no medicine for it. All that was needed was constant care, sufficient rest, soft food and after this cycle, the patients become well. Therefore, I tried my best to keep both of them comfortable, keep them in bed and not feed them anything that might irritate their bowels.

After several days I recognized that I wasn't capable of caring for two ailing people by myself. I began to consider finding a woman to come and attend to Yafa and Susan's needs during the day, but when the caregivers were informed that there were two typhoid patients, she would quickly back out. I was also very concerned that my other two children might become ill.

I was very distraught and concerned. Unfortunately, there was no vacation time that I might use because it was the end of the year (Persian New Year is the first day of spring) and I had to personally complete all unfinished paperwork and submit them to the oil company. During my lifetime I have come to realize that at the darkest moments and the most hopeless of times there is a mysterious hand that reaches and pulls me to safety and saves me from disaster.

As I wrote before, we sold our first house, the small house, to a family that consisted of an older mother, two sons and daughters and a daughter-in-law. This family was honest, kind-hearted and somewhat poor. The eldest son and I were in the service together and we had become very good friends. After the service the only contact we had was we would see each other occasionally in the street. When I was in that desperate, hopeless situation I thought perhaps I might be able to acquire some help from the elderly mother of my friend, whose name was Elisafan. Early one morning I knocked on their door. The mother, who was very cordial, greeted me at the door and asked me in. She was very surprised to see me and she asked, "Mr. Nemat, what has brought you to our home this early in the morning, could my children and I do something for you?" She recognized that something was troubling me. Apologetically, I explained my predicament. Upon listening to my problem, she hit herself on the head and said, "How could you and your family be in so much turmoil and not ask for help from me and my children?" Then she dashed inside the house and summoned her two daughters and explained to them my family situation. She grabbed her chador, and as she ran past the door advising her daughters, "Come over later." We both rushed to my home and as we entered the house this concerned woman asked in which room is my wife and daughter. She entered the room, tossed her chador aside and sat down by my wife's bed and began talking to her like a very caring mother, saying, "My dear Yafa, why have you not called on me sooner, I am so sorry to see you two in this condition."

She bent over and kissed Yafa's head that was burning with fever and then she went and hugged and kissed my daughter Susan. With tears in her eyes she turned to me and told me, "Please go to work and leave everything to me and my two daughters, we will take care of them." As I watched this divine woman with her kindness and her unselfishness I felt that I was in the presence of my mother; I knew then that my family was in good hands and it was reassuring to know this woman would nurture my wife and daughter as well as my mother. My mother was in Tehran at this time and when she returned home and had heard about this woman she was very thankful but not very surprised. That facts being, this divine woman had involved herself for the same reason that she was compelled to comfort others, without any expectations. She had come to understand this as her duty. The elderly lady neighbor was about the same age as my mother and she also had suffered the loss of her husband and she devoted herself to taking care of her young children and grandchildren.

This type of compassion and self-sacrifice was a characteristic of the middle classes in those days, but at present unfortunately, among the educated people who claim to be very civilized and progressive, this characteristic would be rare. Regrettably, today's housewives or other women that work outside the home are so entangled in problems of the day that there is no time for reaching out to lend a hand to their neighbor and fellow mankind. It appears that there is no time for unselfish kindness or sincerity between friends and it is difficult to stumble on anyone who is willing to give a helping hand to a friend or a neighbor during a crisis. Back in the day, it was considered a tradition and a moral issue to aid and support

Nemat's family before his wife Yafa and his daughter Susan became ill with typhoid, from left his oldest son Iraj, Yafa with Susan in her lap and youngest son Jahangir, c. 1946

one another. The old traditional values and the restrictions of society are gone, and people feel free to ignore the old requirements.

In any case, this kind lady and her two daughters took total responsibility of caring for their two patients and the household chores without expecting any compensation. They remained with my wife and daughter until they felt that their patients were well and completely out of danger. Yafa became well 10 days after Ms. Elisafan and her two daughters (Tuba and Neima) came to help. But Susan had to remain in bed for several more days until she was completely well.

In the previous pages I wrote that most of us are not able to control what is in the future for ourselves. There is a mysterious force from beyond that aids and rescues us from disasters. What I am trying to say is we should not completely rely on our power and expect to solve and overcome all of our problems. The human race has not been able to withstand the problems and forces of nature and has not been able to successfully face the complex natural happenings not even one in a thousand.

One day when I came home from work, Yafa informed me that Susan was not doing well and she appeared as if in a coma. I rushed to her bed and I realized from one side of the bed she did not hear nor respond to me. I examined her further and discovered that she was blind in one eye. I am sure those of you who are parents know how I felt and what a sinking feeling it was. However I kept my composure, I did not want to alarm Yafa. I went to another room and got down on my knees and while I was sobbing I prayed for her. The next day I confronted our doctor and inquired of him what would become of my daughter. He promised that everything would be all right and explained to me it was "a usual reaction for patients who have had a severe illness." Fortunately everything worked out well and Susan regained her sight, and thank God, she became well again. Thank God, today, May 22, 1978, as I am writing, Susan is married, has a wonderful son, Chad, and she has just moved into a new home in Lexington, Kentucky, and she is very happy.

The much needed help from the Elisafan family resulted in our families becoming much closer and we saw each other often. This friendship continued with the two daughters even after Ms. Elisafan passed away, until Tuba immigrated to Israel. In Israel my Uncle Yehanan's grandson, who was a widower at the time, married Tuba. Neima, the younger daughter of Mrs. Elisafan, lived in Tehran for a few years and we continued to have contact with her until she also immigrated to Israel. Elisafan, my service buddy and my friend, after having several sons and daughters, at age 50 developed cancer and died. My understanding is that his wife did not want to disrupt the children's education and some of them were educated in the United States. Two of the sons, after the completion of their education, opened a Persian rug store in Atlanta, Georgia, and they are preparing to have their mother reside there.

Nemat's family c. 1959 From left his wife Yafa, standing in the back his oldest daughter Susan, Nemat and in front youngest daughter Simin, Nemat's sons were in the United States

As the reader notices, I have written in detail my share of trials and tribulations that were mostly caused by my family and the few token happy days that I experienced. I will try not to bore you with all my adversities but I beg your indulgence to allow me to write about just a few more.

CHAPTER **15**

My Life's Journey from the Depth of Despair to the Sweetness of Success

Fundamentally I am not a person who is indifferent to others' quandaries and misfortunes. I have never been able to ignore other people's problems and sit on the sidelines and watch people suffer. I am especially sensitive to my family and friends' crises and I jump in with both feet in an attempt to be a degree of support for them.

My first bout with adversity was when my father and my brother declared they were bankrupt. The next adversities were my father's untimely death, my oldest sister Javaher becoming a widow, followed by her family becoming destitute. I was somewhat dejected and incapacitated by these three events before I was married. After I was married I began to forget these unpleasant times when my youngest brother Joseph became very ill, and the situation became so dire that it dragged my mother and I to the edge of despair. His illness continued until he was married and had children, at which time he became completely well. The detailed story about his illness is too painful to describe. Unfortunately, for the last eight years he has had severe depression and he spends most of his time in bed.

Next it was my sister Sinoor and her husband Nissan's poverty, the welfare of their numerous children and the responsibility of supporting them. Then it was the situation of her marital relationship with her husband, and his unfaithful behavior that itself is a long story. I also endured this difficulty and I moved on. For a few years I had to put up with my sister Tauce and her husband, Noorollah, and his lack of financial support for his family. The problems that Noorollah would create were complex and often not solvable. My sister, unfortunately, did not help much and had no appreciation for the difficulty I would go through to help her

Tauce, Noorollah Tauce's oldest daughter Parvaneh & Nasser

Tauce's son Parviz & Mikhah   *Tauce's youngest daughter Forough & Eli Weiner*

and her family. She thought that I was financially so well off that I could support her family in addition to my own family. Because of this she often purposely would annoy me and would create situations that were disturbing and give me sleepless nights. Unlike her, my sister Sinoor was very proud, and regardless of how destitute or the degree of difficulty she endured in her life she would never want others to have pity on her even though her poverty caused her to lose her small child.

She fought her troubles away with a commendably high spirit, raised her children and saved them from the depths of despair. Thank God, all her children are doing very well. Her husband died not long ago. Today my sister lives in Jerusalem with her two daughters. Unfortunately, in my opinion her children do not appreciate her selfless sacrifices.

My youngest sister Hosna was only three years old when my father died. She was raised without her father's affection and care and it was during the worst famine. She had to endure many adversities and do without many material effects. With her determination and sheer willpower she was able to graduate school and she received her diploma. It was unlikely that she would marry, to no fault of her own; she had no father and no dowry. She struggled with every adversity and supported herself by teaching and sewing, unbeknownst to her, God had a bright future planned. Finally God sent her a husband who was a perfect match, and even though he was not well off they worked together relentlessly and overcame many hardships until their situation improved and they became successful. Their life was the envy of others.

I felt that I was continually under pressure and stress due to my anticipation of potential future problems that might arise for Hosna and her

Azizian family, from left Hosna, her son Keyoomars (Robbi) and her husband Khalil

husband. However, God gave me the strength to overcome these worries and lend support to my sister if she ever needed it. Thanks to God a thousand times, her two sons are in college in

England, and Keyoomars (Robbi) who studied electronics will graduate this year.

I was pushing forty years of age when the oil company asked me to transfer to Arak (a town approximately 340 kilometers from Esfahan). This was shortly after buying my sister Sinoor a house next to Aziz's house. Before I left Esfahan I gave Yafa a power-of-attorney to sell the house and bring the children to Arak. It was early morning in December of 1951when I left Esfahan and late the same day I arrived in

Hosna's oldest son Keyoomars   Hosna's youngest son Kamran
  & his wife Farzaneh   & his wife, Sima

Arak. The car that I hired drove me to Arak and I was dropped off at a garage. There was thick snow on the ground and it was a bitter cold. I did not expect it to be so frigid, my fingers tips felt numb. I grabbed my luggage and began walking, hoping to find a hotel on one of the major streets closer to town to spend the evening. Unfortunately, on that cold and dark night there was no one in the street nor was there a flicker of light from any store. Cold, dark and alone I could not locate a living soul to direct me to the whereabouts of a hotel or a place to spend the night. After two hours of wandering in the dark and cold I finally found a hotel and awakened the owner to give me a room. The windows and the door to this room had so much air leakage that even though the oil heater was turned up to its maximum I could not warm up the room, and I shivered to my bones until morning no matter how many blankets I covered myself with.

With much difficulty I endured the night, and early the next morning after having a small breakfast I locked up my hotel room and again on foot I started for the oil company. Fortunately, the heavy overcoat that I had packed from Esfahan was adequate enough to keep me warm. When I reached the oil company I was plenty warm because of my swift pace. There I discovered the outdoor temperature that I had walked in was minus 26° Celsius (minus 15° Fahrenheit) and that was a record low temperature for Arak.

At the oil company, my manager introduced me to everyone and then I returned to town (the oil company was outside town) searching for permanent housing. That day and another two days I looked for housing until I found two rooms in a relatively new and respectable house. I moved the very few belongings that I had to the new place.

The person that rented the rooms to me was an ordinary, devoutly religious man. He was very respectful and kind to me. Every morning before I had a chance to awaken from my bed, he would bring me breakfast and he would sit on the floor with his legs folded and patiently wait for me to finish my breakfast, he would then remove the tray and the dishes from my room. This very shy and quiet man had charmed me with his actions would attempt anything to please me hoping he could benefit in some way by my association. He was no more than fifty years old and was married to a fifteen- or sixteen-year-old girl whom he kept virtually a prisoner in a room all day and would not allow her to come out. Once or twice when I went home unexpectedly I noticed that she would sneak out of her room to breathe in fresh air if her husband was not home. A few times she even inquired into how I was doing, but with each request she would ask me not to repeat anything to her husband about her emergence from her room.

There were many people like my landlord in Iran, especially in the Arak territory. On the surface these people seem very simple and harmless. However, if someone who is not familiar with their culture behaves in a way that is construed as different or disrespectful to their beliefs, or converses with their women too often and creates suspicion, he could be killed instantly. It is quite possible for them to go into a rage and also kill their own family members. These somewhat-civilized people are problematical and volatile to deal and live with and it is prudent to exercise caution in interacting with them.

Nemat in his office at INOC

Even though my landlord was very respectful to me, there was no doubt in my mind he would not hesitate to throw me out if he had discovered his wife had said hello to me two or three times.

After one and a half months, I received word from Yafa that her travel to Arak was imminent. I began to prepare for her, even though we were 45 days into winter, the ground was covered with thick snow and it was very cold. I knew that she would bring Susan, who was five years old with her, and I knew about what time they would arrive at Qum (less than eighty miles northeast of Arak). I went to Qum and waited at the Esfahan gate. I remained from eight in the morning until five o'clock in the afternoon and I was very careful not to miss them and I visually inspected every vehicle that stopped and unloaded people. I was getting worried; the sun was setting and I did not know what to do. I was uncertain whether I should go back home, but I could not remain in the street much longer. I was worried that their bus might have had an accident. Luckily the last bus pulled in and stopped in front of the police station. Even though I was very doubtful that they were on board, I began looking for them. I was so elated and surprised to see Yafa holding the steel passenger bar waiting her turn to exit the bus. After they exited the bus we waited at the gate to Arak for a short while until a car returned and we got a ride to Arak. In a few days Yafa became very friendly with the wife of the landlord and in a conversation she had told the wife that we were Jewish, not knowing how the landlord felt about the Jews.

Late that night we heard a knock at our door. The landlord was standing in the doorway, he was very angry. He walked in pointing his finger at me, telling me, "I want you out of here early tomorrow, otherwise you are responsible for the consequences."

The man, who treated me like a master until a few days ago, now was looking at me as if I was the lowest creature on earth and could not tolerate me even for a minute more. I repeatedly asked him why, but he would not allow me to utter a word edgewise. Later I found out that his wife had conveyed to him that we were Jewish. The next day I was desperate, I looked everywhere until late in the day I found an upper floor apartment in a large circular square, from an Armenian man called Khodadad, and we moved later that day.

We resided in this apartment for two years and then I was transferred to Tehran. After Yafa was certain that the new apartment suited our needs, she returned to Esfahan to sell our house and bring the boys. I was alone again in Arak. There was no other way; it had to be that way until all of my family was able to join me. Fortunately, my mother was in Esfahan, and this valiant woman was a much appreciated help to Yafa during the sale of the house and packing of our belongings.

I ate out often, but I cooked for myself the night my family was supposed to arrive. I made an omelet for myself. I am ashamed to admit that I never learned how to cook, I could not cook even a simple omelet. I began eating the eggs before they were cooked and they tasted awful, but I ate everything and with little concern because I was famished. A bit later I paid a big price — I developed a severe stomachache and I was nauseated. While I was twisting and wreathing on the floor in agony, suddenly I heard my mother's voice outside calling "Nemat". At first because of my condition I thought I was dreaming, but as I listened carefully I realized that it was my mother calling my name loudly "Nemat". Then I heard a knock on the door, I forgot all about my condition and rushed downstairs to open the door, where I found my mother, whom I called "Monnie Joon," and my oldest son Iraj. She was so happy that she had found me.

My mother and Iraj simply got on the truck and came to Arak without knowing the address. All they knew was that I lived in that square where all the doors looked like storefronts. It was late and all the stores were closed. Iraj was in the carriage in the center of the square, while my mother stood in the square looking aimlessly around her, not knowing which door to knock on. She called out my name loudly "Nemat" several times and decided she had to select a door to knock on. It so happened that the first door that she walked to was the door to my apartment. It was a miracle!

My mother took this as a good omen and she walked in and was elated. Iraj and I began to move their luggage in. It was then that I realized how much Iraj had grown during the past few months. My children, from the time they were very young, were taught to be responsible children. They always tried to be helpful to their parents as I had trained them.

After Monnie Joon and Iraj were settled in I began feeling ill once more and my mother noticed the waves of nausea on my face. She was insistent that I disclose to her exactly what happened and what I ate. She did not care how awful I was feeling, she needed to know everything. I conveyed to her how I had undercooked and consumed the eggs and she shook her head and said, "You need to vomit everything you have eaten and get rid of the poisoned food." From childhood I remember my mother had shown us how to induce vomiting, I inserted two fingers in my throat and after a few times I was successful and emptied my stomach out. Within a couple of hours my stomach ache and nausea went away and I began feeling well.

I have no doubt that if my mother had not come to my aid I would have died. Maybe it was not my time yet.

It is necessary to explain that my mother was illiterate and an ordinary woman. But she was very intelligent, a nonconformist and a valiant woman; these qualities overcame her lack of education. For example, she could recite the Old Testament by heart. She was knowledgeable and worldly in solving many problems. Through the years she had learned of many remedies and treatments for a multitude of diseases. It has happened in our family that doctors or medical personnel had conceded defeat in the treatment of our children. After my mother implemented her knowledge and remedies on them, they began their recovery in a few days.

I remember well my sister Sinoor's eldest son caught typhoid and after a few days his three siblings also were infected. My sister was distraught; their poverty had made it impossible to receive medical care. The treatment of typhoid patients was difficult; however, my mother rolled up her sleeves and delved in, "We do not need a doctor, I will care for all four of them, God willing, and they will all be well soon."

One could only imagine the kind of bravery and self-assured confidence it took to assume the responsibility of having four children's lives in her hands and not be remiss in view of the consequences. She remained with her four grandsons until they were well and on their feet and released from the jaws of death. Now that I am transcribing my memories and I reflect back, I am enormously proud of my mother and I have a tremendous respect for her. God bless her soul.

The following day the truck showed up with our furniture and a few days later Yafa, Jahangir (John) and Susan arrived at Arak. We resided there for two years and the only significant event that occurred was the pregnancy of Yafa and the birth of Simin. I need to indulge on your kindness so I may relate to you briefly the delivery of Simin and the help of an Armenian family and a lady. This is so I may properly thank and pay tribute to them for their unselfish and devoted help. The reason this world is so bearable is because there exists people who are willing to assist others with no expectations of anything in return. Helping and administering to others is their nature, their hearts are pure and when in the presence of an individual such as this, one feels peace, love and harmony. I have often advised my children to be extend themselves for others and try to lend a hand when someone is in need.

It was a couple of months after Yafa and my children had arrived in Arak when we found out that Yafa was pregnant. I was surprised and worried about her because there were no substantial medical facilities in Arak and I had no knowledge where Yafa would deliver the baby. For days and weeks I contemplated this dilemma and tried to find a solution. One day I discovered that there was an educated Armenian midwife in

Arak. We immediately visited with her and requested her
services during the pregnancy and delivery of the baby. She
assured us that everything would be fine. I was feeling
somewhat better but I was still concerned about the time of
delivery and who would be assisting the midwife I went to the
Jewish ghetto hoping to find a woman; unfortunately I could not
find anyone even though I was willing to pay handsomely.

When I arrived at Arak I found out that there were no more
than 20 Jewish families in town and no one knew where these
families had migrated from. It was obvious that these families
were not the descendants' of Jews that have inhabited this area
for centuries. Just about all of them were uneducated, indigent
and unworldly. Their homes were nothing but mud huts; all
they had was their total devotion to Judaism. Whenever I
attempted to approach these people they were uncomfortable
and preferred their own kind, they considered me an outsider.
When I asked them for help, their standard answer was, "We
have no one who can come to your house and help you." No
matter how often I insisted and I was willing to pay
handsomely, I received the same answer. I called on them a few
times, but I had come to the realization that I had to find another
solution to my problem. I knew under no circumstances could I
not contact the Muslim community for help because they were
so devout. They were mostly uneducated, and it was forbidden
to them to make a social call at a Jewish person's house. I am
sure that all the Jewish families in that town have migrated to
Israel by now.

The closer we came to the delivery date the more concerned
I became until one day the landlord's wife, who was a wise,
kind and caring woman, offered help and said, "Your wife is
getting close to having her baby and no one knows whether it
will be during the day or night; call us any time. Mrs. Sirvart
and I will be there right away." Mrs. Sirvart was another
Armenian lady that was renting a room from my landlord. Her
husband, Markar, was a truck driver and was away most of the

time. He drove a heavy truck throughout the country and because of this, his wife was alone most of the time. He was a heavy opium user and his interests revolved mostly around making enough money to support his habit and he had no regard for his wife. Mrs. Sirvart over the years had adapted to the situation and the loneliness. They had no children and both of them had accepted that. I was like a blind man who someone had just offered his sight. I quickly accepted their offer and thanked them and promised that at the first sign of labor pains I would call them. She went and came back with Mrs. Sirvart to demonstrate how both were interested to help.

It was a bitter cold February night and there was several inches of snow on the ground when Yafa woke me up and exclaimed, "It is time, I am having my labor pains." Mrs. Sirvart's room was directly under one of our rooms, and as we

From left Nemat's wife Yafa, Yafa's sister, Tamara and Sirvart
Sitting left Tamara's daughter Liza, Yafa's youngest daughter Simin

had previously arranged it, I was supposed to thump my foot on the floor to alert her that it was time. Not long after, both kind Armenian ladies appeared at our door ready to help. They urged me to run and bring the midwife and they indicated that after this I would not be needed. By the time I fetched the midwife, the ladies had boiled water; they had a fire going and had prepared plenty of fresh towels. They previously had everything ready for the baby. These three ladies hand in hand helped with the delivery on that frigid cold night, in a room that was so difficult to get warm. There were many windows in this room, single pane with many large cracks. Even though we had tried to plug the holes with cotton, it could not keep the cold out.

They instructed me to remain in the other room and take care of the other three children who had woken up and were concerned about their mother. I went out of the room confident that my wife was in good hands. I waited in the other room until I was called in. The three women gave me the news that our baby girl was born. Simin was born healthy in spite of the

From left Noorollah, Rachel & her daughter Dalia, Enayat & his wife Turan, Simin, Yafa, Nemat, Aziz and Yafa's brother Joseph visiting from Italy

weather and all other adversities. I have never forgotten the kindness of these two ladies and I have tried to repay their kindness. Mrs. Sirvart often did not have money to cover her everyday expenses; over the years I have tried to help her in any way possible. We tried to be there for her and her husband. She was always a part of our family in Arak and later in Tehran. When she first came to Tehran we moved her to our house and gave her a room of her own.

Yafa's breast swelled while nursing Simin and it became infected. It took more than a one year to heal, with much difficulty and at an exorbitant cost. No sooner was she cured of this problem she then developed diarrhea and stomach distress that would not alleviate itself for years. She was treated over the course of time in Arak, Tehran and in the United States, costing huge sums of money and a lot of heartache.

It is no exaggeration Yafa has been enduring health problems ever since we were married 40 years ago and she has been treated continuously. To date she has had five surgeries, two of them major. One was a hysterectomy; the other was to examine a growth on one of her lungs. After that she was in the hospital intermittently until she was diagnosed with high blood pressure. She was also diagnosed with an enlarged heart; this may have been caused by a lack of care for rheumatism in early life. She frequently complained of pain in her shoulder and back. Unfortunately, Yafa has a low threshold for pain, and with the slightest malaise she runs to a doctor. That explains why in our home one would find many bottles of pills, some half full, others that had never been opened. In spite of all these obstacles, Yafa is vibrant and very youthful in appearance. Maybe one reason for this is that Yafa copes with everyday problems much better than I ever could and she does not easily become hopeless and discouraged.

The people of Arak in my opinion appear relaxed and unworldly, as compared to the populace of other larger cities in Iran. They were hardly industrious and the vast majority of their work is relegated to the Persian Rug industry. Unfortunately this industry is on the brink of decline due to inferior quality and negligible detail in their workmanship. The carpet weavers day begins somewhere between 7:00 or 8:00 in the morning and concludes at sun set as everyone dashes home until the next morning. Many young people that inhabit Arak are or seek employment elsewhere. Fortuitously, my family and I never developed an attachment or a fondness while residing in Arak.

My family and I departed Arak on a very frigid and snowy evening on December 19, 1953 and boarded a train to Teheran. We arrived in Teheran the next day and we settled in with my brother Aziz for a few days until we moved to a rented apartment. Our furniture that was shipped via a moving truck arrived coincidently as we found an apartment. The apartment was undersized with only two rooms and we managed to stay there for three months in discomfort until my two brothers and I leased a house in Ab-e-Sardar (آب سردار) district near Jaleh Street . My two brothers and my family dwelled in this house for about 15 months and then I purchased a house in Bagh-e-Saba district near Shemiran Avenue and we moved in on October 14, 1955. After we settled into this house, Yafa put aside one room for Mrs. Sirvart and invited her to move in with us. She was a part of our family; she was a great help to Yafa in house hold chores and assisted in rearing our children. She was like a sister to Yafa and a mother to our children. We lived like a happy family.

Susan and Simin, c.1958   *Family at a wedding in Louisville, KY*

Nemat's four children, each one before entering college From left in birth order, Iraj (David, the translator of Dardashti), youngest son Jahangir, oldest daughter Susan and youngest daughter Simin

My son Iraj graduated Hadaf High School in Tehran in 1957 and on October 24, 1957, departed for the United States to continue his education. Iraj had been accepted into several highly qualified colleges and universities, and in his letters to me and Yafa, he had made the prudent decision of attending the University of South Carolina because this had suited his needs well with his budget and engineering degree that he pursued. My son Iraj David was the first of the Dardashti lineage to go abroad to continue his higher education degree. Yafa and I were very proud of him, he prepared all of his paperwork in applying for college entries, passport and visa, and all the appointments required to government offices to accomplish the vast amount of paperwork needed for such a huge undertaking. He completely handled this on his own, even though his ability to speak and write in English was very limited. Most of our relatives joined us at the airport in Tehran to see Iraj off to the United States.

It was then that the relationship between Yafa and Mrs. Sirvart became strained and sometime later we had to ask her to move out. The reason for this was Yafa was distraught over her son Iraj being far away from home and long distance telephone calls were too difficult and costly. Writing letters was the only means of communication. I wrote letters to Iraj several times a week. Yafa sobbed almost every day and became short tempered and the smallest thing would irritate her. She even was irritated at her good friend and companion, Mrs. Sirvart, and life became unbearable with these two women in one house. It was difficult to ask Mrs. Sirvart to vacate our home, she had conducted herself impeccably and without question whatsoever, there was no wrongdoing by either account. However, when we sold this house it was a good opportunity to notify Mrs. Sirvart that we all had to vacate the house and that her kind help to Yafa and our family was not needed. Mrs. Sirvart quickly found another room in one of her friend's home and moved out. After Mrs. Sirvart moved out, she and Yafa renewed their friendship again and the years that we remained in Tehran they had a very cordial relationship. We lost contact with this kindhearted woman and I do not know what has happened to her since we moved to the United States.

In the late 1970's Yafa was diagnosed with breast cancer and she had a radical mastectomy on one breast including all the surrounding lymph nodes. Yafa was in the hospital for a few days following the surgery and we had one of the worst snow storms in Lexington. I was staying at my son Iraj's house when we received a distress call from the hospital from Yafa urging us to go rescue her before she is killed at the hospital. Iraj and I tried to shovel the car out of the snow and by the time we reached the hospital four hours had passed, even though the hospital was a distance of just a few miles.

Today when I look back at the many adversities that I was faced with, I thank God that everything worked out well and everyone is doing well. As I recollect these events my comprehension of the hardships of disease, famine, poverty of the family and the prejudicial environment which surrounded us were out of our control. I do not claim by any means that I was solely responsible for finding solutions and eliminating my brothers' and sisters' predicaments.

The things that I criticized and moaned about concerning my family was because of the damage that was inflicted on my spirit and annoyed me most of my life, to a point that I would become fed up with them. The fate of their future and their well-being was a constant source of worry for me, and it was always a thorn in my side to a point that would deprive me of an opportunity to enjoy my life. The misfortunes and problems were never-ending which always would lead my thoughts to be entangled in a web of distress. No matter how much I tried, I could not free my arms and legs out of the web and I would totally neglect my wife and children. At this writing, in the late 1970's, I would never have dreamt of the positive changes that have occurred in my lifetime and in my homeland Iran. I am very thankful to be able to enjoy the fruits of my ancestor's constant toil and strife and to see the entire extended family, including my own, have conditions that allowed us access to education, a skill, a profession or a business. In the Jewish ghettos where we were forced to reside, living conditions were constricted and sparse. There was no alternative but for entire families to reside in one or two rooms due to the restrictive nature of the ghettos. It amazes me with the occurrences of the famine, typhoid, diarrhea, and other illnesses we managed to survive.

I feel lucky to witness the exponential improvements regarding humanitarian, social and economic conditions for Iranian Jews. For a brief moment the Jews were allowed to be educated and were given the freedom to pursue their dreams and their aspirations. The results were astounding and just about every Jewish family tried to educate their children. Unfortunately most of the Jews emigrated from Iran to other countries with a heavy heart; those who were born in Iran loved their country dearly and would have preferred to remain in Iran to further advance the move to greatness.

Epilogue

My father, Nemat Shakib, died on December 2nd, 1993, in Lexington, KY at the age of 84, about 15 years after he wrote this book. My mother, Yafa died on June 3rd, 2007, several days shy of her 88th birthday. Nemat's four children were married and he had eight grandchildren and three great grandchildren at the time of his death. He was well respected, loved and revered by his family and he is sorely missed even to this day. His family has prospered in the United States and his children and grandchildren are all college graduates; as teachers, engineers, physicians, software developers, lawyers, accountants, business managers and builder/developers. He always held the United States in the highest esteem for the opportunities granted for his children and grandchildren to become successful and flourish.

My father had tremendous respect and love for his mother, known to us grandchildren as Monnie-Joon. I was fortunate to be her favorite grandchild (I, being the first born grandson of her own son, Nemat) in which I inexplicably had certain privileges. At times I accompanied her on her sales calls along the Zayandeh River to several of her wealthy Muslim customers. Some of these were the same customers that supplied food for Monnie-Joon's family during the horrendous famine and these women were very affectionate to me. I too, had similar euphoric experiences as my father did regarding outings along the river. Monnie-Joon and I carried our lunch and picnicked along the banks of the river. The air was sweet, the sky was always blue and sunny and this was an oasis in the desert—I remember those days as if it were yesterday, at the time I was 6 or 7 years old.

My memory recollects of only one unpleasant incident in the many ventures she and I took. I might have been 10 years old when Monnie-Joon asked if I would accompany her to one of her Muslim customers' homes to collect a debt in the middle

of the Muslim district. It was two o'clock on a summer
afternoon, and due to Esfahan's arid location in a high altitude,
most everyone partakes of an afternoon nap. We walked passed
Maidon-e-Shah and through the Gold Bazaar and Persian
Carpets Bazaar and entered the heart of the Muslim district. We
walked to the front door of grandmother's customer that was
located at the end of a long narrow alleyway. Monnie-Joon
knocked on the heavy door several times but no one answered.
She pushed on this heavy door and surprisingly the door swung
open. She began calling the name of her customer, the lady of
the house, "Sekinh Khanum (سكينه خانم) are you there". Several
more times she bellowed, still no one answered. Monnie-Joon
walked into the yard where there were rooms on all four sides
and the roofs were flat and connected to other neighboring
buildings. One could walk for miles bounding from roof to roof.
She repeatedly called out Sekinh's name, but to no avail.
Suddenly without warning a half asleep man in his under
garments ventured out of one of the rooms as he was rubbing
his eyes in order to awaken himself. He was surprised this
elderly woman and her grandchild were in the middle of his
yard. He inquired "Who are you and what are you doing in my
house?" My grandmother with a kind word greeted the master
of the house, "Salam" she said, and proceeded to explain her
purpose for her untimely intrusion into this man's home. "I
have sold jewelry to your wife Sekinh Khanum and I am here to
collect the money for it". The drowsy man, with agitation in his
voice asked my grandmother "Are you a Jew". My
grandmother, always fearless and never ashamed of her heritage
quickly replied "Yes". The man became furious and shouted at
my grandmother "Why you Jew, the Nejes (a very demeaning
phrase meaning "dirty Jew") why have you put your dirty Jew
feet in my house". I stood there, completely stunned. As I
looked up, within minutes there were throngs of people on the
flat roofs above us and they were observing what was taking
place in their neighbor's yard. The man, completely disgusted

with my grandmother and me for setting foot on his property, demanded we vacate his home immediately otherwise he

Mohtaram, Rahoullah
& his daughter Orly

threatened to strangle us both. I was scared and I was begging my grandmother for us to leave as I tugged on her chador. My brave grandmother had other plans and had no intentions of leaving the premises without collecting her money. As the events unfolded, I could feel the many wide eyed onlookers up on the roofs as they chanted, "Kill the Jews, kill the Jews". Finally my grandmother reluctantly deferring to my pleas, decided to vacate the premises as we heard rocks that had been thrown in our direction landing in the yard.

My aunt Javaher Shakib Benji, the first born sibling of my father's family, was widowed early in life which left her destitute with several children.   Her oldest daughter Mohtaram followed in her foot steps and bore many children without having the means of caring for them. Fortunately Motaram's first born Rahoullah Ahdoot;   a   very   determined,

Rahmatollah & Rosa's
Wedding Yahuda &
his three children

courageous and hardworking man became the savior of the Ahdoot and Benji families. He not only saved his brothers and sisters from the depths of poverty and despair, his uncles and aunts also benefited from his assistance. Before the Iranian Revolution he had a thriving consumer electronic business in Tehran. After the revolution he migrated to Los Angeles, California established himself firmly. He then assisted his mother, siblings, aunts and uncles to migrate to the United States where again he established his successful consumer electronic business in Los Angeles.

My father wrote in detail about the trials and tribulations of his older brother, Aziz, my eldest uncle. Although my father's comments were brusque and not always complementary, he sincerely loved and respected his brother. My father and I had several heated discussions on this matter. Some of my father's criticism of Uncle Aziz arose due to my father's extremely high expectations of a young man at the age of twenty, through no fault of his own, was placed in a situation of tremendous responsibility to earn, educate and care for his younger siblings upon the untimely death of their father Yaeir. My father had envisioned Uncle Aziz guiding this orphaned family seamlessly through the obstacles of life and all the decision making that is required. My Uncle Aziz was a hard working Industrialist and vastly ahead of his time. He initiated the industrialization of my home town, Esfahan, and established multiple factories. I remember fondly in my childhood, the first occasion we had electricity, its source was the surplus power from the Nakhtob (نختاب)Factory, and this was his foremost project. Nakhtob was the first textile factory for spinning cotton threads in Esfahan. Uncle Aziz's encouraging nature towards me and my brother Jahangir was endless, no challenge was insurmountable; this was his life lesson to us. He was my inspiration in pursuing the engineering field. At an early age I was fascinated by his many factories and I would beg my father incessantly for us to please visit some of my uncle's factory locations. My uncle was very attentive to the family. He helped many people, friend or family, monetarily or with his personal time. I recollect that when I was 14, I was visiting Tehran during the summer for several weeks. Even though he was very busy, Uncle Aziz assisted me with my English studies and he accompanied me to the bus station when I was departing for Arak; he hugged me with tears in his eyes as he was regretfully obliged to see me off on the bus. Uncle Aziz's two daughters, Homa and Heshmat and their respective families, migrated to the United States and are residing in Los Angeles, California.

My youngest uncle, Uncle Joseph, died c. 1988 in Iran after battling brain cancer for several years. In 1986 he and his wife, Aunt Parri, visited the United States and their daughters in the New York area. He was a very sweet man and the essence of kindness. At that time I worked in Purchase, New York, and I visited with him. I had not seen Uncle Joseph in 27 years and I was so elated to see him again. His wife, Aunt Parri passed away last year. Uncle Joseph's oldest daughter Fleur and his youngest daughter Forouz continue to reside in Long Island in the New Yew area with their families. His middle daughter Fereshteh and her family reside in Los Angeles, California. My three cousins and their families are well educated and have prospered in the United States.

From left Iraj David, Joseph's youngest daughter Forouz, Joseph's oldest daughter Fleur, Joseph, his wife Parri, Fleur's daughter Romina, Fleur's husband Houshang, Fleur's son Ronan, Standing Forouz's husband Behzad and their daughter Bianca

Sinoor and all of her children except her youngest daughter Maheen (مهین) migrated to Los Angeles, California after the revolution of 1979. She passed away in the mid-1980. Maheen departed Iran in the late-1950's for Israel and at this writing, March 2013, she resides there with her family. One of Sinoor's sons, Goleh (گوله) died of cancer in the 1990's. One son, Faizollah died at the age of 14 or 15, when I was 6 or 7 years old. I have many fond memories visiting with him at his home or at his place of work in downtown Esfahan. He was extremely kind to me and my brother Jahangir (John).

Tauce and Noorollah lived in Israel until they both passed away. Their youngest daughter, Forough also resides in Israel with her family. Their son Parviz, who traveled to Israel in 1959 to continue his education, married a North African Orthodox Jewish girl and migrated to Los Angeles, California, a few years later. He passed away from cancer and suffered from years of depression. Tauce's older daughter, Parvaneh migrated to Los Angeles, California, before the revolution. She worked very hard to make sure her children were well educated.

My youngest aunt, Hosna, was like a second mother to me and my siblings. She and my mother were like two sisters and tried to be there for each other. When I was very young my aunt lived with us and she loved me like her own. She was a very hard working person and from a young age she had to fend for herself. I remember her while she was in high school and I remember her teaching herself how to sew. For years she supported herself by sewing dresses and tutoring. She married late in life and in poverty. I remember once I helped her move to a rented room in someone's home. Her total belongings fit into a very small cart that was pulled by a man. She and her husband, Khalil, were very resourceful and they managed to pull themselves out of poverty, send their two sons to England for higher education and finally come to the United States. I have many fond memories of her.

My father's nature was to help everyone in need. He was always very fond of my Aunt Tamara, my mother's sister; she was instrumental in my father meeting my mother. I recollect my aunt and my father being very jovial, they laughed loudly as they would take turns telling jokes, ribbing one another and playing cards, they were the best of friends. Our families enjoyed visiting each other and my father often played chess with my half cousins, Monsieur Gabbay's two sons from his

Standing from left M. Omidvar, Tamara's son Eli, B. Mohaber, E. Laad, sitting from 2nd left Tamara's daughter Zolaikha Omidvar, Khaleh-Jan (Tamara) & grandchildren, Tamara's oldest child Rachel, & Tamara's daughter Turan Laad

previous marriage, Albert and Jojo. When my cousin Rachel, the first born of Aunt Tamara, was getting married, Monsieur Gabbay's insurance business, Lloyds of London, was not doing well. My father was very instrumental in assisting my aunt and managed to put together a dowry. Thankfully all went well and she was married. Rachel and her family migrated to the United States and they also reside in Los Angeles.

Late in 1985 my mother, Yafa was rushed from Dr. William Maxson's office (our long time personal physician, a wonderful, skilled physician) to St. Joseph Hospital for heart surgery. The doctor had detected that she was in the process of having a massive heart attack. My mother was submitted and underwent a quadruple bypass surgery on her heart. I lived in Stamford, Connecticut, and worked for IBM in Purchase, New York and I was returning to work after visiting with my parents and my family for the weekend. I had arrived at work in Purchase, New York and within a few minutes I was informed there was a family emergency back in Lexington, Kentucky. I returned immediately to Lexington, and by the time my mother was being wheeled into surgery, I arrived to wish her well. The surgery lasted about 8 hours. It took many months of therapy before she was completely well. Before the surgery my mother was always grim and could not walk or climb stairs. Upon her post surgery, she became the same vibrant "Yafa" we all knew. My father was elated with her recovery and her new found demeanor. However, my mother's heart surgery had a profound effect on my father and thereafter he concluded his writings and abruptly ended his book.

As the eldest in my family, similar to my father, I too have witnessed the drastic changes that have taken place and I was very fortunate to be the first wave of Jewish children to go abroad to continue my higher education. I thankfully experienced a mild version of the prejudicial world that my father experienced and wrote about. Many of my cousins that were raised in absolute poverty had prospered over the years and acquired large factories and businesses by the time the 1979 Iranian Revolution came about. Many of them, like my family, came to the United States and are well educated and enjoy very affluent lives.

Phyllis and David, 1987   *From left Nematollah, Yafa,*
and David sitting

From left Monnie, Keith, Darren and sitting David   Keith's son Ryan

Anne & Darren, 1990 (David's son)   Denise & Monnie, 2002
(David's Daughter)

From left Darren's Son Dale-Joon, Darren,   From left Monnie's daughter,
Darren's daughter Aria, Darren's   McKenna, Monnie, Denise
wife Anne, Darren's son, Nathan,   & Monnie's son, Ethan
Darren's mother Sallie

John and Martha, 1965   *John and Sherene, 1999*
(John's daughter)

*Left picture, from left John, Nicholas, Alexander & Sherene Right picture,
from left Sherene's sons Alexander & Nicholas, Chris' Daughter & son
Ashley & Evan*

*Left picture, John's son, Chris   Right picture, from left Sherene's sons,
Alexander & Nicholas, Chris, Chris' Daughter & son Ashley & Evan*

Left picture, Susan & Bob, 1971   Right picture, Susan, Bob, Susan & Bob's son, Chad, his wife Jennifer & their three children

Chad & Jennifer, 2001   From left Kate, Jennifer, Cole, Chad & Brooke

Simin & Tom, 1973   From left Leslie, Simin, Jamie & Tom

Jamie & Ryan, 2002   *From left Grant, Jamie, Ryan & Lucy*

Leslie her husband Jamie, 2013,   *Jamie's daughter, Abbe, front, Leslie's*
children Alex & Samantha

From left Parri, Joseph, Nemat in 1986 in Lexington, KY Fleur & Houshang

Fereshteh & Syruce's,   *from left Joseph, Parri, Fereshteh*
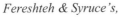
(فرشته,Ferry), Syruce (سیروس), in front Desiree

From left Yafa, Madlen, Parvin, Martha, Phyllis, David, Homa, Simin &
Roya (Heshmat's youngest daughter)

The family reunion couple of years after my father passed away
From left back row David, my oldest son Keith, Susan's son Chad, David's
2nd son Darren and Susan's husband Bob, from left standing Simin's
husband Tom, Simin, John, David's wife Phyllis, Cindy, Simin's youngest
Daughter Leslie, Darren's wife Anne, John's daughter Sherene, David'
daughter Monnie, friend, John's wife Martha and Susan, from left sitting
Simin's oldest daughter Jamie, Amy, Michael, Laura and my mother Yafa

Family Trees

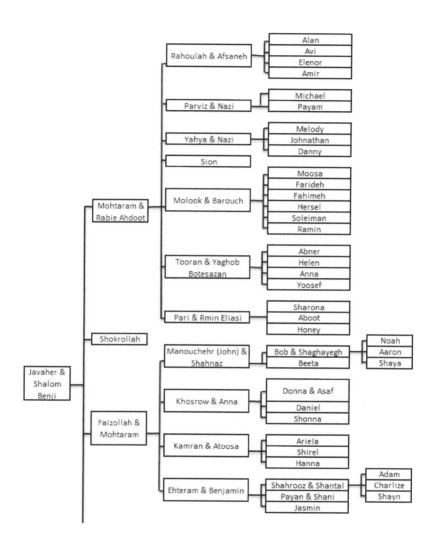

Javaher Benji Family Tree (continue to next page)

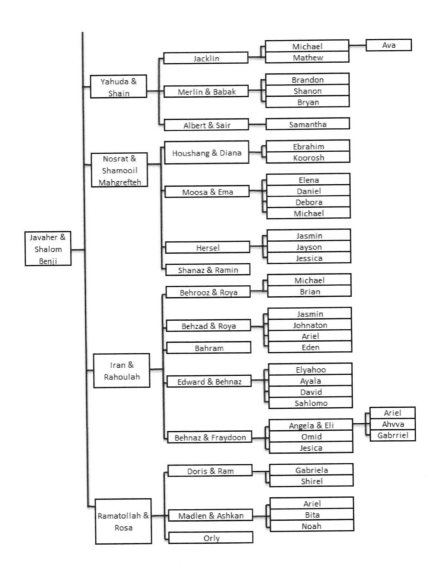

Javaher Benji Family Tree

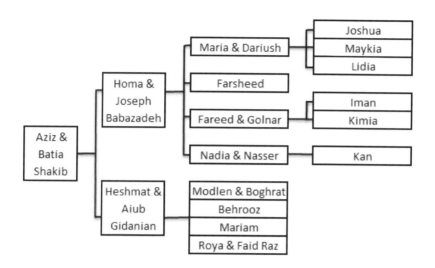

Aziz's Family Tree

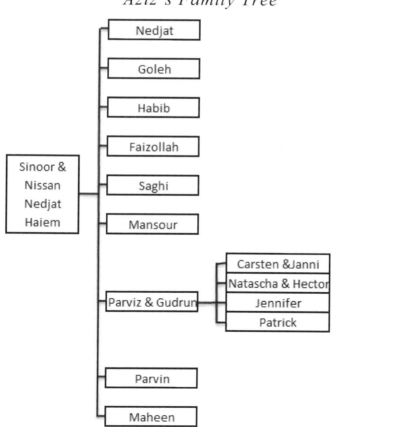

Sinoor's Family Tree

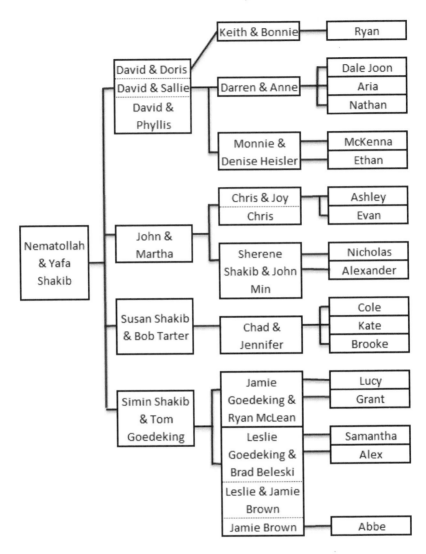

Nematollah Shakib's Family Tree

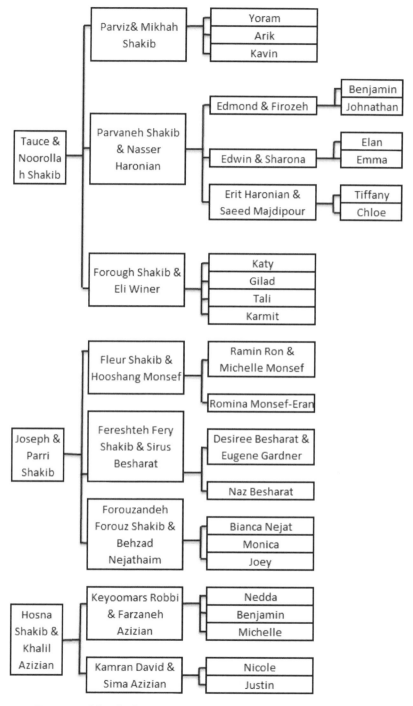

Tauce Shakib's, Joseph Shakib's & Hosna Shakib Azizian's Family Trees

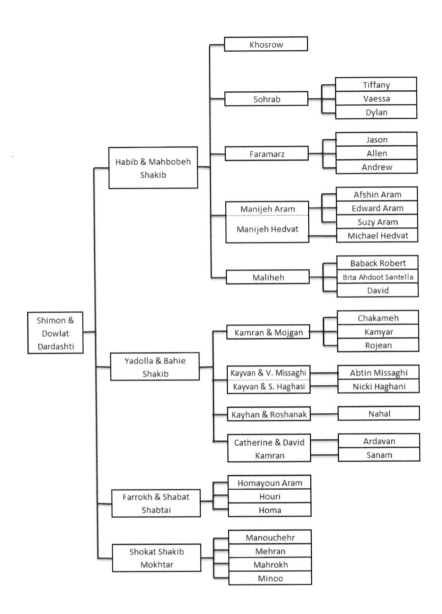

Shimon's Family Tree

Made in the USA
San Bernardino, CA
27 June 2013